Cognitive Linguistics Research ... ER Mo... gv

Walter de Gruyter 1749

250

Berlin · New York

1999

# Cognitive Linguistics Research
# 15

*Editors*
René Dirven
Ronald W. Langacker
John R. Taylor

Mouton de Gruyter
Berlin · New York

# Cognitive Linguistics: Foundations, Scope, and Methodology

*Edited by*
Theo Janssen
Gisela Redeker

Mouton de Gruyter
Berlin · New York 1999

Mouton de Gruyter (formerly Mouton, The Hague)
is a Division of Walter de Gruyter GmbH & Co. KG, Berlin

♾ Printed on acid-free paper
which falls within
the guidelines of the ANSI
to ensure permanence and durability.

*Library of Congress Cataloging-in-Publication Data*

Cognitive linguistics, foundations, scope, and methodology /
edited by Theo Janssen, Gisela Redeker.
    p.   cm. − (Cognitive linguistics research ; 15)
    Includes bibliographical references and index.
    ISBN 3-11-016163-X (alk. paper) − ISBN 3-11-016164-8
    (pbk. : alk. paper)
    1. Cognitive grammar.   I. Janssen, Theodorus Albertus
Johannes Maria, 1944−  II. Redeker, Gisela.  III. Series
    P165.C643   1999
    415−dc21                            99-056747

*Die Deutsche Bibliothek − Cataloging-in-Publication Data*

**Cognitive linguistics** : foundations, scope, and methodology /
ed. by Theo Janssen ; Gisela Redeker. − Berlin ; New York :
Mouton de Gruyter, 1999
    (Cognitive linguistics research ; 15)
    ISBN 3-11-016163-X Gb.
    ISBN 3-11-016164-8 brosch.

# Acknowledgments

The idea for this volume originated in the Organizing Committee of the *5th International Cognitive Linguistics Conference* (Amsterdam 1997). We could never have realized it without the enthusiasm and cooperation of the plenary speakers at that conference, who agreed to focus their plenaries on foundational and methodological issues of Cognitive Linguistics, and most of whom then prepared a chapter for this volume.

The initial versions of the chapters and of the Introduction were read by Melissa Bowerman, Bill Croft, Gilles Fauconnier, Dirk Geeraerts, Peter Harder, Ron Langacker, John Nerbonne, Chris Sinha, Eve Sweetser, and Marjolijn Verspoor. We are very grateful for their thorough and constructive commentary.

We wish to thank the Series Editors and Anke Beck, Christiane Graefe, Katja Huder, and Monika Wendland of Mouton de Gruyter for their support, patience, and helpful advice; the *Department of Language and Communication* at the University of Groningen and the *Stichting Neerlandistiek* of Vrije Universiteit Amsterdam for their material and financial support; and, last not least, Rogier Nieuweboer, Nel Courtz, and the Helpdesk staff of the Faculty of Arts at the University of Groningen for their technical advice and assistance.


Theo Janssen and Gisela Redeker

# Contents

# Introduction

## Gisela Redeker and Theo Janssen

### 1. Background

Cognitive Linguistics established itself as a coherent, identifiable approach about a decade ago, marked by the first *International Cognitive Linguistics Conference* (Duisburg, Germany, 1989) and by the founding of the journal *Cognitive Linguistics*, which first appeared in 1990. By that time, the major theoretical foundations had been laid and a substantial amount of empirical data had already been gathered to support and develop those theories, resulting in a number of scholarly publications that have since become widely-cited classics: George Lakoff and Mark Johnson's (1980) *Metaphors We Live By*, Leonard Talmy's (1983) "How language structures space", Charles Fillmore's (1985) *Frames and the Semantics of Understanding*, Gilles Fauconnier's (1985) *Mental Spaces*, George Lakoff's (1987) *Women, Fire and Dangerous Things*, Ronald Langacker's two-volume work on the *Foundations of Cognitive Grammar* (1987, 1991; paperback edition 1999), Leonard Talmy's (1988) *Force Dynamics in Language and Cognition*, Brygida Rudzka-Ostyn's (1988) *Topics in Cognitive Linguistics*, George Lakoff and Mark Turner's (1989) *More than Cool Reason*, Eve Sweetser's (1990) *From Etymology to Pragmatics*, and the first volume in the *Cognitive Linguistics Research* series, Ronald Langacker's (1990) *Concept, Image, and Symbol*.

All these authors and a steadily increasing number of scholars world-wide have taken up the challenge of mapping out the structure and dynamics of language in use from a cognitive perspective. That perspective entails a concern for contextualized, dynamically constructed meanings and for the grounding of language use in cognitive and social-interactional processes.

Against the background of diversification and consolidation of cognitive linguistic research, the plenary talks at the *Fifth Interna-*

*tional Cognitive Linguistics Conference* (Amsterdam 1997) were focused on examining the theoretical and methodological foundations of cognitive linguistics. Most of those plenaries have been elaborated into chapters for this volume; in addition, a contribution was invited from Chris Sinha. The authors each present their particular view of cognitive-linguistic methodology and of the foundations and scope of the field.

## 2. Scope and methodology of Cognitive Linguistics

The first four papers focus on issues and theories belonging to the programmatic core of Cognitive Linguistics: What is it trying to describe and explain, and by what methodological principles is it guided? Ronald Langacker and Gilles Fauconnier illustrate and discuss cognitive-linguistic methodology as applied in the research paradigms of Cognitive Grammar and Mental Spaces/Conceptual Integration Theory. William Croft and Eve Sweetser each extend those discussions by showing the relevance of this research to, in Croft's case, language typology, and in Sweetser's, the problem of compositionality.

Ronald Langacker, in his paper *Assessing the cognitive linguistic enterprise,* outlines and discusses the major tenets of formalist and functionalist approaches to the study of language, and argues that a comprehensive account of language and language structure will cover both the descriptivist and the functionalist research agendas, which should therefore be pursued as synergistically as possible.

An important implication of the functional agenda is methodological diversity, as functionalists (including Cognitive Linguists) have to cover such diverse domains as language change, typology, acquisition, and the neurological basis of language. The most important guiding principle to choose among methodologies and approaches is the principle of *converging evidence.*

In Cognitive Grammar, this principle is applied in proposing and motivating basic descriptive constructs in the following way: Show the necessity of a construct for the adequate *semantic* description of multiple phenomena in various languages, seek *psychological* evidence, and demonstrate that the same construct needs to be referred to for optimal *grammatical* descriptions. Langacker illustrates this for the concept of *profiling* and then along the same lines explores the proposal of the concept of *focal prominence* for the characterization of subject and object.

William Croft, in *Some contributions of typology to linguistics, and vice versa*, assesses the nature of grammatical knowledge and the relation between form and meaning from a typologist's point of view. He finds agreement between typologists and Cognitive Linguists in identifying as the basic linguistic units not the syntactic components themselves, but rather the constructions they occur in, that is, the symbolic units that (more or less tightly) bundle different types of linguistic information into complexes of forms and functions. Croft discusses how certain kinds of variation across and within languages pose fundamental problems for distributional analysis unless the assumption of syntactic primitives is abandoned in favor of what he calls a *radical construction grammar*.

Concerning the relation between syntactic structure and semantic structure, Croft dispels 'radical semantic relativism', but also shows that the reverse, a determination of syntactic structure by semantics, would ignore the dynamic tensions present in any living language. He argues for a more complex interplay between form, meaning, and experience, where syntactic structure does reflect semantic structure, but where the experience of immanent conflicting conceptualizations can also lead to reconstrual of the semantic structure.

Gilles Fauconnier, in *Methods and generalizations*, describes Cognitive Linguistics as a 'science of meaning construction and its dynamics'. He discusses three major areas where this approach has yielded new insights: economy, operational uniformity, and cognitive generalization. *Economy* refers to the fact that meanings are not contained in linguistic forms, but are filled in by context and 'backstage cognition'. If we ask the right questions, we find *operational uniformity* at all levels of linguistic structure; one such very general operation is *blending*, the conceptual integration of elements from different domains as found in metaphors, framing effects, and so forth, but also in the simple default mappings involved in the under-standing of relational information as in *the top of the building* or *Sally's father*. If language is understood as embedded in cognition, it can in turn serve as a 'window to the mind' and yield *cognitive generalizations*: The processes of meaning construction as reflected in language can be generalized to other cognitive domains.

The conceptual integration (blending) operations proposed in mental space theory were conceived to explain semantic phenomena, but they extend straightforwardly to accounts for non-compositional meanings of compositional syntactic forms, as in the *NP be NP of NP*-construction discussed in Fauconnier's chapter.

This last point is argued for in detail in *Compositionality and blending: semantic composition in a cognitively realistic framework* by Eve Sweetser. She shows how blending accounts for a very broad range of relations that can be expressed in English Adjective-Noun (A-N) modification constructions, from the most mundane cases like *red ball* through cases that obviously require some kind of scenario, like *safe beach* (what or who is "safe" here?), to cases like *possible textbook* or *fake gun*, the interpretation of which must make reference to the speaker's ongoing epistemic processing. Traditionally, the first of these cases is considered unproblematically compositional, but an analysis based solely on the lexical meanings cannot account for the fact that *red* here can mean any number of different things: a red surface, but also any other kind of redness suitable to identify the ball in question *in a particular context*.

Sweetser thus shows that semantic compositionality can be achieved easily and elegantly for even the most creative combinations, if it is recognized that compositional semantic interpretation does not involve just combining lexical meanings, but combining conceptualizations from diverse kinds of spaces, whose cognitive construction is prompted by the lexical meanings of the forms used in that context. Sweetser's account of A-N modification extends Langacker's (1987, 1990, 1991) concept of *active zone* to include not only aspects of the entity itself, but also parts or aspects of the frames associated with the entity in the context of utterance. This is one of an increasing number of instances where different cognitive linguistic approaches have been brought together to yield more unified accounts.

There are several issues and paradigms central to what we have called the programmatic core of Cognitive Linguistics, which are not covered or only marginally considered in the chapters in this volume. Most importantly, we might mention cognitive neurolinguistics, spearheaded within Cognitive Linguistics by George Lakoff *c.s.* (cf. Lakoff and Johnson 1998); psycholinguistic approaches focusing, for instance, on issues of polysemy (cf. Cuyckens and Zawada, to appear); and, last not least, the growing tradition of cognitive-linguistic work on Signed languages, and the growing awareness in the Cognitive Linguistic community of the importance of visual-gestural languages for understanding the cognitive basis of grammatical structure (see, e.g., Armstrong, Stokoe and Wilcox 1995; Liddell 1998; Taub 1997; Van Hoek 1997).

## 3. Philosophical foundations

The remaining three papers in this volume explore basic philosophical issues. First, Dirk Geeraerts places ongoing discussions between "schools" in Cognitive Linguistics into the perspective of the age-old "idealism-empiricism" debate. Peter Harder then questions the status of the qualification "cognitive"[2] and argues that a cognitive approach to language implies the recognition that language is an essentially social (interactional) phenomenon. Chris Sinha elaborates a quite similar argument and presents additional convincing evidence for the inherently social nature of language.

Dirk Geeraerts, in *Idealist and empiricist tendencies in cognitive semantics*, begins by discussing the problem of radical subjectivism raised by Cognitive Semantics' adherence to the principle of *internal realism*. He then reframes the opposition between idealist subjectivism and empiricist objectivism in terms of Dilthey's problem of what constitutes a legitimate interpretation of natural language expressions. Geeraerts concludes that the "empiricist" approach to seek maximal empirical grounding for posited interpretations (cf. Langacker's concept of converging evidence) seems a better safeguard against arbitrariness than the "idealist" quest for a vocabulary of allegedly universal concepts. The idealist approach to Cognitive Linguistics shares with formal semantics the reliance on a "representational" strategy for imposing restrictions on interpretations. It differs (along with empiricist Cognitive Linguistics) from formal semantics in the desire to describe the full range of semantic phenomena that play a role in natural language use.

Peter Harder, in *Partial autonomy: ontology and methodology in cognitive linguistics,* proposes to recast the question of autonomy versus continuity of different levels of language and between language and other cognitive structures, in terms of partial autonomy in functional hierarchies. He illustrates the asymmetry of causal and functional grounding in such hierarchies using economics and biology as examples. Consider, for instance, the mutual dependency between physical and biological facts, as in anatomy and physiology: Properties of the physical substratum causally support the higher-level organization, while the functional role of physical elements (such as oxygen) can only be understood with reference to the biological level of organization. Note that the physical substratum may remain intact when the higher level collapses, while this does not hold the other way round.

Analogously, cognition is *causally grounded* in the biology of the organism and *functionally grounded* in the interaction between organism and environment. The ontological levels related to understanding language form a functional hierarchy and thus should be considered as partially autonomous: syntactic items, for instance, are not simply meaning-bearing elements; their role is bound up with the task of assembling the whole-clause meanings in service of communication.

Chris Sinha, in *Grounding, mapping and acts of meaning,* warns against confusing Cognitive Linguistics' fundamental hypothesis that meaning involves motivated mappings from conceptualization to expression, with what he calls the 'Reificatory Semantics doctrine of meaning-as-mental-object'. Adopting that doctrine means admitting the dilemma between objectivism and subjectivism, and Cognitive Linguistics is then seen as subjectivist (cf. Geeraerts).

Sinha urges us to reject the representational theory in favor of a practical-communicative view of meaning as communicative action, thereby embracing a *referential realism*. Starting from an analysis of the primordial discourse situation of intersubjectively joint attention, he distinguishes *embodied grounding, discursive grounding,* and the *specifically linguistic mediational means* by which articulated conceptualizations get mapped onto articulated expressions. Importantly, conceptualizations are not seen as uniquely grounded in embodied experience (as Lakoff's, 1987, *experiential realism* might suggest), but as motivated by, on the one hand, embodied grounding, and on the other fundamental discourse construction principles.

The chapters by Geeraerts, Harder, and Sinha each call for a reflection on fundamental ontological and epistemological questions associated with the Cognitive Linguistic enterprise. Harder and, even more radically, Sinha challenge some deeply-seated implicit assumptions in Cognitive Linguistics and call on Cognitive Linguists to take the commitment to language *use* seriously by acknowledging and accounting for its functional dependence on the social-interactional (and not just the more narrowly cognitive) context. Sinha in addition suggests (similar to, e.g., Dan Slobin and Melissa Bowerman before him), that the constructivist Cognitive Linguistics he envisages could and should contribute to and be informed by the study of language development and cognitive development.

## 4. Conclusion

After a decade of growth, exploration, and consolidation (preceded by another decade or so during which a number of Cognitive Linguistic paradigms were being developed and elaborated), Cognitive Linguistics has now definitely come of age. There are firm (if diverse) methodological principles, the arguably most important of which is the principle of *converging evidence*, which implies a constrained methodological pluralism; and there is a large and fast-growing body of knowledge that can be seen as constituting the substantive core of the discipline.[3]

Another important development of the past decade is the increased mutual reception and appreciation of diverse, more or less functionalist approaches and a certain amount of "rapprochement" between functionalist and formalist traditions. Cognitive Linguistics has informed and has been informed by many strands of research, as evidenced in the author index to this volume and the discussions in the chapters. It is our hope that this volume will help to further stimulate fruitful dialogues and collaborations across the boundaries of disciplinary paradigms.

To help our readers locate Cognitive Linguistics research on the Internet, we have compiled a small webliography, which is appended to this introduction.

## Notes

1.  Selected papers from the Amsterdam conference are being published in various thematic volumes (i.a., Cuyckens and Zawada, in press; Foolen and Van der Leek, to appear; Gibbs and Steen 1999; Horie, to appear; Panther and Radden 1999; Van Hoek, Kibrik and Noordman 1999). Other recent monographs and collections in which cognitive linguistic research is presented include Achard (1998), Allwood and Gärdenfors (1999), Blank and Koch (1999), Hiraga, Sinha and Wilcox (1999), Koenig (1998), Lakoff and Johnson (1998), Langacker (1999), Stadler and Eyrich (1999) and Talmy (in press). We cannot begin to give a more comprehensive overview here; in particular, we had to leave out all publications before 1998. We refer the reader to references in these recent volumes and in the chapters of the present volume, and to articles in *Cognitive Linguistics* and other linguistic, literary, and cognitive science journals.
2.  For a discussion of the label "cognitive" in "Cognitive Linguistics" see Peeters (1999).
3.  Another sign of the maturity of the approach is the publication of Cognitive Linguistics textbooks (e.g. Ungerer and Schmid 1996, Dirven and Verspoor 1999).

# References

Achard, Michel
  1998    *Representation of Cognitive Structures: Syntax and Semantics of French Sentential Complements.* (Cognitive Linguistics Research 11.) Berlin/New York: Mouton de Gruyter.
Allwood, Jens, and Peter Gärdenfors (eds.)
  1999    *Cognitive Semantics: Meaning and Cognition.* (Pragmatics & Beyond New Series 55.) Amsterdam: Benjamins.
Armstrong, David F., William C. Stokoe, and Sherman E. Wilcox
  1995    *Gesture and the Nature of Language.* Cambridge/New York: Cambridge University Press.
Blank, Andreas, and Peter Koch (eds.)
  1999    *Historical Semantics and Cognition.* (Cognitive Linguistics Research 13.) Berlin/New York: Mouton de Gruyter.
Cuyckens, Hubert, and Britta E. Zawada (eds.)
  in press *Polysemy in Cognitive Linguistics. Selected Papers from the 5th International Cognitive Linguistics Conference, Amsterdam, 1997* (Current Issues in Linguistic Theory 177.) Amsterdam: Benjamins.
Dirven, René, and Marjolijn Verspoor (eds.)
  1999    *Cognitive Exploration of Language and Linguistics.* (Cognitive Linguistics in Practice 1.) Amsterdam: Benjamins.
Fauconnier, Gilles
  1985    *Mental Spaces.* Cambridge, MA: MIT Press [Rev. ed. Cambridge/New York: Cambridge University Press 1994.]
Fillmore, Charles
  1985    Frames and the semantics of understanding. *Quaderni di Semantica* 62: 222-253.
Foolen, Ad, and Frederike van der Leek (eds.)
  to app.  *Constructions in Cognitive Linguistics. Selected Papers from the 5th International Cognitive Linguistics Conference, Amsterdam, 1997* (Current Issues in Linguistic Theory 178.) Amsterdam: Benjamins.
Geeraerts, Dirk
  1995    Cognitive Linguistics. In: Jef Verschueren, Jan-Ola Östman, and Jan Blommaert (ed.), *Handbook of Pragmatics,* 111-116. Amsterdam: John Benjamins.
Gibbs, Raymond W., Jr., and Gerard J. Steen (eds.)
  1999    *Metaphor in Cognitive Linguistics. Selected Papers from the 5th International Cognitive Linguistics Conference, Amsterdam, 1997.* (Current Issues in Linguistic Theory 175.) Amsterdam: Benjamins.

Hiraga, Masako, Chris Sinha, and Sherman Wilcox (eds.)
    1999    *Cultural, Psychological and Typological Issues in Cognitive Linguistics. Selected Papers of the Bi-annual ICLA Meeting in Albuquerque, July 1995.* (Current Issues in Linguistic Theory 152.) Amsterdam: Benjamins.
Horie, Kaoru (ed.)
    to app.    *Complementation: Cognitive and Functional Perspectives.* (Converging Evidence in Language and Communication Research 1.) Amsterdam: Benjamins.
Koenig, Jean-Pierre (ed.)
    1998    *Discourse and Cognition: Bridging the Gap.* Stanford: Center for the Study of Language and Information.
Lakoff, George
    1987    *Women, Fire and Dangerous Things: What Categories Reveal about the Mind.* Chicago: University of Chicago Press.
Lakoff, George, and Mark Johnson
    1998    *Philosophy in the Flesh: The Embodied Mind and its Challenge to Western Thought.* New York: Basic Books.
Lakoff, George, and Mark Turner
    1989    *More than Cool Reason. A Field Guide to Poetic Metaphor,* Chicago/London: University of Chicago Press.
Langacker, Ronald W.
    1987    *Foundations of Cognitive Grammar, Vol. 1: Theoretical Prerequisites.* Stanford: Stanford University Press.
    1990    *Concept, Image, and Symbol: The Cognitive Basis of Grammar.* (Cognitive Linguistics Research 1.) Berlin/New York: Mouton de Gruyter. [paperback edition 1991]
    1991    *Foundations of Cognitive Grammar, Vol. 2: Descriptive Application.* Stanford: Stanford University Press.
    1999    *Grammar and Conceptualization.* (Cognitive Linguistics Research 14.) Berlin/New York: Mouton de Gruyter.
Liddell, Scott
    1998    Grounded blends, gestures, and conceptual shifts. *Cognitive Linguistics* 9: 283-314.
Panther, Klaus-Uwe, and Günter Radden (eds.)
    1999    *Metonymy in Language and Thought.* (Human Cognitive Processing 4). Amsterdam: Benjamins.
Peeters, Bart
    1999    Does Cognitive Linguistics live up to its name? Paper presented at the 6th International Cognitive Linguistic Conference, Stockholm, 1999. (An undated written version of this paper is available on the Internet at http://www.tulane.edu/~howard/LangIdeo/Peeters/Peeters.html).

Rudzka-Ostyn, Brygida (ed.)
  1988    *Topics in Cognitive Linguistics.* Amsterdam: Benjamins.
Stadler, Leon de, and Christoph Eyrich (eds.)
  1999    *Issues in Cognitive Linguistics.* (Cognitive Linguistics Research 12.)
          Berlin/New York: Mouton de Gruyter.
Sweetser, Eve E.
  1990    *From Etymology to Pragmatics: Metaphorical and Cultural Aspects of
          Semantic Structure.* (Cambridge Studies in Linguistics 54.) Cam-
          bridge: Cambridge University Press.
Talmy, Leonard
  1983    How language structures space. In: Herbert L. Pick and Linda P.
          Acredolo (eds.), *Spatial Orientation: Theory, Research, and Applica-
          tion,* 225-282. New York etc.: Plenum.
  1988    Force dynamics in language and cognition. *Cognitive Science* 2: 49-
          100.
  in press *Toward a Cognitive Semantics, Vol. I: Concept Structuring Systems.*
          Cambridge, MA: MIT Press.
  in press *Toward a Cognitive Semantics, Vol. II: Typology and Process in
          Concept Structuring.* Cambridge, MA: MIT Press.
Taub, Sarah
  1997    Language in the body: iconicity and metaphor in American Sign
          Language. Ph.D. dissertation, University of California, Berkeley.
Ungerer, Friedrich, and Hans-Jörg Schmid
  1996    *An Introduction to Cognitive Linguistics.* (Learning about Language
          Series.) London: Longman.
van Hoek, Karen
  1996    Conceptual locations for reference in American Sign Language. In:
          Gilles Fauconnier and Eve Sweetser (eds.) *Spaces, Worlds, and
          Grammar,* 334-350. Chicago: University of Chicago Press.
van Hoek, Karen, Andrej A. Kibrik and Leo Noordman (eds.)
  1999    *Discourse Studies in Cognitive Linguistics: Selected Papers from the
          5th International Cognitive Linguistics Conference, Amsterdam, 1997.*
          (Current Issues in Linguistic Theory 176.) Amsterdam: Benjamins.

## Cognitive Linguistics Webliography

*International Cognitive Linguistics Association*
        http://www.let.rug.nl/orgs/icla/
*6th International Cognitive Linguistics Conference, Stockholm 1999*
        http://bamse.ling.su.se/iclc99/

*5th International Cognitive Linguistics Conference, Amsterdam 1997*
      http://ohrid.cca.vu.nl:8000/ICLC97/
*ATT-Meta Project Databank: Examples of Usage of Metaphors of Mind*
      http://www.cs.bham.ac.uk/~jab/ATT-Meta/Databank/
*Blending and Conceptual Integration*
      http://www.wam.umd.edu/~mturn/WWW/blending.html
*Center for the Cognitive Science of Metaphor Online*
      http://metaphor.uoregon.edu/metaphor.htm
*Conceptual Metaphor Home Page*
      http://cogsci.berkeley.edu/
*Neural Theory of Language project*
      http://www.icsi.berkeley.edu/NTL/
*Newsletter of the Center for Research in Language*
      http://crl.ucsd.edu/newsletter/
*Pedagogical Quarterly of Cognitive Linguistics*
      http://pqcl.indstate.edu/

# Assessing the cognitive linguistic enterprise

## Ronald W. Langacker

In accordance with the theme of this volume, I will offer a personal assessment of cognitive linguistics with respect to both its place and its character. I will first consider how cognitive linguistics, and cognitive grammar in particular, relate to the broader functionalist tradition and to the field of linguistics as a whole. I will next discuss certain methodological principles that have guided research in cognitive grammar. The application of these principles will then be exemplified by an extended case study, pertaining to the proposed characterization of subject and object.

## 1. Cognitive, functional, and formal linguistics

I would be the first to acknowledge the gross distortions and over-simplifications inherent in the commonplace distinction between formalist and functionalist traditions in linguistics, as well as the increasing irrelevance of any such division. If its limitations are recognized, the distinction is nonetheless useful for the general discussion of some important intellectual differences. On this basis, the movement that has come to be known as cognitive linguistics belongs to the functionalist tradition. Cognitive grammar (as described in Langacker 1987a, 1990a, 1991) is one approach to cognitive linguistics.

It is sometimes asked whether functional linguistics as a whole is defined by anything other than a common opposition to generative grammar. I believe it is, despite the multiplicity of research agendas, methodologies, and theoretical outlooks it comprises. At the risk of preaching, I would say that the various strands of cognitive and functional linguistics are complementary, synergistically related facets of a common global enterprise. Their diversity is a natural consequence of central ideas shared by most practitioners.

Most basically, cognitive and functional linguists believe that language is shaped and constrained by the functions it serves and by a variety of related factors: environmental, biological, psychological, developmental, historical, sociocultural. This alone, of course, does not necessarily distinguish them from formalists. The crucial difference appears to be the following: functionalists tend to believe that an understanding of these factors is *prerequisite* and *foundational* to a revealing characterization of linguistic structure, whereas formalists tend to regard them as *subsequent* or *ancillary* to such a characterization. Stated at this abstract level, the contrast is a matter of emphasis and degree; it sounds inconsequential, which it may in fact prove to be over the long term. In the short term, however, it leads to strikingly different practices and often incommensurate ways of thinking in all phases and at all levels of linguistic investigation.

What are the functions and related factors whose foundational or ancillary status is at issue? As I myself see it, language serves the *semiological function* of allowing conceptualizations to be symbolized by means of sounds and gestures, as well as a multifaceted *interactive function* involving communication, manipulation, expressiveness, and social communion. The semiological and interactive functions are not distinct and independent, but are better seen as two sides of the same coin. Although we can certainly exploit the semiological function of language for purposes of silent thought, we acquire language through social interaction, and verbal thought is not unreasonably regarded as derivative—a kind of mental discourse with oneself or an imagined interlocutor. Conversely, it is primarily by virtue of the symbolizations it affords that language is able to serve its interactive function. Interaction is critically dependent on the embodied minds that engage in it, and cannot be properly understood or described without a detailed characterization of the conceptions they entertain, including their conceptions of the interaction itself and of the interlocutor's conceptions.

A number of other factors have an essential role in shaping linguistic structure. Here I can only devote a few words to each, in hopes of expressing attitudes widely shared among cognitive and functional linguists:

*Environmental factors*
We live in a structured environment that in many fundamental respects is essentially alike for virtually all humans (the constant force of gravity, interaction with physical objects, the alternation of night and day, etc.). We have presumably evolved to accommodate this environment, which provides a common experiential basis for the development of conceptual (and thus semantic) structure.

*Biological factors*
Such factors—anatomical, physiological, perceptual, neurological, genetic—determine and constrain the range of our abilities and the quality of our mental experience. Most obviously, they define a range of possible speech sounds and the parameters for their characterization. They likewise define and structure conceptual space (the basis for meaning and grammar). What we posit for language ought to be plausible from the biological perspective.

*Psychological factors*
What we posit for language must also be psychologically plausible. While linguistic constructs and descriptions have to be posited and justified on linguistic grounds, they ought to be broadly compatible with what is known from psychological studies, and linguistic claims must at some point be confronted with actual psychological evidence. Linguistic descriptions should not be shielded from such findings by apriori assertions of strict modularity, encapsulation, competence versus performance, and so forth.

## Developmental factors

The structure of a linguistic system (for a given speaker, at a given time) is the product of language acquisition, which is one facet of cognitive development. In fact, cognitive and linguistic development represent the basic phenomenon to be accounted for—even for mature speakers, the notion of an established linguistic system constitutes a non-innocent, distorting idealization. The nature of linguistic reality is not adequately captured in the "cross-section" representing one "time slice" along the developmental axis.

## Historical factors

The same distortion inheres in the notion of a synchronic linguistic system. A language at any one time is not just the product of diachronic change, but is also—and more accurately—seen as being in the midst of such change. It is inappropriate, for example, to view the study of grammaticalization as pertaining merely to the antecedent sources of grammatical elements. Rather, it constitutes the study of grammar itself, as all aspects of a grammatical system are at some stage of an ongoing grammaticalization process.

## Sociocultural factors

Whatever may be the extent to which language structure is universal, innately specified, or shaped and constrained by factors common to all speakers, the specific conventions of a given language are culturally transmitted through social interaction, which is also the crucible of their constant evolution. Language is an essential instrument and component of culture, whose reflection in linguistic structure is pervasive and quite significant.

A particular linguistic system (as manifested in a given speaker at a given time) represents one possible resolution of the potential, the constraints, and the shaping pressures that stem from these factors. In the functionalist view, therefore, investigation in all these areas contributes directly to the formulation of a comprehensive linguistic theory and is pertinent even to the most basic and central issues of grammar.

It follows that linguistic investigation, as properly conceived and executed from the functionalist perspective, is an extremely complex and multifaceted enterprise. It has at least the facets listed in (1), all of which are valid and important.

(1)   Domains of linguistic investigation:

| a. *Descriptivist agenda* | b. *Functionalist agenda* |
|---|---|
| structure | function |
| sentences | discourse |
| cognitive representation | actual speech behavior |
| synchronic language structure | language change |
| individual languages | typology and universals |
| acquired linguistic system | acquisition process |
| psychological manifestation | neurological basis |
| theory and description | practical application |

One description of formalism versus functionalism is that formalists tend to believe in the validity of these dichotomies, and assume the priority of the domains in (1)a, constituting what I will call the *descriptivist agenda*. Functionalists tend to do the opposite, believing that these are false dichotomies, and that if anything the domains in (1)b, constituting what I will call the *functionalist agenda*, take precedence.

If we consider just the domains in (1)a, collectively and autonomously, they define the classic enterprise of generative grammar: describing, as a discrete and separate psychological entity, the synchronic sentence grammar of an adult speaker of an individual language. In very broad terms, this enterprise comprises a single methodology. On the other hand, if we recognize the artificiality of that enterprise, and the importance of the domains in (1)b for arriving at a viable characterization of linguistic structure, the number of essential methodologies increases dramatically, since each domain requires one or several very different kinds of investigation. As functionalists, we ought to expect to be doing a large number of very different things. The methodological diversity comes with the territory.

Does functional linguistics have an overall coherence or unity? I believe it has, and ironically, I believe that generative grammar provides an important clue. With all due qualifications—and they are by no means trivial—we have to recognize that the primary target of generative description does exist: a person qualifies as a fluent speaker of a particular language, at a given point in time, by virtue of certain aspects of psychological organization constituting the ability to construct and understand expressions in accordance with conventional patterns. That is, speakers do learn languages, and linguists have to discover their structure and describe them.

Generative grammarians have always recognized and accepted this primary descriptive obligation, even if they have gone about it incorrectly. I believe they are wrong, for example, in viewing the linguistic system as discrete and autonomous. I believe they are wrong about the nature of linguistic structure (e.g. the nature of rules, or the relation between meaning and grammar). I believe they are wrong about the independence and priority of the descriptivist agenda. Nonetheless, they have always accepted the importance of proposing and justifying specific descriptions of language structure.

Functionalists have not always evidenced full acceptance of the descriptive obligation. This is quite understandable, given their strong and correct concern with investigating the domains in (1)b. Still, one should not throw the baby out with the bathwater. Language structure is neither distinct nor autonomous vis-à-vis these domains, and cannot be properly elucidated without taking them into account in a serious way, but it does exist. Moreover, language structure provides the coherence of cognitive-functional linguistics, for it is the place where these domains all come together. In language acquisition, there is something that is being acquired, resulting in more or less stable cognitive structures (or abilities, to use a more dynamic term) that are invoked and manifested in actual speech behavior. Structural patterns sanction expressions used in the construction of discourse. The patterns acquired and used are the product of historical change, which in turn is driven by acquisition and use, yet a substantial structural core is by and large stable and conventional during the life span of a given individual. Typological/universal investigation is naturally dependent on the description of individual languages, as are practical applications such as language teaching.

To help focus the issue, let me quote a brief passage from T. Givón's insightful book *On Understanding Grammar*:

> "The coherence structure of this book resembles a circle. Language sits at the center, defiant and wide open. The various chapters straddle the rim, focusing upon the elusive center from different perspectives" (Givón 1979: xiii).

In my review of this book, I responded as follows:

> "The problem, as I see it, is that G never does attack the center or render it any less elusive. Though he has much of validity and importance to say about the functional motivation of grammatical structure, he is almost totally silent about the character of this structure and the nature of a viable framework for describing it...Explanations for why grammar has the properties it has will be more convincing and firmly grounded when we have some clear idea about precisely what these properties are supposed to be" (Langacker 1981: 444).

In sum, a language does have a conventionally determined structure that children have to learn specifically and linguists have to describe explicitly. However great its functional *motivation*, the structure of a language cannot be *predicted* in full and precise detail on the basis of the motivating factors. Moreover, it has some kind of cognitive representation: major aspects of linguistic structure reside in individual minds.

Functionalists have sometimes been hesitant to take cognition seriously, but I think they have to if they want to achieve a viable account of the phenomena that most concern them. Some arguments I have encountered for resisting this point are listed in (2).

(2)  Invalid arguments against a cognitive approach:
   a. Language structure is strongly shaped and motivated by communicative and discourse factors.
   b. Certain aspects of language have a distributed representation and are not represented in individual minds.
   c. A language is never fixed or static; its elements are continually being "renegotiated" in social interaction.
   d. Linguistic elements are not object-like entities lodged in the brain, but consist rather in patterns of neurological activity.
   e. A linguistic element is generally not static or monolithic, but has numerous contextually-induced variants. In a sufficiently fine-grained account, an element assumes a unique value on every occasion of its use, and every such occasion has some impact on its cognitive representation.
   f. No two speakers have precisely the same inventory of linguistic elements, nor the same values for the elements they share.

To believe that these positions are in conflict with a cognitive account would however be both gratuitous and incorrect. (Most of them, in fact, are clearly stated and defended in Langacker 1987a.) They are not valid reasons for eschewing the descriptivist agenda, but rather conditions on how it ought to be pursued.

My assessment, then, is that the research programs defined by the descriptivist and functionalist agendas are both essential, and that they are interdependent. Language structure is a valid and necessary target of description. It is not however autonomous, nor can one describe it properly without drawing extensively on findings from the domains in (1)b. Conversely, investigation in those domains cannot proceed very far without a viable description of language structure viewed as an integral facet of cognition. It is not a matter of choosing between the two agendas or deciding their relative importance or priority. The problem is rather to pursue both agendas in a compatible and mutually informing manner. Ideally, investigation in all the domains in (1) will proceed synergistically and converge on a coherent understanding of language in all its aspects.

I would characterize my own efforts in formulating cognitive grammar as an attempt to reconcile the two agendas. Certainly I have emphasized the descriptivist agenda, as defined in (1)a. However, I have tried to describe language structure in a way that would mesh with and support the functionalist agenda in (1)b. Even a cursory reading of some basic works in cognitive grammar should make it evident that the pairs in (1) are viewed in graded rather than dichotomous terms, that the descriptive enterprise cannot proceed autonomously, that language is not a discrete and separate psychological entity, and that a "linguistic system" is neither static nor clearly delimited.

The myriad structural patterns a speaker learns and uses vary greatly in their entrenchment, stability, and conventionality. They are dynamic, both in the sense of residing in processing activity (cognitive routines), and also in the sense of constantly being reinforced, refined, adjusted, and adapted to new circumstances, resulting in complex and ever-evolving networks of related patterns. Still, each such pattern has a certain structure at a given point in time, which we must in principle be able to characterize, in order to explicate both its current use and its status as a product of the functions and related factors discussed earlier. Moreover, a substantial number of patterns are stable enough, for a long enough span of time, across a large enough population of speakers, that we can take them as constituting a "linguistic system" susceptible to coherent description. But to the extent that we find it useful to do this, we must resist any tendency to reify such patterns into a discrete and autonomous object of study. While practicality dictates that we must always focus on selected patterns, we must never lose sight of the artificiality of any particular delimitation.

I believe the descriptive apparatus being developed in cognitive grammar can accommodate the complexity, variability, and dynamicity of language structure. In any case, I have always conceived of it as one part of a global enterprise encompassing both the descriptivist and the functionalist agendas. Its overall goal is a comprehensive linguistic theory with the components listed in (3).

(3)  Facets of a comprehensive linguistic theory:
     a. A body of constructs, descriptive notions, and so forth, adequate for the explicit characterization of any element or construction that might be encountered in natural language (being quite general, this would not in itself be strongly predictive).
     b. An enumeration of structures that appear to be prototypical (unmarked, natural, universal, etc.) in language, including their relative degree of prototypicality (likelihood of instantiation).
     c. A functional explanation of the findings at levels a and b.

Cognitive grammar has thus far focused primarily on level a. Research in typology and language universals contributes directly at level b. Many kinds of functional linguistic investigation are aimed at level c. I view research on these three levels as being complementary, simultaneous, interdependent, and mutually informative.

If research on cognitive grammar has so far emphasized the descriptivist agenda, those paying proper attention will nonetheless realize that the functionalist agenda has not at all been ignored. The descriptive apparatus is sufficiently flexible that it should be able to handle the substantial diversity in language structure revealed by typological and cross-linguistic investigation. I and others have used it to investigate grammaticalization and other aspects of language change (e.g. Langacker 1990b, 1992, 1998a; Ryder 1991, 1994; Carey 1994; Rubba 1994; Israel 1996). Despite the focus on structure, function has not altogether been neglected (*pace* Harder 1996). For instance, Langacker (1991) examines a parallel set of semantic functions fulfilled by both noun phrases and finite clauses irrespective of their varied structural manifestations. I am also happy to say that notions of cognitive grammar are starting to be applied to problems in acquisition (Tomasello 1992), neurolinguistics (Kellogg 1994, 1996), language teaching (Taylor 1993), and cultural anthropology (Palmer 1996).

Let me say just a word about discourse. Cognitive grammar has never been a theory of sentence structure (indeed, I have never even tried to define a "sentence"). The sentence has no privileged position in the framework, and basic notions like construal and constructional schemas are potentially applicable to discourse structures of any size (they could even be used in a "dyadic" grammar of the sort DuBois has recently been advocating—cf. Ono and Thompson 1995). An excellent example of cognitive grammar transcending the boundary between sentences and discourse is Karen van Hoek's analysis of pronominal anaphora (1995, 1997). She has not only examined extensive discourse data, but has shown that the same principles (based on reference-point/dominion organization) govern pronoun-antecedent relationships at both the sentence and discourse levels. I should also note the growing body of work combining cognitive linguistic perspectives, especially mental space theory (Fauconnier 1985; Fauconnier and Sweetser 1996), with textual analysis (e.g. Verhagen 1992; Cutrer 1994; Sanders 1994; Sanders and Redeker 1996; Schilperoord 1996; Cornelis 1997).

## 2. Some methodological principles

Because cognitive-functional linguistics has so many important facets of diverse character, there is no unique or uniquely privileged way of pursuing it. For example, I would resist a possible claim that the only data properly used for linguistic description be drawn from actual speech behavior, collected by audio or video recording. I like to think that I am working on real problems, even if I do not go around with a tape recorder, but at the same time I am awfully glad that a lot of people do just that. Lakoff has emphasized the importance of what he calls "grounding explanations", based on neural modeling and the study of metaphor systems and their acquisition. It certainly is important that we pursue these avenues, even though neural modeling and metaphor analysis are quite different, in virtually all respects, from the task of recording actual speech data in a natural setting. Not everybody can engage in typological studies, or psycholinguistic experimentation, but surely we need major research programs in these areas. A division of labor is obviously unavoidable. The most we can realistically expect, in practical terms, is that those pursuing a given line of investigation maintain a certain level of awareness of what is happening in the others, and that serious efforts of coordination and integration be made when feasible.

Because cognitive and functional linguists do so many different things, the methodological principles they all share are limited to general ones applicable in any branch of science. I have in mind very basic principles, for instance, concern with the integrity of one's data, the need for precise formulations leading to testable hypotheses, the desirability of accounting for a wide range of phenomena with a limited set of constructs, and so forth. Two such principles that I have emphasized in cognitive grammar are *conceptual unification* and a kind of *restrictiveness* in regard to what the analyst can validly posit.

In most realms of science, conceptual unification and the reduction of diverse phenomena to a common basis is considered desirable. If it is viable (which I personally regard as having been clearly demonstrated), cognitive grammar achieves a remarkable unification and reduction. To fulfill its semiological function, a language must at least comprise semantic (conceptual) structures, phonological structures, and symbolic links between the two. Cognitive grammar claims that only these elements are necessary. It attempts to show that lexicon, morphology, and syntax form a gradation fully describable as configurations of symbolic structures (form-meaning pairings). It thus achieves the unification of grammar with lexicon and their reduction to symbolic relationships. One should think that linguistic theorists would be delighted at the prospect of such a sweeping conceptual unification as well as the reduction of grammar and lexicon to something more fundamental. I take it to be the default position, which ought to be abandoned only with the greatest reluctance under the force of overwhelming evidence. I have no idea why this attitude is not universally shared.

It should perhaps be emphasized that the *reduction* of grammar to symbolic assemblies is not the same as its *elimination*. Grammar does exist, and has to be described as such as a higher-order phenomenon. It is simply claimed that the elements which figure in such a description are not irreducible grammatical primitives, but can be characterized in terms of more fundamental notions. This is analogous to the description of water as consisting in a certain configuration of hydrogen and oxygen atoms—accepting this reduction does not amount to denying that water exists and has higher-order properties (e.g. wetness, phase changes, chemical properties). Of course, knowing its atomic composition is likely to be helpful in explicating these properties.

The kind of restrictiveness I have in mind pertains to the relationship between actual language data, in the form of occurring expressions, and the mental structures ascribable to speakers as a characterization of their linguistic "knowledge" (or ability). The intent is to limit such structures to those for which a straightforward acquisitional account can in principle be given. I assume two very basic and general cognitive abilities, namely *abstraction* or *schematization* (i.e. reinforcement of the coarse-grained commonality inherent in multiple experiences) and *categorization*. The restriction is that all putative linguistic structures be derivable from the primary data via these mechanisms. This amounts to a sort of "grounding" in Lakoff's sense—a requirement that we have a plausible story of how the structures we posit could actually arise.

The means of implementing this restriction is the *content requirement*, stated in (4).

(4) The only elements ascribable to a linguistic system are:
   a. semantic, phonological, and symbolic structures that are (part of) overtly occurring expressions (hence directly apprehended);
   b. abstractions (schematizations) of permitted structures; and
   c. categorizing relationships between permitted structures (e.g. the relationship between a schema and a specific structure that instantiates it).

Of course, I am not assuming pure induction starting from a blank slate. The acquisition process is part and parcel of the physical, cognitive, social, and cultural development of the language learner, and reflects an innate predisposition to acquire language. This predisposition most likely represents the specialization and adaptation for language of more basic and general structures and abilities. Together with embodied experience, it provides a rich matrix for language acquisition that incorporates the biases we characterize in terms of prototypicality.

Perhaps the most fundamental methodological principle I follow is to look for *converging evidence* from multiple sources. This is especially important considering the diversity of the cognitive-functional enterprise. An essential source of guidance and empirical support for work in any one area is its broad compatibility, and hopefully its convergence in specific details, with the findings of others. Ideally, as a long-term goal, we can aim toward a comprehensive account of language and language structure encompassing all the domains constituting the descriptivist and functionalist agendas. We can hope that these accounts achieve an overall coherence, such that everything fits together in tightly interlocking fashion.

On a more modest scale, I have followed the principle of converging evidence in proposing and motivating some basic descriptive constructs of cognitive grammar. A primary working strategy (explained and illustrated in Langacker 1993a) has been to seek converging evidence from three different sources. First, particular descriptive constructs (e.g. profiling, trajector/landmark alignment, immediate scope, search domain) are shown to be necessary for the adequate semantic description of multiple phenomena in various languages. Second, it is argued that these constructs are commensurate with (if not identical to) independently observable cognitive abilities. Third, it is demonstrated that the same constructs—psychologically natural and semantically necessary—are critical for the explicit characterization of varied grammatical phenomena.

Consider *profiling*. It can first be proposed and strongly motivated as a construct necessary for achieving viable semantic descriptions. One component of this demonstration is to show that an expression's meaning invokes a certain body of conceptual content but cannot be identified with that content taken as a whole. Thus the term *hypotenuse* evokes as the basis for its characterization the conception of a right triangle, but clearly its meaning cannot be equated with that conception per se. A necessary aspect of its meaning is that the expression designates or refers to a particular substructure within that conceptual *base*. Likewise, a term like *aunt* evokes as its base the conception of a certain set of kinship relations, but it *profiles* just one element within it. This is shown in Figure 1 below, where heavy lines indicate profiling.

The need to adopt profiling as a descriptive construct is especially evident in sets of expressions that evoke essentially the same content but contrast in meaning because they designate different facets of it, for instance, *husband* versus *wife*, or *cry* versus *tear*. Profiling affords a principled way of characterizing the meaning difference among sets of expressions that are otherwise very similar if not identical in meaning, and does so for numerous and diverse examples. Thus it has strong motivation from the standpoint of semantic description, in and of itself.

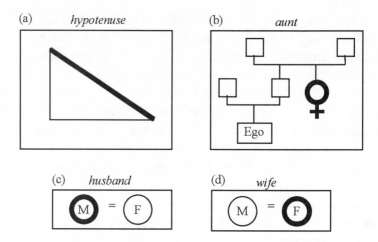

*Figure 1.* Profiling

The next step in the working strategy is to show that the construct in question is plausible, if not independently supported, from the psychological standpoint. Here it is evident that profiling represents a kind of focusing of attention, obviously a basic and well-established cognitive ability. That may not be sufficient, for there may be different kinds and levels of attention, whose cognitive basis is not in any case fully understood. Still, attentional phenomena clearly exist, and profiling is reasonably taken as one of their linguistic manifestations.

The third step in the working strategy is to show that this construct—semantically necessary and psychologically natural—also plays a role in grammatical description. Of course, profiling turns out to be quite fundamental to grammatical structure. For one thing, slight differences in profile/base organization allow a straightforward description of the similarities and differences among subtly contrasting grammatical encodings of comparable situations. Consider the verb *melt*, the participle *melted*, and the adjective *liquid*, as exemplified in (5). *Melt* occurs in (5)a as a transitive verb; in (5)b it is intransitive, exemplifying the "patient-subject" construction (van Oosten 1977), where it co-occurs with adverbs like *easily*; and in (5)c it is a simple change-of-state intransitive. The stative-adjectival participle *melted* in (5)d is comparable grammatically to the adjectival *liquid*, in (5)e.

(5) a. *I **melted** it.*
   b. *It **melted** easily.*
   c. *It **melted** in the heat.*
   d. *It is finally **melted.***
   e. *It is now **liquid.***

The semantic characterizations of these elements are respectively sketched in Figures 2(a)-(e). Circles stand for things (participants). A double arrow indicates causation or the transmission of energy. A single arrow inside a circle represents a participant undergoing an internal change of state. Quite adhocly, I have portrayed a liquid state as a box labeled L. Recall that heavy lines indicate profiling.

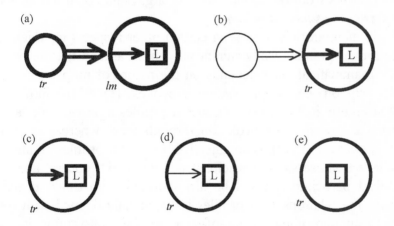

*Figure 2.* Alternative base and profile options

The transitive *melt*, sketched in Figure 2(a), profiles the entire *action chain* including both the causation and the change leading to the resultant state (that of being liquid). In 2(b), representing the patient-subject construction, only the patient's change of state is profiled. However, if only due to the adverb *easily*, the agent's causation is still evoked as an unprofiled facet of the base. The construction therefore retains a force-dynamic construal even though the verb is intransitive (having only a single profiled participant). The simple intransitive construction in 2(c) has the same profile, limited to the change of state, but lacks the causative component. The contrast between the intransitive *melt* and participle *melted* is a matter of alternate profiles on the same base: *melt* profiles the change resulting in the state of liquidity, whereas *melted* profiles the resultant state itself (i.e. the situation of the single participant having the property of being liquid). Finally, *melted* contrasts with the adjective *liquid* by virtue of incorporating the change of state as an unprofiled aspect of its base: something can only be *melted* if it has undergone the process of melting, but something can be *liquid* regardless. Observe that *liquid helium* results from the solidification of a gas and could not normally be referred to as *melted helium*.

I will mention only in passing certain other respects in which profiling proves grammatically significant. I have argued that an expression's grammatical class depends on the nature of its profile in particular, not on the overall content it evokes. Hence the intransitive *melt* in Figure 2(c) is a verb because it profiles a *process*, i.e. a relationship followed in its evolution through time, whereas *melted* in 2(d), like *liquid* in 2(e), is an adjective because it profiles an atemporal relation whose single participant is a thing. (Of course, a stative-adjectival participle can still be distinguished from other adjectives because the relationship it profiles is specifically defined with reference to an unprofiled change-of-state-process constituting its conceptual base.) I have further argued that a *head*, in a particular grammatical construction, is describable as a component structure whose profile is the same as the construction's composite structure profile. Also, a *subordinate clause* is one whose profile is overridden at higher levels of grammatical organization (Langacker 1991: 10.1).

Profiling thus illustrates a specific application of the working strategy based on converging evidence from three sources. Another example of this is *trajector/landmark* organization, pertaining to the relative prominence of participants in a profiled relationship. In a profiled relationship, it is usual for one participant—called the *trajector (tr)*—to be singled out for primary focal prominence, in the sense of being the entity the expression is concerned with locating, characterizing, or assessing in relation to others. If another participant is accorded secondary focal prominence, it is called a *landmark (lm)*. As seen in Figure 2, if there is just a single focal participant it functions as the trajector. The examples also show that trajector status is not tied to any particular semantic role. It is useful to invoke the metaphor of spotlights of focal prominence that can be directed at different elements within a scene.

What is the motivation for adopting these constructs? First, in accordance with the first step in the working strategy, they are necessary for mere descriptive adequacy in the semantic characterization of relational elements. There are, for instance, pairs of relational expressions that invoke the same conceptual content and profile the same relationship, yet contrast semantically. A stock example is *above* versus *below*, diagrammed in Figure 3. Since their content and reference are the same, some additional construct is needed to account for their difference in meaning. The trajector/landmark asymmetry accomplishes this in a way that seems intuitively natural.

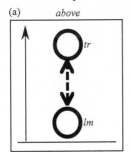 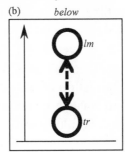

*Figure 3.* Trajector/landmark alignment

What about psychological plausibility, the next step in the working strategy? I have suggested that it is very much akin to the perceptual phenomenon of figure/ground organization, proposing that a trajector be characterized as *primary figure* in a profiled relationship, and a landmark (when present) as *secondary figure*. The contrast between *above* and *below* would then be an instance of figure-ground reversal, which seems right to me intuitively. In any case, we certainly do have the ability—independently of language—to focus selectively on one participant in an interaction. If I watch a boxing match, for example, I can focus on one boxer to observe his techniques, which hand he favors, his footwork, even the number of blows he absorbs (this is analogous to a passive construal). Moreover, as I do so the other boxer naturally becomes a kind of secondary focus: I am following boxer$_1$ mostly in relation to his interaction with boxer$_2$, and only in a peripheral way with the referee, his corner, or the audience. Thus, while there may be questions about the precise psychological characterization of trajector/landmark organization and how it relates to other kinds of attention (like profiling), we have good reason to think that the kind of cognitive ability being appealed to does in fact exist.

We must now ask whether this construct—semantically necessary and psychologically natural—plays a role in grammar. I have long maintained that it provides a conceptual basis for the subject/object asymmetry. I characterize the *subject*, at a given level of grammatical organization, as a nominal element which specifies the trajector of the relationship profiled at that level. An *object* is a nominal element which specifies the landmark at a given level. Illustration is given in (5) and Figure 2, for verbs and clauses, and in Figure 3 for prepositions and prepositional phrases. I personally find it hard to imagine why this characterization of subjects and objects should be in any way controversial, but since it apparently is, I will discuss it extensively.

First, though, I would like to consider one more example of converging evidence, pertaining to the notion *search domain* (Miller and Johnson-Laird 1976: 384; Hawkins 1984). A search domain is defined as the region to which a locative expression confines its trajector, i.e.

the set of trajector locations that will satisfy its specifications. This construct is necessary for the semantic characterization of prepositions and comparable elements. Diagrams like Figure 3 are at best only first approximations, since they show the trajector in just one location vis-à-vis the landmark. However, a preposition or prepositional phrase does not pin down the trajector's location with full precision—it merely identifies a general region (fuzzily bounded) in which one can find it, this region being the search domain. The extent of the search domain, as well as its position with respect to the landmark, have to be described as part of a full, explicit semantic description of prepositional elements. In Figure 4, the approximate search domains of *in* and *above* are shaded.

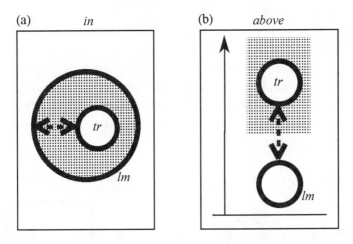

*Figure 4.* Search domains

Does this construct correspond to an independently attested psychological phenomenon? I think it reflects a basic aspect of our ability to find things in space. Obviously, we have the ability to scan through a region in order to find something, and we can single out that region by first locating a salient landmark. In an unfamiliar town, for example, I might use the cathedral tower, visible almost everywhere, as a landmark for getting back to my hotel nearby. I feel secure in knowing that I need only walk to the cathedral and then search the area around it. Thus a typical locative relationship involves three distinct elements: a landmark, a search domain accessible via the landmark, and the target of search.

The focal participants of a preposition represent the landmark and the target of search (the trajector); the search domain per se is not explicitly coded or directly mentioned. I have shown, however, that it has numerous grammatical manifestations and is required for the explicit characterization of various constructions (Langacker 1993a). For example, many speakers accept sentences like these:

(6)  a. *Near the fire is warmer.*
    b. *Under the bed is all dusty.*

I analyze them in terms of the profile of the prepositional phrase being shifted from the locative relationship per se to the search domain implicit in that relationship, as sketched in Figure 5. Hence the search domain becomes explicit, the intended referent of *near the fire* or *under the bed*. In accordance with their subject function, then, these expressions profile a type of thing (a spatial region) and qualify as (derived) nouns by the cognitive grammar definition.

(a)    Relationship Profiled       (b)    Search Domain Profiled

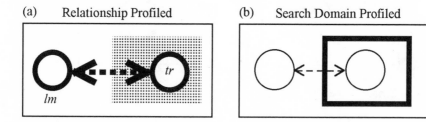

*Figure 5.* Shift of profile to search domain

The search domain also becomes grammatically "visible" with "two-way" prepositions in German, i.e. those whose objects can occur with either accusative or dative case, as in (7).

(7)  a. *Wir wanderten in den (DAT) Bergen.*
        'We wandered around in the mountains.'
     b. *Wir wanderten in die (ACC) Berge.*
        'We wandered into the mountains.'
     c. *Das Auto steht hinter dem (DAT) Baum.*
        'The car is standing behind the tree.'
     d. *Er stellt das Auto hinter den (ACC) Baum.*
        'He parks the car behind the tree.'

The correct generalization is represented in Figure 6: accusative case is used when the trajector's path reaches and enters the search domain, making it the goal in terms of a source-path-goal image schema, and dative case when this is not so (e.g. when the trajector's motion is entirely confined to the preposition's search domain). Hence this construct is needed for an explicit characterization of these case-marking constructions.

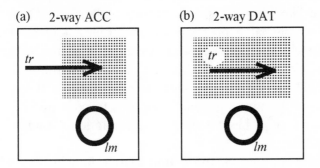

*Figure 6.* Role of search domain in determining case

The notion of a search domain receives additional support from both typological and diachronic considerations, and thus illustrates converging evidence of broader scope. There are many languages, for instance Mixtec (as described by Brugman and Macaulay 1986), in which the function typically served by adpositions is instead fulfilled by nominal elements, often transparently related to body-part nouns. To cite just one example:

(8) *nikązáa   ini        ndúčá*
    drowned  stomach  water
    'Someone drowned in the water.'       [Mixtec]

The Mixtec data is often cited as a striking example of systematic body-part metaphor, as well as metonymy, and I myself have described in detail how constructions like this are put together (1999b). Here, though, I merely want to observe that the entity explicitly coded by a relational noun like *ini* 'stomach' in (8) corresponds to the search domain of adpositional expressions. I suggested earlier that a typical locative relationship involves three distinct elements: a landmark, a search domain accessible via the landmark, and the target of search. An adpositional construction makes salient the landmark and the target of search (i.e. the trajector), leaving the search domain implicit. A language like Mixtec instead chooses to highlight the search domain, via a nominal expression which profiles it, and while other nominals specify the landmark and the target of search, there need be no separate element which profiles the locative relationship and takes them as focal participants. In short, we can make a typological distinction based on how a language chooses to code and highlight the various facets of a basic locative configuration (landmark, search domain, and target).

Diachronic support for the notion search domain comes from the recurrent path of grammaticization whereby relational noun constructions evolve into adpositional constructions. Rubba (1994) discusses this with reference to modern Aramaic, which has a series of locative constructions representing different points along this trajectory. (Of course, there are clear traces of it in English prepositional expressions like *beside* and *in front of*.) Abstracting away from many details, we can note that the overall development involves an initial stage where the major content element profiles a thing, and eventuates in one where it profiles a relationship, for instance, the nominal 'belly' becomes the relational 'in'. In gross terms, this development is sketched in Figure 7:

*Figure 7.* Evolution of body-part noun to preposition

A noun like 'belly' is easily construed as naming a *location* (as opposed to a participant—see Langacker 1993a). To the extent that we construe it as a location, the idea of something occupying that location becomes relevant, as indicated by the dashed-line circle in the middle diagram. The potential for this to occur is part of the very notion of a location. Three elements thus figure in the conception of a body part construed locationally: the host individual (a kind of landmark), the body part itself (a spatial location, hence a potential domain of search), and contingently, an object found in that location (a target of search). These are all of the components of an adpositional relationship. The change from a locational noun to an adposition is therefore just a matter of shifting the profile within the same conceptual base—from the domain of search to the relationship between the landmark and the target of search. (This is, of course, the inverse of the shift described in Figure 5.) Hence the search domain construct proves central to explicating a recurring kind of diachronic development. We can see emerging the basic outlines of an account in which typological, diachronic, and synchronic descriptions converge and achieve an overall coherence where everything fits together in a tightly interlocking fashion.

## 3. Case study: subject and object

I turn now to the proposed characterization of subject and object in terms of focal prominence. The topic is vast and just about the most vexed and controversial in linguistics. It is unlikely that I will resolve it here to anyone's satisfaction but my own. I consider it mainly to illustrate the methodological principle of converging evidence as applied in cognitive grammar. To simplify, I will often limit the discussion to subjects. Extending it to objects is largely a matter of referring to both *primary* and *secondary* focal elements.

It should first be made clear that I am not trying to export Standard-Average-European-type subjects to all languages. Nothing in the proposed description (primary focal participant) specifically ties it to SAE. Though I do offer it as a general and universal characterization of subjects, the degree of its universality has yet to be firmly established and will depend on how it is ultimately applied to particular constructions and various kinds of languages. That is, I am not taking the precise extension of the category "subject" as being given beforehand. The actual strategy is rather different. It starts with a suggested characterization that is arguably appropriate not just for some but for all subjects (including those in "marked" constructions, like passives) in languages for which positing subjects is relatively straightforward. This characterization is sufficiently abstract and flexible that it has a very good chance of being appropriately applied to phenomena in other kinds of languages, for instance, the "topic" or "trigger" in Tagalog (Schachter 1976, 1977; Wouk 1986), and perhaps the "absolutive" in ergative languages. SAE-type subjects are thus regarded as a special case of an aspect of linguistic organization having a wider range of instantiations.

A preliminary question needs to be addressed: Why seek a general description in the first place? Would it not be sufficient to establish a prototype for the subject category? The simplest response is that sound linguistic methodology obliges us to look for a general characterization. I suggest, moreover, that positing a prototype is not sufficient for descriptive purposes.

Language exhibits patterns at all levels of generality. I believe that the preponderance of grammatical knowledge resides in lower-level schemas, that productive patterns characterized at high levels of schematicity constitute a distinct minority. Still, if I am going to describe a language there are times when I will want to refer to subjects or objects—and likewise, to such elements as nouns or verbs—as a class. In some cases a correct generalization that speakers appear to employ makes reference to a high- or even the highest-level schema rather than the category prototype per se. The pattern of "subject-auxiliary inversion" in English questions, for example, applies productively to essentially any kind of subject noun phrase, not just prototypical ones or to the prototype plus a certain set of extensions. A fully productive morphological pattern, such as the "regular" English plural, is applicable to any count noun, not just the prototype and certain extensions. (Needless to say, the existence of an accessible general pattern does not rule out its being preempted by more specific, entrenched alternatives.)

Suppose a pattern is freely and productively applicable to any subject noun phrase. How do I formulate it? If I simply refer to the category prototype, let us say "agent", I am not capturing the generalization that I believe to be valid and operative in the language. It might be argued that a pattern applying to the prototype would tend to be applied by speakers to non-prototypical instances, for one aspect of prototypicality is serving as a model for other members. However, relying on such analogy would not seem sufficient to account for the crisp, secure, essentially categorical behavior that at least some patterns exhibit. Moreover, if a fully general pattern is stated with reference to the category prototype (as opposed to a high-level schema), how can such a pattern be distinguished from one applicable only to the prototype?

In thinking about grammar I often find it useful to consider analogous problems in phonology. The extensive parallels I find between them (Langacker 1987a) is a kind of coherence and converging evidence that I take as supporting basic ideas of cognitive grammar. Phonological constructs like consonant, vowel, and syllable are reasonably considered analogous to grammatical constructs like noun, verb, subject, and object: fundamental and universal notions for which schematic characterizations applicable to all instances are difficult to formulate, though one feels it should be possible. Phonologists often propose rules that apply to all consonants or to any vowel, as in (9)a. They would not find it satisfactory to state such generalizations only with reference to the category prototype. Assuming that [t] is identified as the prototypical consonant, and [a] as the prototypical vowel, the rule in (9)b would not be considered adequate to express the generalization in (9)a, nor could it then be distinguished from a rule applying specifically to the sequence [ata].

(9)  a.  A consonant is voiced between two vowels.
     b.  [t] is voiced between two occurrences of [a].

There may be ways around these problems. One could, for example, treat noun, verb, subject, and object as purely formal categories in an autonomous syntax. But assuming that option is rejected, anyone suggesting that we can do without schematic characterizations of basic notions like these must at least think about the consequences for actually describing certain patterns speakers apparently learn and use.

A further motivation for positing a schematic characterization of subject and object is a general working hypothesis that has emerged over the years in my consideration of different facets of grammatical structure. I have come to believe that fundamental and universal grammatical notions—notably subject, object, noun, verb, and possessive—instantiate inborn *cognitive abilities* and bear natural affinities to experientially grounded *conceptual archetypes*. The abilities are initially manifested in the archetypes, making possible the structured experience which constitutes them, and are subsequently extended to other domains. The abilities and archetypes respectively function as schematic and prototype characterizations of the resulting categories. This view is outlined in Table 1.

*Table 1.* Basis for some fundamental and universal categories

| Category | Basic Cognitive Abilities | Conceptual Archetypes |
|---|---|---|
| Noun | Grouping; conceptual reification | Physical object |
| Verb | Conceiving of a relationship; sequential scanning | Agent-patient interaction |
| Possessive | Invoking a reference point to access another entity | Ownership; kinship; whole-part |
| Subject | Focusing on one participant in a relationship | Agent; theme/patient |
| Object | Focusing secondarily on another participant | Theme/patient |

Nouns, for example, are characterized schematically in terms of the ability to *group* constitutive entities (on the basis of contiguity, similarity, or other factors) and to *reify* a group, i.e. manipulate it as a unitary entity for higher-order cognitive purposes (Langacker 1987c). These abilities are initially manifested in the conception of physical objects, the category prototype, and subsequently extended to cases where their application is less automatic and their effect is thus more visible (e.g. collective nouns like *stack* and *archipelago*). For possessives, the schematic characterization pertains to our ability to invoke the conception of one entity as a *reference point* for purposes of establishing mental contact with another (Langacker 1993b). The prototypes of ownership, kinship, and whole-part relations are conceptual archetypes in which the reference-point function is quite evident. For subject, the basic cognitive ability affording a schematic characterization is figure/ground organization, more precisely our capacity to focus selectively on one participant in conceptualizing a relationship. In events considered prototypical, an agent's activity makes it the obvious choice, although a patient or theme, as the participant in which a change is most evident, is also a serious candidate.

I cannot be sure this story is right, but it is interesting and at least as plausible as any other I have heard, accommodating both embodied experience and the inborn basis needed to ever have that experience. Thus, while I do not claim that schematic characterization (applicable to all members) is possible for every complex category, I believe it is for the categories listed. Moreover, an additional factor strengthens this conviction in the case of subject, object, and possessive.

Recall that a subject is characterized as a nominal expression that specifies the trajector of a profiled relationship, and an object as one that specifies its landmark. The notions trajector and landmark can in turn be informally described in various ways: (i) as primary and secondary figure; (ii) as the participants a relational expression is primarily and secondarily concerned with locating or characterizing ("internal topics"); or (iii) as the first and second participant accessed in building up to the full conception of the profiled relation. These descriptions are meant to be complementary and mutually compatible. For instance, the figure in a scene (i) is the element that first catches our attention (iii), and also the one seen as moving or having a location in relation to the ground (ii).

Description (iii) pertains to a general view of conceptual and grammatical structure I have been exploring in recent years (Langacker 1997a, To appear), which goes by the name of *dynamic conceptualization*. It holds that conceptual structure is not static but emerges and develops through processing time, this temporal dimension being inherent and essential to its characterization. As one aspect of this dynamicity, the conception of a complex structure comprises numerous *natural paths* (cognitively natural orderings of elements), which may or may not coalign. The origin of a natural path can be called a *starting point*. As shown in Figure 8, a natural path often consists of a chain of *foci*, with each focus, $F_i$, evoking a *context*, $C_i$, in which the next focus can be found.

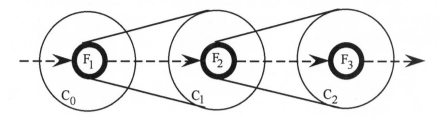

*Figure 8.* Focus chain

A *focus chain* is the same as what I have elsewhere called a *refer-ence-point* chain (Langacker 1993b). The context evoked by a focus or reference point is its *dominion*, and the next focus—found in that dominion—is the *target*. I should note that the temporal sequencing being posited pertains to the inherent organization of dynamic con-ceptions and is no doubt idealized relative to the actual complexities of on-line processing. (A helpful analogy may be reading, where the eye movements that actually occur obscure the ideal, inherent organi-zation based on a single linear progression through the written text.)

I have analyzed numerous grammatical phenomena as being special cases of focus chains or reference-point organization, each pertaining to a different level or dimension of linguistic structure. With respect to symbolization, for example, an expression's phonological pole can be thought of as an initial focus, which evokes a context—the expres-sion's conceptual base—and directs attention to the next focus—the profile—found within it. With respect to the conceptual archetype of localization (finding things in space), the initial focus can be identified as a salient landmark, the context evoked as the search domain asso-ciated with that landmark, and the subsequent focus as the target of search, found within the search domain. Similarly, possessive relation-ships are analyzed in terms of the possessor defining a dominion in which the possessed is found; topic constructions in terms of a propo-sition being integrated in the domain of knowledge evoked by a nomi-nal element; and pronoun-antecedent relationships in terms of a nomi-nal reference point setting up a dominion within which an appropriate pronoun is freely interpretable as being coreferential to it (van Hoek 1995, 1997). The expressions in (10) exemplify focus chains in the dimensions of possession and localization.

(10) a. *Tom's wife's cousin's friend's lawyer*
   b. *In the garage, on the workbench, beside the vise lay a giant dead rat.*

If trajector/landmark organization is a kind of focusing, and the prominence hierarchy *trajector > landmark > other* is a kind of focus chain, what dimension of conceptual or linguistic organization does it pertain to? I suggest that it pertains to the internal structure of a relational conception per se. Since a relationship is *conceptually dependent* with respect to its participants (i.e. its conception presupposes and incorporates that of the participants), we can reasonably posit a natural path given by the order in which participants are evoked or accessed in building up to its full conceptualization. Trajector and landmark can then be characterized as the first and second foci on such a path. The trajector is a starting point, creating the potential for the conception of relationships which are thereby construed with reference to it. A second focus, the landmark, is often evoked to support the conception of a specific relationship "anchored" by the trajector. For example, conceptualizing a person creates the potential for conceiving of that person engaging in some activity, which may involve its interaction with another salient entity. In the case of clauses, typical kinds of interaction include an agent affecting other entities via the transmission of energy, an experiencer establishing mental or perceptual contact with them, and a mover whose path of motion reaches them.

A rather impressive amount of evidence—some circumstantial, some more direct—converges to support the type of characterization proposed. I will first discuss some general considerations and then cite a certain amount of psychological, discourse, and grammatical evidence.

Note first that the trajector/landmark asymmetry is independently motivated as a necessary construct for the semantic description of relational expressions. As seen in Figure 3, it is needed to account for the semantic contrast between *above* and *below*, and for many other such pairs. Moreover, it is not just a characteristic of lexical items, but holds at all levels of structural organization. Complex expressions manifest the same asymmetry as individual prepositions; for instance, *above the house* shows the same asymmetry as *above*, construing the house as a landmark for purposes of locating its schematic trajector. A clause-level manifestation is therefore predicted as well. The subject/object asymmetry is just what we should expect if we take the kind of asymmetry responsible for the semantic contrast between *above* and *below* and apply it *mutatis mutandis* to clausal relationships. If this is correct, it underscores the need for a schematic characterization in terms of focal prominence, since prototypes like agent and patient are only appropriate for verbs and clauses (which describe events), and not, say, for prepositions and prepositional phrases. They do not afford a unified description of the asymmetry between relational participants across levels and across grammatical classes.

A second general consideration is the strong tendency for a clause with only one focal participant to code it as the subject, even when its semantic role is comparable to that of a transitive object, as seen in (5) and Figure 2. Without getting into the explanations and analyses needed to sustain it, let me suggest that the following cross-linguistic generalization will ultimately prove valid: a landmark presupposes a trajector, but not conversely. This follows from the characterization of trajector and landmark as primary and secondary foci. There cannot be a secondary focal participant unless there is also a primary one (otherwise it would itself be primary).

A final general consideration is that the proposed characterization affords sufficient flexibility to accommodate the full range of subject choices. It accommodates both active and passive subjects, as well as the focusing of any participant along an *action chain* leading from agent to patient. In fact, the characterization of subject as initial focus in building up to the full conception of a profiled relationship affords a basis for predicting (rather than merely stipulating) the hierarchy *agent* > *instrument* > *patient,* which Fillmore advanced many years ago (1968) to account for the subject choice in data sets like (11). It merely requires the assumption that the flow of energy along an action chain tends strongly to be adopted as the motivating factor in assigning focal prominence to clausal participants. Now different segments of an action chain can be put in profile, as indicated by the formulas in (11). We observe that the subject is in each case the *head* (initial element) of the *profiled* portion of the action chain. Thus, choices of subject follow from (i) the fact that energy is conceived as flowing from agent to instrument to patient, (ii) different options for profiling, and (iii) the characterization of subject as initial focus in the conception of a profiled relationship.

(11) a. *Sam sliced the salami with a sharp knife.*
$$[\ \mathbf{AG_S} \Rightarrow \mathbf{INSTR} \Rightarrow \mathbf{PAT_O}\ ]$$
   b. *This knife easily sliced the salami.*
$$[\ \mathrm{AG} \Rightarrow \mathbf{INSTR_S} \Rightarrow \mathbf{PAT_O}\ ]$$
   c. *This salami slices easily.*
$$[\ \mathrm{AG} \Rightarrow \mathrm{INSTR} \Rightarrow \mathbf{PAT_S}\ ]$$

However, not every clause is devoted to describing force-dynamic events. Other clause types have other conceptual and discourse motivations, leading to other rationales for subject choice. Here I will merely note the prevalence of constructions which choose as subject an entity construed as the *setting* for a relationship (Langacker 1987b). Various kinds are illustrated in (12).

(12) a. *The next decade will see many amazing new technologies.*
   b. *The garden is swarming with bees.*
   c. *There were several fiddlers on our roof.*
   d. *It appears that interest rates are going up.*

There is no reason at all why focal prominence cannot be conferred on a setting, rather than a participant in the narrow sense. In fact, one kind of natural path—a path of localization, exemplified in (10)b—takes a setting for its starting point: by first directing our attention to a particular setting, we are able to locate a process occurring within it. It is this natural path that motivates the choice of setting as initial focus in setting-subject constructions.

Let me say a word about the so-called "dummy" subjects in (12)c-d. I analyze *there* and *it* as profiling *abstract settings*, perhaps to be thought of as abstract *presentational frames* within which something is going to be introduced. If focal prominence is correctly character-ized as *initial focus* in building up to the full conception of the pro-filed relationship, then presentational elements like *it* and *there* would seem to qualify quite well. A presentational frame in which something is to be introduced functions as a starting point and initial focus al-most as a matter of definition.

Let us turn now to some psychological evidence for the proposed characterization. From one perspective, I described trajector and landmark as primary and secondary figure in a profiled relationship. We should thus expect a certain correlation between the properties of figure/ground organization on the one hand, and trajector/landmark alignment on the other. Perceptually, the figure in a scene "stands out" against the background and initially attracts our attention. The element selected as figure tends to be small, compact, and mobile relative to the ground. But even in cases having a clear asymmetry along these lines, with some effort we can effect a figure-ground reversal and impose an alignment that runs counter to these factors.

Quite some time ago, Talmy (1978) pointed out that what I call the trajector tends to have figure-like properties. Thus in (13)a, the bicy-cle represents the natural choice of figure by virtue of size and mobil-ity. Often, however, when the asymmetry is less drastic, an alternate choice of trajector is possible. I thus regard alternations like *above* versus *below*, and also active versus passive, as cases of figure-ground reversal. As in perceptual figure-ground reversal, one alternative seems less effortful and functions as a kind of default. Thus an active is unmarked relative to a passive, and in (13)b, the first member of each pair tends to be used unless there is some specific reason to override this default choice. It is worth pointing out that the default member in each case chooses as trajector the participant that, in perceptual terms, is likely to be more visible, or is first encountered.

(13) a. *The bicycle is next to the church* vs. *?\*The church is next to the bicycle*
    b. *above* vs. *below; in front of* vs. *in back of; over* vs. *under; on top of* vs. *underneath; before* vs. *after*

My proposed characterization of trajector (initial focus, first participant accessed in building up the conception of a profiled relation, starting point anchoring the conception of a relationship thereby construed with reference to it) is quite reminiscent of a notion proposed by MacWhinney, who also used the term starting point:

> "The speaker uses the first element in the English sentence as a starting point for the organization of the sentence as a whole...Starting points serve as bases for the ACTIVE CONSTRUCTION OF AN ACTIVE PERSPECTIVE" (MacWhinney 1977: 152).

He supported his proposal with experimental results from tasks involving rating, recall, elicited production, comprehension, problem solving, and verification. Observe that MacWhinney defined a starting point in terms of linear order, as the first element in a sentence, not specifically as the subject. In most of his examples, however, the subject was in fact the initial element. While it may be hard to sort out whether particular effects are due to initial position or to subject status, either way they support the general notion of dynamic conceptualization and the importance of sequential access, with respect to which my characterization of trajector represents a special case.

The same holds for what Gernsbacher and Hargreaves call the *structure building framework*, based on the *privilege of primacy*:

"According to the Structure Building Framework, comprehension involves building coherent, mental representations or **structures**...Building mental structures involves several cognitive processes. The first cognitive process is laying a foundation...The next cognitive process is mapping: Incoming information that coheres or relates to previous information is mapped onto the developing structure. It is the process of laying a foundation that...underlies the primacy effects...Laying the foundation for a mental structure requires some mental effort..." (Gernsbacher and Hargreaves 1992: 87-88).

They cite abundant evidence showing that elements occurring early in a sequence take longer to process than those occurring later, but are better in cueing recall.

A striking bit of experimental evidence is provided by Russ Tomlin (1995), who tested the hypothesis in (14), which I interpret as being fully consistent with my proposed characterization:

(14) At the time of utterance formulation, the speaker codes the referent currently in FOCAL ATTENTION as the SYNTACTIC SUBJECT of the utterance.

He tested this by controlling the attention of experimental subjects as they observed a two-participant event, specifically one fish swallowing another, which they then encoded verbally with either an active or a passive sentence. Attention was directed to one of the fish (by means of an arrow flashed on the screen) just 150 ms. prior to the swallowing—too brief an interval for attention to wander in between. Tomlin thus predicted that attention focused on the swallowing fish would lead to the production of an active sentence (e.g. *The red fish swallowed the blue fish*), while attention focused on the swallowee would lead to production of a passive (*The blue fish was swallowed by the red fish*). This happened nearly 100% of the time.

Let me also mention some experimental work by Verfaillie and Daems (1996) suggesting that agents—prototypical subjects—are accessed faster than patients in visual event perception. They relate this to the cross-linguistic tendency for subjects to precede objects in canonical word order.

I turn now to some discourse evidence. One facet of the proposed characterization of trajector identifies it as the participant a relational expression is primarily concerned with locating or characterizing. It follows that if we ask where something is, the answer should express that entity as the subject or trajector, not, say, as a prepositional object. The data in (15)-(16) is thus predicted:

(15) a. *Q: Where is the alarm button?*
   b. *A: The alarm button is just above the light switch.*
   c. *A: \*The light switch is just below the alarm button.*

(16) a. *Q: Where is the light switch?*
   b. *A: The light switch is just below the alarm button.*
   c. *A: \*The alarm button is just above the light switch.*

Someone who has examined actual discourse data much more extensively and seriously than I have, namely Wallace Chafe, has come to essentially the same conclusion concerning the nature of subjects. He even uses the term *starting point* to describe them:

> "...The function of a grammatical subject is to express a starting point to which other information is added" (Chafe 1994: 92).

He notes that in actual, natural conversational discourse, subjects are almost always "light": they are usually given or accessible, but if new they are generally "trivial" in the sense of being mentioned only incidentally and in passing, and are not at all important in the discourse that follows. This "light subject constraint" accords well with the starting point characterization, in that it is natural to build from given or accessible elements. If an initial element takes longer to process, it is advantageous to start with one that can easily be disposed of or taken for granted, rather than one we are forced to dwell on as a sustained center of attention. In this connection, we might note the awkwardness of clausal subjects, especially in conversation. Thus (17) a would normally be avoided in favor of (17)b.

(17) a. *That rent controls restrict the supply of housing is obvious.*
    b. *It is obvious that rent controls restrict the supply of housing.*

Lastly, I return to grammatical evidence, adding a few observations to the points already made. Starting with Keenan and Comrie (1977), linguistic theorists have not uncommonly posited hierarchies headed by subject, followed by object, to account for various grammatical phenomena. Often they are described in terms of "prominence" or "accessibility". To the extent that any hierarchy of this sort is motivated, it supports my proposal, for it is in terms of prominence—explicated as accessibility—that subject and object are most fundamentally characterized. I should observe that the prominence and accessibility of subject and object are inherent in my account, not ad hoc or in need of stipulation.

I have mentioned van Hoek's analysis of pronoun-antecedent relations in terms of reference-point organization. In a viable relation of this sort, the antecedent establishes itself as a reference point (or focus) for purposes of referential identification, and the pronoun occurs in the dominion (or context) accessible via that reference point. Central to van Hoek's analysis is the long recognized importance of subject and object status in this regard. Within a clause, a subject establishes itself as reference point for all other nominal participants and their modifiers. An object establishes itself as reference point for all other non-subject nominal participants and their modifiers. The examples in (18) illustrate these relationships, which directly corroborate the focal prominence ascribed to subject and object.

(18) a. *Tom likes his mother.*
    b. *\*He likes Tom's mother.*
    c. *Jenny put the kitten in its box.*
    d. *\*Jenny put it in the kitten's box.*

I have suggested that subject, topic, and possessor are all to be analyzed as reference points, or initial foci. As nominal reference points, they should have a lot in common, as they do. They nonetheless differ in terms of dimension of structure, level of organization, and the nature of the target found in their dominion. A possessive relationship (e.g. *Tom's wife*) holds between two things, and since it serves the purpose of identifying a nominal referent, it holds at the level of a noun phrase. A topic relationship holds between a nominal element specifying a domain of knowledge and a proposition meant to be integrated in that domain, hence it holds at the clausal level and above. A subject relationship is more intrinsic to a process, hence it is clause-internal. It is the relationship between a profiled process and a thing accessed as starting point for the very purpose of arriving at the full conception of that process. (Thus clause-internal topicalization, being extrinsically motivated by discourse factors, does not per se result in a change of subject—that requires a redefinition of the clausal profile, based on a different inherent starting point.)

Since they all involve nominal reference points, the analysis predicts that subject, topic, and possessive constructions ought to show special affinities to one another. It is of course well known that they do (Langacker 1998b, 1999a). Possessive constructions, for example, are commonly used to specify both the trajector and the landmark of a nominalized verb, as in (19). This is actually predictable from the characterization of trajector and landmark, as well as possessives, in terms of reference-point relationships. When a process is reified and conceived as an abstract thing, the inherent reference-point relation between a focal participant and the process becomes a relation between two things, which is precisely how possessives are described.

(19) *the army's destruction of the city; the city's destruction by the army*

Further support for characterizing subject in terms of prominence and accessibility is the strong tendency for a subject quantifier to assume wide scope with respect to others. What it means for a quantifier to have "wide scope" is that any other quantifier is part of the common property ascribed to each of the individuals quantified. The individuals it quantifies are *directly accessed*, whereas other individuals are accessed only via these, as part of a *process type*, instances of which are distributed across them (Langacker 1991: 3.3, 1996, 1997b). Thus (20) would usually be interpreted as introducing five specific students and saying that each participated in an instance of the process type 'X read three novels'. No specific novels are mentioned.

(20) *Five students read three novels.*

We can see this as a special case of the tendency noted by Keenan (1976) for subjects to have "autonomy properties", such as independent existence and autonomous reference.

The subject also has privileged status in equational sentences, which specify the identity of nominal referents. Although identity per se is a symmetrical relationship, these sentences display an asymmetry that I ascribe to the status of subject as initial point of access. This asymmetry is most evident with plural generics:

(21) a. *Kangaroos are marsupials.*
    b. *\*Marsupials are kangaroos.*

I analyze these as equational sentences that establish identity between sets of indefinite size, comprising "arbitrary instances" of the nominal categories (Langacker 1991: 2.2). Since the extension of kangaroos is included in the extension of marsupials, a set of kangaroos (even the maximal set) can always be equated with a set of marsupials, but not conversely. Thus (21)a will always be valid, for it initially focuses on a set of kangaroos and describes it as coinciding with a set of marsupials. But if we start with a set of marsupials, as in (21)b, its coincidence with a set of kangaroos cannot be assumed.

## 4. Conclusion

The point of this extended exercise has been methodological, to illustrate the principle of converging evidence as it has in fact been practiced in formulating some basic notions of cognitive grammar. Whether or not the demonstration has been successful, it indicates the wide range of considerations that can in principle be brought to bear on specific problems. It is only when evidence converges and interlocks in this fashion that one can start to feel confident about an analysis. Moreover, in working on particular problems one should not lose sight of their place in the global enterprise of describing all aspects of language in cognitive-functional terms. In short, everything has to fit, and everything has to fit together.

## References

Brugman, Claudia, and Monica Macaulay
    1986    Interacting semantic systems: Mixtec expressions of location. *Proceedings of the Annual Meeting of the Berkeley Linguistics Society* 12: 315-327.
Carey, Kathleen
    1994    Pragmatics, subjectivity and the grammaticalization of the English perfect. Ph.D. dissertation, Department of Linguistics, University of California, San Diego.
Chafe, Wallace
    1994    *Discourse, Consciousness, and Time: The Flow and Displacement of Conscious Experience in Speaking and Writing.* Chicago/London: University of Chicago Press.
Cornelis, Louise H.
    1997    *Passive and Perspective.* (Utrecht Studies in Language and Communication 10.) Amsterdam/Atlanta: Editions Rodopi.
Cutrer, Michelle
    1994    Time and tense in narrative and in everyday language. Ph.D. dissertation, Department of Linguistics, University of California, San Diego.

Fauconnier, Gilles
   1985    *Mental Spaces: Aspects of Meaning Construction in Natural Language.* Cambridge, MA/London: MIT Press/Bradford.
Fauconnier, Gilles, and Eve Sweetser (eds.)
   1996    *Spaces, Worlds, and Grammar.* Chicago/London: University of Chicago Press.
Fillmore, Charles J.
   1968    The case for case. In: Emmon Bach and Robert T. Harms (eds.), *Universals in Linguistic Theory*, 1-88. New York: Holt.
Gernsbacher, Morton Ann, and David Hargreaves
   1992    The privilege of primacy: Experimental data and cognitive explanations. In: Doris L. Payne (ed.), *Pragmatics of Word Order Flexibility*, 83-116. (Typological Studies in Language 22.) Amsterdam/Philadelphia: John Benjamins.
Givón, Talmy
   1979    *On Understanding Grammar.* (Perspectives in Neurolinguistics and Psycholinguistics.) New York: Academic Press.
Harder, Peter
   1996    *Functional Semantics: A Theory of Meaning, Structure and Tense in English.* (Trends in Linguistics Studies and Monographs 87.) Berlin/New York: Mouton de Gruyter.
Hawkins, Bruce W.
   1984    The semantics of English spatial prepositions. Ph.D. dissertation, Department of Linguistics, University of California, San Diego.
Israel, Michael
   1996    The *way* constructions grow. In: Adele E. Goldberg (ed.), *Conceptual Structure, Discourse and Language*, 217-230. Stanford: CSLI Publications.
Keenan, Edward L.
   1976    Towards a universal definition of "subject". In: Charles N. Li (ed.), *Subject and Topic*, 303-333. New York: Academic Press.
Keenan, Edward L., and Bernard Comrie
   1977    Noun phrase accessibility and universal grammar. *Linguistic Inquiry* 8: 63-99.
Kellogg, Margaret Kimberly
   1994    Conceptual mechanisms underlying noun and verb categorization: Evidence from paraphasia. *Proceedings of the Annual Meeting of the Berkeley Linguistics Society* 20: 300-309.

1996    Neurolinguistic evidence of some conceptual properties of nouns and verbs. Ph.D. dissertation, Department of Linguistics, University of California, San Diego.

Langacker, Ronald W.

1981    Review of Talmy Givón, *On Understanding Grammar*. *Language* 57: 436-445.

1987a   *Foundations of Cognitive Grammar*, Volume 1, *Theoretical Prerequisites*. Stanford: Stanford University Press.

1987b   Grammatical ramifications of the setting/participant distinction. *Proceedings of the Annual Meeting of the Berkeley Linguistics Society* 13: 383-394.

1987c   Nouns and verbs. *Language* 63: 53-94.

1990a   *Concept, Image, and Symbol: The Cognitive Basis of Grammar*. (Cognitive Linguistics Research 1.) Berlin/New York: Mouton de Gruyter. [paperback edition 1991]

1990b   Subjectification. *Cognitive Linguistics* 1: 5-38.

1991    *Foundations of Cognitive Grammar*, Volume 2, *Descriptive Application*. Stanford: Stanford University Press.

1992    Prepositions as grammatical(izing) elements. *Leuvense Bijdragen* 81: 287-309.

1993a   Grammatical traces of some "invisible" semantic constructs. *Language Sciences* 15: 323-355.

1993b   Reference-point constructions. *Cognitive Linguistics* 4: 1-38.

1996    Conceptual grouping and pronominal anaphora. In: Barbara Fox (ed.), *Studies in Anaphora*, 333-378. (Typological Studies in Language 33.) Amsterdam/Philadelphia: John Benjamins.

1997a   A dynamic account of grammatical function. In: Joan Bybee, John Haiman, and Sandra A. Thompson (eds.), *Essays on Language Function and Language Type Dedicated to T. Givón*, 249-273. Amsterdam/Philadelphia: John Benjamins.

1997b   Generics and habituals. In: Angeliki Athanasiadou and René Dirven (eds.), *On Conditionals Again*, 191-222. (Current Issues in Linguistic Theory 143.) Amsterdam/Philadelphia: John Benjamins.

1998a   On subjectification and grammaticization. In: Jean-Pierre Koenig (ed.), *Discourse and Cognition: Bridging the Gap*, 71-89. Stanford: CSLI Publications.

1998b   Topic, subject, and possessor. *Linguistic Notes from La Jolla* 19: 1-28.

1999a   Double-subject constructions. In: Sung-Yun Bak (ed.), *Linguistics in the Morning Calm 4*, 83-104. Seoul: Hanshin.

1999b    A study in unified diversity: English and Mixtec locatives. *RASK* 9/10: 215-256. [Jacob L. Mey and Andrzej Boguslawski (eds.), *'E Pluribus Una': The One in the Many* (For Anna Wierzbicka), Odense University Press.]

to app.    Dynamic conceptualization in grammatical structure.

MacWhinney, Brian
1977    Starting points. *Language* 53: 152-168.

Miller, George A., and Philip N. Johnson-Laird
1976    *Language and Perception.* Cambridge, MA: Harvard University Press/Belknap.

Ono, Tsuyoshi, and Sandra A. Thompson
1995    What can conversation tell us about syntax? In: Philip W. Davis (ed.), *Alternative Linguistics: Descriptive and Theoretical Modes*, 213-271. (Current Issues in Linguistic Theory 102.) Amsterdam/Philadelphia: John Benjamins.

Palmer, Gary B.
1996    *Toward a Theory of Cultural Linguistics.* Austin: University of Texas Press.

Rubba, Jo
1994    Grammaticization as semantic change: A case study of preposition development. In: William Pagliuca (ed.), *Perspectives on Grammaticalization*, 81-101. (Current Issues in Linguistic Theory 109.) Amsterdam/Philadelphia: John Benjamins.

Ryder, Mary Ellen
1991    Mixers, mufflers and mousers: the extending of the -er suffix as a case of prototype reanalysis. *Proceedings of the Annual Meeting of the Berkeley Linguistics Society* 17: 299-311.
1994    *Ordered Chaos: The Interpretation of English Noun-Noun Compounds.* (University of California Publications in Linguistics 123.) Berkeley: University of California Press.

Sanders, José
1994    Perspective in narrative discourse. Ph.D. dissertation, Department of Language and Literature, Tilburg University.

Sanders, José, and Gisela Redeker
1996    Perspective and the representation of speech and thought in narrative discourse. In: Gilles Fauconnier and Eve Sweetser (eds.), *Spaces, Worlds, and Grammar*, 290-317. Chicago/London: University of Chicago Press.

58    Ronald W. Langacker

Schachter, Paul
  1976    The subject in Philippine languages: Topic, actor, actor-topic, or none of the above? In: Charles N. Li (ed.), *Subject and Topic*, 491-518. New York: Academic Press.
  1977    Reference-related and role-related properties of subjects. In: Peter Cole and Jerrold M. Sadock (eds.), *Syntax and Semantics*, Volume 8, *Grammatical Relations*, 279-306. New York: Academic Press.
Schilperoord, Joost
  1996    *It's About Time: Temporal Aspects of Cognitive Processes in Text Production*. (Utrecht Studies in Language and Communication 6.) Amsterdam/Atlanta: Editions Rodopi.
Talmy, Leonard
  1978    Figure and ground in complex sentences. In: Joseph H. Greenberg (ed.), *Universals of Human Language*, Volume 4, *Syntax*, 625-649. Stanford: Stanford University Press.
Taylor, John R.
  1993    Some pedagogical implications of cognitive linguistics. In: Richard A. Geiger and Brygida Rudzka-Ostyn (eds.), *Conceptualizations and Mental Processing in Language*, 201-223. (Cognitive Linguistics Research 3.) Berlin/New York: Mouton de Gruyter.
Tomasello, Michael
  1992    *First Verbs: A Case Study of Early Grammatical Development*. Cambridge: Cambridge University Press.
Tomlin, Russell S.
  1995    Focal attention, voice, and word order. In: Pamela Downing and Michael Noonan (eds.), *Word Order in Discourse*, 517-554. (Typological Studies in Language 30.) Amsterdam/Philadelphia: John Benjamins.
van Hoek, Karen
  1995    Conceptual reference points: A cognitive grammar account of pronominal anaphora constraints. *Language* 71: 310-340.
  1997    *Anaphora and Conceptual Structure*. Chicago/London: University of Chicago Press.
van Oosten, Jeanne
  1977    Subjects and agenthood in English. *Papers from the Regional Meeting of the Chicago Linguistic Society* 13: 459-471.
Verfaillie, Karl, and Anja Daems
  1996    The priority of the agent in visual event perception: On the cognitive basis of grammatical agent-patient asymmetries. *Cognitive Linguistics* 7: 131-147.

Verhagen, Arie
  1992    Praxis of linguistics: Passives in Dutch. *Cognitive Linguistics* 3: 301-
          342.
Wouk, Fay
  1986    Transitivity in Batak and Tagalog. *Studies in Language* 10: 391-424.

# Some contributions of typology to cognitive linguistics, and vice versa

## William Croft

### 1. Thinking like a typologist (with apologies to Aldo Leopold)

I am both a typologist and a cognitive linguist. What does it mean to be either one of those types of linguists? Being a typologist or being a cognitive linguist are two ways of thinking about language; they are "theoretical styles" (à la "cultural styles" of Pierre Bourdieu). These two theoretical styles are harmonious, along with (discourse) functionalism and variationist sociolinguistics.

One cannot really make explicit a "manual of theoretical style". But I can identify certain ways of thinking that come naturally to me as a typologist but which do not always seem to come naturally to other theoretical linguists (particularly formalists, but also others).

Above all, variation is basic. It is the normal state of language which we have to deal with. It is dealing mainly with cross-linguistic variation that is typology's claim to fame. But typologists have also come to integrate diachronic variation and synchronic language-internal variation into their purview. Everything else about doing typology represents typology's way of dealing with the fact of variation.

The first way in which a typologist deals with variation is accepting that arbitrariness in language should be accepted. Not everything in language can be, or should be, explainable, either in terms of formal or functional general principles, abstract generalizations, and so forth. If it were, all languages would be alike, all languages would be internally invariant, and no languages would change. A typologist endeavors to make his/her language universals explainable (e.g., in functional or cognitive terms), and hence anything arbitrary about language is, we hope, language-particular. But that means that the grammars of particular languages involve some arbitrariness mixed in with the motivated universal principles (Croft 1995: 504-9). This is because the principled motivations compete with each other, and the resolution of the competition for each language is always partly arbitrary. This way of thinking is quite foreign to many non-typological linguists, who seek an explanation for everything in a grammar. Having an eye on the slightly different language across the ocean, or down the road, generally reminds the typologist of the futility of the Leibnizian view.

A typologist also accepts that all things in grammar must pass. Explanations are to be found in the dynamic aspects of language, at the micro-level—language use—as well as the macro-level—the broad sweep of grammatical changes that take generations to work themselves out. Synchronic language states are just snapshots of a dynamic process emerging originally from language use in conversational interaction. This thinking follows from the recognition of arbitrariness. What is arbitrary can change (since it is not dictated by general principles)—and does. What is functional are the "background" universals that govern the dynamic or diachronic universals. Although the dynamic turn in typology is thought of as emerging in the 1970s (e.g. Givón 1971, 1979), in fact Greenberg himself initiated it at the same time that he developed modern typology (Greenberg 1966a, 1969).

Finally, a typologist looks for universals across languages, not within them. The fundamental generalization of typology, an implicational universal, can only be observed by examining a large range of languages. Typological universals exist only across languages. Some universals appear to exist in individual languages as well, namely the so-called absolute universals such as "every language has nouns and verbs". But a careful formulation of absolute universals such as the noun/verb universal reveals that they are really systematic cross-linguistic patterns of variation (in this case, prototypes; Croft 1991, chapters 1-3). The essentially cross-linguistic character of language universals follows from the derivative character of stasis. An absolute universal—"all languages have X"—would be a static one; but no grammatical category or construction stays the same.

In fact, anyone who does typology soon learns that there is no synchronic typological universal without exceptions. But a typologist sees not only the counterexamples—which, after all, must be possible language types, since they actually exist—but also the highly skewed distribution. (Joe Greenberg once said, what is striking is that the more languages you look at, the more familiar they all look. There are fewer surprises in typology than one might think, or hope...) In a diachronic perspective, where every language type comes into existence and passes on to another type with different degrees of frequency and stability, and the gradualness of change means all sorts of "anomalous" intermediate types are found, possibility is much less important than probability. As a result, there has been a shift from constraining possible language types to calculating probable language types.

This, then, is thinking about language like a typologist: variation, arbitrariness, change, probability and the fundamentally cross-linguistic character of universals. In Aldo Leopold's famous essay "Thinking like a mountain" (Leopold 1949), he speaks of his conversion to an ecological approach to the land and its inhabitants upon seeing the fierce green fire die in the eyes of a wolf he has shot and killed. In typology, one also learns upon seeing the fire of a language, any language, die in its last speaker, that something important is lost to the world.

In this paper, I will describe how a typologist approaches two fundamental problems in cognitive linguistics, one on the nature of syntax and the other on the nature of semantics. Thinking like a typologist on these two questions brings new perspectives onto the problems that cognitive linguistics struggles with. I hope that these thoughts will shed new light on the nature of syntax and semantics. They will also reveal how cognitive linguistics has itself made important contributions to how typologists think about these same questions.

## 2. Typology and construction grammar

### 2.1. Constructions in cognitive linguistics

It has now become de rigueur in cognitive linguistics to acknowledge the centrality of constructions in the representation of syntactic knowledge in the human mind. In some cases this is a declaration of principle, and a way to show how cognitive linguistics is fundamentally different from generative grammar. Some cognitive linguists have presented detailed examples of the syntactic analysis of constructions (for example, Fillmore, Kay and O'Connor 1988, Michaelis and Lambrecht 1996), and in a few cases more comprehensive models of syntactic representation in "construction grammar" (Langacker 1987, Fillmore and Kay 1993, Goldberg 1995). From these and other studies of syntax in cognitive linguistics, one quickly sees that there is some variation in what constitutes "construction grammar". But we can also fairly easily draw out some general principles which all cognitive linguistic approaches to constructions appear to have in common.

First, constructions are independent grammatical entities. They exist in the mind as integrated wholes that are greater than the sum of their component categories and relations, even when those categories and relations themselves appear to have an independent psychological representation. This principle follows from one aspect of thinking like a cognitive linguist: redundancy in mental representation should be accepted; it shouldn't be rooted out at its every appearance.

Second, constructions are symbolic units. Although constructions are complex syntactic entities, such as the English double object construction *[SBJ VERB OBJ1 OBJ2]*, they are complexes of form and function. That is, constructions possess distinctive morphology (such as *the* in *the more, the better*, which is etymologically distinct from the definite article), distinctive syntax (such as the two objects in the double object construction), distinctive semantics (such as the complex scalar models required for the *[SENTENCE1, let alone SENTENCE2]* construction described by Fillmore, Kay and O'Connor), and distinctive pragmatics/discourse function (such as the differences between the preposed purpose clause construction and the postposed purpose clause construction described by Thompson 1985, or between the WH-cleft and the *It*-cleft described by Prince 1978). Constructions also have their own sociolinguistic value (such as that associated with the aptly named "Yiddish movement" construction described by Prince 1981) and phonetic/phonological manifestation (such as the difference in reduction of *don't* in *I don't know* and *why don't you* versus ordinary verbal negation shown by Bybee and Scheibman 1997). Another aspect of thinking like a cognitive linguist is what I call "thinking vertically": focusing on linguistic units as complexes of different types of linguistic information bound together, instead of "thinking horizontally", where the different types of linguistic information are separated into levels (or in the more trendy non-orientational metaphor, modules).

Third, constructions exist to varying degrees of schematicity. There is a continuum between lexically completely fixed idioms, such as *[As American as apple pie]* and highly schematic "rule schemas" such as the aforementioned *[SBJ VERB OBJ1 OBJ2]*. All possibilities in between can be found, with so-called idioms of varying degrees of flexibility such as *[pull NP's leg]* or *[come/bring NP to a head, NP be brought to a head]*, and so forth. There is also a continuum between "lexicon", which cognitive linguists think of as merely the one-word, fully specified symbolic units of our linguistic knowledge, and "grammar" in the traditional sense, which are the multiword schematic symbolic units of our language. (Again, this view is compatible with another way of thinking like a cognitive linguist, which can be summed up in the slogan "everything is gradient".)

Lastly, constructions are organized into a network of grammatical knowledge in the mind. The precise nature of this network is a matter of difference of opinion. The "Construction Grammar school" (e.g., Fillmore and Kay 1993) tend to think of it as a knowledge network as found in artificial intelligence research, where constructions and their elements are representational units linked by taxonomic (IS-A) links and meronomic (HAVE-AS-PART) links. The "Cognitive Grammar school" (e.g., Langacker 1987) tend to appeal to distributed, spreading/interactive activation models which are generally associated with connectionism (Goldberg 1995 straddles both schools). I am not particularly concerned with this issue here; the main point is that for both approaches, knowledge of linguistic constructions is organized into a network.

## 2.2. Constructions in typology

### 2.2.1. Constructions as symbolic units

Typologists for the most part have not explicitly advocated some version of construction grammar. However, most typologists begin with the traditional, informal definition of constructions, and so one finds typological studies of the relative clause construction (Lehmann 1984), the passive (Siewierska 1985), the comparative (Stassen 1985), and so on.

There is one important respect in which the typological approach to syntax and the cognitive linguistic approach are similar. Typologists must first confront the question of what grammatical categories and constructions should be identified as "similar" or comparable across languages (Croft 1990: 11-18). From the beginning of modern typology, typologists have identified grammatical structures as similar by virtue of their encoding similar functions (see for example, Greenberg 1966b: 74, Keenan and Comrie 1977: 63, Downing 1978: 377-80, Stassen 1985: 14). That is, it is assumed that categories/ constructions are symbolic units, and the variation in the formal (structural) side of a symbolic unit across languages is rendered analyzable by comparing similar functions or meanings. This is one important respect in which the typological and the cognitive linguistic styles are harmonious.

## 2.2.2. A typological argument for a radical construction grammar

An important problem that arises in typology leads me to the conclusion that in fact the sort of construction grammar that is needed to describe the syntax of the world's languages is more radical than even most cognitive linguists have envisioned. This problem is the definition of the basic categories and relations that are assumed to constitute the elements of a construction. To see what the problem is, and the solution that a typological approach ineluctably pushes us towards, let us begin by illustrating how a category is defined within a single language.

The standard method for defining a category, first codified by American structuralist linguists, is *distributional analysis*. In distributional analysis, categories are defined by their distribution across a class of constructions. I have just described the distribution of a category as being across constructions, but in much of the syntactic literature, distribution is defined in terms of whether the category in question "undergoes a syntactic rule" or whether "a syntactic rule applies to" the category. A syntactic rule such as Passivization has a construction as an output, namely, the passive construction. One need not believe in the transformational approach assumed by this terminology to recognize good old distributional analysis in these approaches. Other terms used to describe constructional distribution are "tests", "arguments" or "criteria" for category membership.

A well-known example of distributional analysis is the set of constructions used to define Subject as a grammatical relation in English (the examples are adapted from Croft 1990: 8, but they follow standard arguments in the syntactic literature). The distribution is illustrated in sentences (1) through (5):

(1)  a. *He congratulated him/*he.*
     b. *He died.*

(2)  a. *Teresa likes/*like horses.*
     b. *Teresa sings.*

(3)  a. *Jack wants to build his own house.*
     b. *Jack wants to leave.*

(4)  a. *Help John!* [addressed to Teresa]
     b. *\*Teresa help!* [addressed to John]
     c. *Sing!*

(5)  a. *John found a ring and took it home with him.*
     b. *\*John found a ring and was gold.* [the ring was gold]
     c. *John got up and left.*

In (1)a-b, the preverbal noun phrase in both transitive and intransitive sentences (labeled A and S respectively in the typological literature), takes nominative case marking, while the postverbal noun phrase (labeled P) is accusative. In (2), A or S triggers verb agreement, while P does not. In (3), the understood (unexpressed) argument of the infinitival complement is A/S, not P. In (4), the unexpressed argument of the imperative is A/S, not P. In (5), the unexpressed argument of the second clause in a conjoined sentence is coreferential with A/S of the first clause, not P. The distributional pattern of A/S versus P is summarized in Table 1.

*Table 1.* Traditional constructional tests for subjecthood in English.

|                                    | I   | II  | III | IV  | V   |
|------------------------------------|-----|-----|-----|-----|-----|
| Preverbal NP (A + S arguments)     | √   | √   | √   | √   | √   |
| Postverbal NP (P argument)         | *   | *   | *   | *   | *   |

I:    case marking
II:   agreement
III:  unexpressed controlled argument of infinitive complement
IV:   unexpressed argument of imperative
V:    unexpressed shared argument in conjoined sentence

While distributional analysis is widely used, certain problems in its application arise again and again. In fact, these problems were recognized by the American structuralists, and are the main subject matter of much of the syntactic literature, where they are described as problems in deciding on the existence or status of particular categories such as Subject, Noun, Head, Subordination in individual languages. The main problems can be grouped under three main headings.

First, the constructions that are used for defining categories in one language may be absent in another language. For example, Vietnamese almost entirely lacks the morphological inflections that are used for distinguishing lexical-syntactic categories such as Noun, Verb, Adjective, Auxiliary and so on (Thompson 1965/1987). Wardaman lacks coordination and infinitival complements, and allows unexpressed (null) arguments of all kinds, so the constructions III-V in Table 1 for Subject in English simply do not apply to syntactic arguments in Wardaman (Merlan 1994). As Nida wrote, in listing typical morphological criteria for word classes, "There are so many languages in which the following generalizations do not hold that one is tempted to avoid such statements altogether" (Nida 1949: 149, fn 30).

The problem is that there is no a priori way to decide between choosing another construction and assuming it defines the same universal syntactic primitive Noun or Subject across languages, or to conclude that the primitive category does not exist in, or is irrelevant for, that language. Different linguists take different approaches, but neither approach is a priori justified. The choice depends more on the linguist's theoretical beliefs about universal categories. If s/he believes in universal syntactic primitives, s/he will find some constructions to define them in every language. If s/he believes that the language in question lacks the categories, s/he will not look for other constructions that might define the category.

Second, when the same (or similar) constructions are found in two different languages, sometimes there is a wildly different distribution from one language to another. For example, in English, the category Verb is defined largely on morphological inflectional grounds, and a class of words denoting processes such as *dance* or *break* and stative relations such as *love* or *need* is found. But in Makah, words of all semantic classes can be inflected morphologically (Jacobsen 1979). This is illustrated below for what in English would be verbs (6), nouns (7), adjectives (8) and adverbs (9):

(6)  *k'upšil*                    *baʔas*        *ʔu·yuq*
     point:MOM:INDIC:3    house        OBJ
     'He's pointing at the house.'

(7)  *babałdis*
     white.man:INDIC:1SG
     'I'm a white man.'

(8)  *ʔi·ʔi·x̣ʷʔi*
     big:INDIC:3
     'He's big.'

(9)  *huʔaxis*                      *haʔukʷ'ap*
     still:INDIC:1SG        eat:CAUS
     'I'm still feeding him.'

The problem here is that there is no a priori way to decide whether to call the Makah category Verb, and conclude that almost all lexical items are verbs (as does Hengeveld 1992 for instance); or to choose some other construction(s) to distinguish a category Verb not that different from the more restricted English category (as does Jacobsen 1979).

Third, there is often a mismatch in distribution between constructions within a particular language. This can be illustrated for the category Direct Object in English. This category is typically defined using two constructions: the encoding of the Direct Object as a pre-positionless postverbal NP, and the occurrence of the Direct Object as the Subject of the counterpart Passive construction. In (10) and (11), the two constructions coincide in their distribution, thereby defining Direct Objects and Obliques. But in (12) through (14), the two constructions do not coincide in their distribution.

(10) a. *Jack kissed Janet.*
     b. *Janet was kissed by Jack.*

(11) a. *The old man walked with a cane.*
     b. *\*The old man walked a cane.*
     c. *\*A cane was walked with by the old man.*

(12) a. *Jack weighs fifteen stone.*
     b. *\*Fifteen stone is weighed by Jack.*

(13) a. *1997 witnessed the demise of 18 years of Tory rule in Britain.*
     b. *\*The demise of 18 years of Tory rule in Britain was witnessed by 1997.*

(14) a. *Claude Debussy lived in this house.*
     b. *\*Claude Debussy lived this house.*
     c. *This house was lived in by Claude Debussy.*

72     William Croft

Every possible distributional pattern of the two constructions is attested, as can be seen in Table 2:

*Table 2.* Distribution of argument types across "tests for direct objecthood"

|        | Prepositionless postverbal NP | Passive subject |
|--------|-------------------------------|-----------------|
| 10     | √                             | √               |
| 11     | *                             | *               |
| 12, 13 | √                             | *               |
| 14     | *                             | √               |

Here, the problem is that there is no a priori way to decide whether to select one criterion—the choice taken by S. Anderson 1976 in defining "deep subjects"—and if so, which one(s); or whether the anomalous cases (i.e. those where the other criterion fails) are a subclass of the category in question or not; or whether there are in fact four categories, as defined by the cross-cutting distributional patterns given in Table 2.

This problem seems more serious because it occurs within a single language. Most linguists (other than typologists) tend to analyze one language at a time, and devote most of their analyses to identifying the categories of the language. Bloomfield and Harris were aware of this problem:

> Form-classes are not mutually exclusive, but cross each other and overlap and are included one within the other, and so on. (Bloomfield 1933: 269)

> ...in many cases the complete adherence to morpheme-distribution classes would lead to a relatively large number of different classes. (Harris 1946: 177)

> If we seek to form classes of morphemes such that all the morphemes in a particular class will have identical distributions, we will frequently achieve little success. It will often be found that few morphemes occur in precisely all the environments in which some other morphemes occur, and in no other environments. (Harris 1951: 244, discussing analysis of a corpus)

The problem is that the distributional method in itself does not provide any justification for deciding which distributional criteria are the "right" ones for establishing syntactic primitives (categories and relations) demanded by contemporary syntactic theories.

The real problem is not in the distributional method itself, however. The real problem is that there is a fundamental theoretical conflict between the distributional method and the assumption that the categories and relations defined by constructions are the syntactic primitives used to represent grammatical knowledge. There is a logical fallacy in the relationship between the distributional method and the formal syntactic model of representation that the distributional method is alleged to support. Constructions are used to define categories—this is the distributional method. But then the categories are taken as primitives which define constructions—this is the standard syntactic model of representation. This approach is circular.

Does this mean that the distributional method is wrong, and should be discarded in favor of another method? I think not. Yet what Bloomfield, Harris and their successors have done is essentially to abandon the distributional method. In the continuation of the passages cited above, Bloomfield and Harris both advocate the selective use of the distributional method:

> ...a system of parts of speech in a language like English cannot be set up in any fully satisfactory way: *our list of parts of speech will depend upon which functions we take to be the most important.* (Bloomfield 1933: 269 [emphasis mine])

> ...we change over from correlating each morpheme with all its environments, to *correlating selected environments (frames) with all the morphemes that enter them.* (Harris 1946: 177 [emphasis mine])

Selecting some distributional environments (constructions) to define primitive syntactic categories and ignoring others is empirically irresponsible: it is throwing away facts about the language in order to preserve the notion that constructions are built out of atomic syntactic primitives (that is, categories such as Noun or Subject). The distributional method is perfectly valid: it accurately and completely describes the grammatical patterns of a language. There is no proper alternative to distributional analysis.

Instead, we should abandon the assumption that syntactic structures are made up of primitive categories and relations (whether these are language-universal or language-particular). This move may appear difficult or discomforting at first, but it is not impossible or illogical. In fact, it leads to a truly radical construction grammar (see Croft in preparation).

In a radical construction grammar, constructions, not categories and relations, are the basic, primitive units of syntactic representation. Constructions are conventional units consisting of one or more subunits in relation to each other, with meanings associated with the whole and with the subunits and relations. All that is necessary to identify constructions is the ability to analyze a syntactic structure into subunits and relations. It is not necessary to treat those units and relations as independent primitives of the language, let alone as cross-linguistic universal categories. (Constructions are themselves also language-particular in their structure—there is no universal "passive" construction, for example—but they are functionally comparable across languages, as was noted in §2.2.1.)

In this view, the grammatical knowledge of a speaker is knowledge of constructions (as form-meaning pairings), lexical items (also as form-meaning pairings), and the mapping between lexical items and the constructions they fit in, which is many-to-many. It is not necessary to posit grammatical categories as primitive units. Moreover, this view of grammatical knowledge is quite compatible with the connectionist-style network models that are favored by most cognitive linguists. Research in connectionist modeling (and also statistical natural language processing) demonstrates that it is not impossible to model distributional knowledge directly, that is, without positing primitive grammatical categories such as Noun or Subject.

Grammatical categories (of the necessary-and-sufficient sort) are derivative, in fact epiphenomenal. They can be defined either construction-specifically—the class of lexical items that fits into a single construction—or word-specifically—the class of words that has an identical distribution across all constructions of the language. Construction-specific definition of categories corresponds to defining categories by the columns in Tables 1 and 2; word-specific definition of categories corresponds to defining categories by the rows in Tables 1 and 2. But it is the tables themselves—the full pattern of distribution of words in constructions—that is basic in syntax.

If a radical construction grammar is accepted, it would explain one puzzle about the relationship between "formalist" syntactic models and "functionalist" (typological, cognitive, discourse-pragmatic etc.) models of grammar. It has often been noted that formalist theories and functionalist theories appear to be talking about very different things. Formalists devote much of their time to perfecting the set of primitive elements and relations and the constraints on their combination for syntactic representation. Functionalists devote little time to that task, instead looking at the form-function relation, discourse context, and cross-linguistic variation and change. Some have suggested that formalism and functionalism are complementary to each other, and perhaps should even be combined. But radical construction grammar explains why to most functionalists, formalist syntactic models seem irrelevant to the search for universals of grammar. They are.

## 2.2.3. Some contributions of cognitive linguistics to typology

Where are the universals of grammar, then? Here we may see how cognitive linguistics has made significant contributions to typology. The universals of grammar, the universals which are associated with parts of speech and grammatical relations for instance, are not to be found in an inventory of universal syntactic primitives, whether they are found in all languages or form a smorgasbord of primitives which particular languages choose from. They are found instead in the universal patterns of variation referred to in §1. These patterns can be formulated as interlocking sets of implicational universals that hold across languages; but what has attracted the greatest interest of typologists are those wider patterns. The two most common patterns are grammatical hierarchies and prototypes. The latter in particular is a major contribution of cognitive linguistics (and its psychological antecedents) to typology.

The cross-linguistic universals must themselves be explained; they are typological generalizations which are manifestations of deeper patterns. Grammatical universals are to be explained as maps of conceptual space, organized so that particular-language categories/constructions cover functions in a coherent region of the cognitive map. Prototypes represent focal points on the conceptual map, while hierarchies define dimensions in conceptual space. This approach to universals of grammatical categories was pioneered by Lloyd Anderson (L. Anderson 1974, 1982, 1986, 1987), and has come to be used more frequently in syntactic typology (Croft, Shyldkrot and Kemmer 1987; Croft 1991; Kemmer 1993; Haspelmath 1997; Stassen 1997; van der Auwera and Plungian 1998). Also, Bybee's research in morphology (Bybee 1985) depends crucially on a notion of semantic distance (which she calls relevance in the 1985 book). The notion of conceptual space is another illustration of the central role that cognitive approaches to language have played in typological research.

We may now briefly return to the distributional patterns within languages. My description of syntactic facts in the preceding section may make it appear to the reader that there is no regularity in the distributional patterns of elements across constructions within a single language. This is not true. There are patterns; it is just that they cannot be described in terms of discrete atomic primitive categories. The striking fact however is that the distributional patterns of grammatical elements across constructions in a single language conform to the same functional principles and the patterns across languages that typologists have found. And they can be explained in the same way, in terms of the structure of the conceptual space possessed by speakers.

## 3. Typology, semantics and conceptual structure

### 3.1. Iconicity vs conceptualization?

Both typologists and cognitive linguists assume that there is a close relationship between syntactic structure and semantic structure. In typology, the close relationship is characterized as one of *iconicity*, which can be defined as follows:

> the structure of the language reflects in some way the structure of experi-ence, that is to say, the structure of the world, including (in most function-alists' view) the perspective imposed on the world by the speaker (Croft 1990: 164)

The principle of iconicity implies that there is a parallelism between syntactic structure and semantic structure. It also suggests that se-mantic structure determines or, better, motivates grammatical struc-ture.

Cognitive linguistics also recognizes iconicity. Traditional gram-marians and generative grammarians have analyzed many grammatical elements as being "meaningless". If this were true, the existence of these elements would be problematic for iconicity, since they have no counterparts in semantic structure. One of the more significant hy-potheses of cognitive linguistics is that most if not all grammatical elements in fact do have meaning. But the meaning contributed by these elements (and in fact all elements) is conceptual; that is, it repre-sents a way of conceptualizing experience in the process of encoding it and expressing it in language:

> Meaning reduces to conceptualization...Semantic structures incorporate conventional "imagery", i.e. they construe a situation in a particular fash-ion...The lexical and grammatical resources of a language are therefore

not semantically neutral—inherent to their nature is the structuring of conceptual content for symbolic purposes (Langacker 1988: 49, 50, 63).

Now, a radical interpretation of this approach (not Langacker's, I
believe), such as that expressed in Sasse (1991), suggests that grammatical structure determines semantic structure—the opposite assumption from typology. Thus, there appears to be a conflict between
typology and (a radical interpretation of) cognitive linguistics, despite
the claim in §1 that the two styles are harmonious. In fact, as typological investigation reveals, there is some truth in both views.

## 3.2. Problems with radical semantic relativity

The radical relativist conclusion, that syntactic structure determines
the conceptualization of experience manifested in semantic structure,
involves a series of hidden assumptions. I explored those assumptions
in an earlier paper (Croft 1993); here I focus on the most important
hidden assumptions and offer a more detailed analysis of the resolution of the apparent conflict noted in §3.1.

### 3.2.1. Monosemy vs. polysemy

Sasse mostly argues for relativity in grammar: grammatical elements
and constructions impose their conceptualization on the lexical items
that occur in them. In order for such an argument to follow logically,
it must be assumed that the grammatical element has the same meaning in all its uses. This is the first hidden assumption (Hidden Assumption #2 in Croft 1993): All analyses of linguistic forms must
posit monosemy or monofunctionality.

In fact, Sasse does refer to this assumption, albeit in a footnote:

A methodological question is being touched on here, which I cannot discuss in detail due to lack of space. One of the fundamental heuristic strate-

gies in linguistic analysis should be the attempt to find a uniform function or meaning for each formal linguistic phenomenon, i.e., not to assume *a priori* that there are irregular mapping relations between form and function (homonymy, etc.), but to proceed from the assumption that there is, *in principle*, a 1:1 relation, each form having one and only one basic function, the subfunction being determined by and explainable in terms of the environment. Assuming of homonymy is acceptable only as the result of the inability to discover a uniform meaning, i.e., as a last resort, so to speak, but never as an acceptable working principle. (Sasse 1991: 94, fn. 8)

However, monosemy is not the only possible analysis of word, morpheme or constructional meaning. An alternative analysis of the meaning of a linguistic element distinct from homonymy (see e.g. Lakoff 1987, Croft 1998) is polysemy. A polysemy analysis argues that two uses of a form are semantically related to each other by a semantic process (such as metaphor)—which occurred historically and may still govern the speaker's knowledge of the two uses—without those two uses being semantically identical (= having a single overarching meaning).

Polysemy analyses play a central role in cognitive linguistics; Lakoff (1987) for example discusses them in detail, calling them radial categories. The contribution of typology here is more modest, namely to provide another sort of argument in favor of polysemy analyses of grammatical elements. A simple and clear example of the typological argument for a polysemy analysis is found in a discussion of Russian and Finnish cases by Dahl (1987). Russian and Finnish use different cases to distinguish location and motion. For location, Russian uses the locative case (15)b and Finnish uses a set of cases, including the inessive (15)c; for motion, Russian uses the accusative case (16)b and Finnish a different set of cases, including the illative ([16]c; Dahl 1987: 151-52):

(15) a. *John lives in London.*
    b. *Džon živët v Londone.*    [locative]
    c. *John asuu Lontoossa.*    [inessive]

(16) a. *John went to London.*
    b. *Džon poexal v London.*    [accusative]
    c. *John meni Lontooseen.*    [illative]

However, for a class of predicates including 'remain', 'stay' and 'leave [something somewhere]', Russian uses the locative case (17)b while Finnish uses the illative case ([17]c; Dahl 1987: 151-52):

(17) a. *He remained in London.*
    b. *On ostalsja v Londone.*    [locative]
    c. *Hän jäi Lontooseen.*    [illative]

Dahl first entertains a monosemy analysis of the two cases in each language, exploiting the spatial and temporal properties of the predicates involved. Location involves one point in time and one place (i.e. one point in space). Motion involves at least two points in time and at least two different places: one moves from one place to another over an interval of time. The anomalous predicates involve just one place, but over an extended time period, i.e. at least two points in time.

Given this semantic analysis of the predicates, one can formulate the following monosemy analysis of the cases in Russian and Finnish:

Russian:    *accusative* = involves at least two different places ('go')
               *locative* = involves only one place ('live', 'remain')
Finnish:     *inessive etc.* = involves only one point in time ('live')
               *illative etc.* = involves at least two points in time ('go', 'remain')

One effect of the monosemy analysis of the Russian and Finnish cases is that the cases appear to be defined on completely different semantic parameters, the Russian cases on space and the Finnish cases on time. From a typological perspective, this appears odd; one would expect more similarity in case systems than this analysis provides. But in fact there are greater difficulties.

There is a major shortcoming of monofunctional/monosemy analyses: It is almost impossible to find necessary *and sufficient* conditions for category membership. Without sufficient conditions, speakers' knowledge of their language is not captured by the analysis (see also Cruse 1992). For example, the aforementioned Russian and Finnish cases have many other uses than those illustrated in examples (15)-(17), and those uses cannot be subsumed under the monosemous definitions given above. The cases must be polysemous in a broader perspective, which raises the possibility that they are polysemous in (15)-(17) as well.

Dahl offers an alternative polysemy analysis for both the Russian and Finnish cases, which we can illustrate graphically in the following diagram:

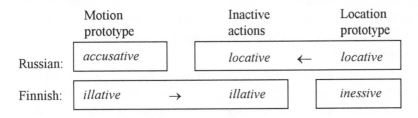

*Figure 1.* A universal prototype analysis of Russian and Finnish cases.

There is a motion prototype, defined as involving at least two points in both time and space. The Russian accusative and Finnish illative both encode the motion prototype. There is also a location prototype involving only one point in both time and space. The Russian locative and Finnish inessive both encode the location prototype. Then there is an intermediate non-prototypical category, which I have called *inactive actions* elsewhere (Croft 1991: 97), which involves one point in space but at least two in time. In Russian, the case for the location prototype is extended to inactive actions, based on its similarity with respect to spatial features. In Finnish, the case for the motion prototype is extended to inactive actions, based on its similarity with respect to temporal features.

The prototype analysis has a number of desirable features. It captures our intuition that motion and location are more common or salient spatiotemporal situation types. It suggests that grammars of many if not all languages are designed by their speakers to encode the more salient situations that they encounter. This is the respect in which a semantic universal (the prototype) is expressed in language—in DuBois' aphorism, "grammars code best what speakers do most".

The less prototypical situation type varies in its expression across languages (probably arbitrarily—not a problem for a typologist). The prototype analysis also makes a theoretical prediction. The three situation types define a simple one-dimensional conceptual space. Languages are predicted to have categories defining continuous regions in conceptual space. Thus, it is predicted that a language type that coded the location argument of "go" and "live" in the same way, but coded the location argument of "remain" differently will not occur. (This is a nonvacuous competing motivations analysis; see Croft 1990: 193.)

The prototype analysis suggests that it is the properties of the situation type, as encoded by the lexical item, that influences the choice of grammatical case, not that the grammatical case imposes a "spatial" or "temporal" construal of the situation type. A prototype analysis undermines a radical relativist position, unlike the monosemy analysis. It is possible that Russian and Finnish speakers have both analyses simultaneously, that is, they distinguish the prototype and its extension but also form a monosemous semantic category for the cases. This may be the case; but it would only apply to the subset of uses described here, as noted above. And the existence of the prototype-extension pattern that implies there are universals of the encoding of meaning by form, and also universals of the diachronic extension of forms, which can be attributed to universal human conceptualizations.

## 3.2.2. The Semantic Uncertainty Principle

A polysemy analysis is often plausible and would suggest that the radical relativist position described in §3.1 is too strong. But the heart of the matter in analyzing radical relativism is a logical flaw in the argumentation (just as a logical flaw in argumentation leads from distributional analysis to radical construction grammar).

Sasse argues that certain languages lack a noun-verb distinction, that is, all semantic classes of words take the same inflections and can occur as referring expressions or as predications. However, not all such languages behave alike. According to Sasse, Tongan is a language in which all clauses are nominal phrases, as illustrated by his "literal translation" of the following example (Sasse 1991: 79):

(18) *na'e   ui        'a         Sione*
     PRET  call(ing)  ABS/GEN  Sione
     'It was calling of Sione.'  [= 'Sione called/was called.']

Cayuga, on the other hand, is a language in which all words are verbal sentences in Sasse's view, again illustrated by his "literal translation" of the following example (Sasse 1991: 84):

(19) *a-      hó-          htǫ:'   ho-      tkwę't   -a'*
     PAST-  3SGN/3SGM-  lose    3SGN-  wallet   -NOM
     *nę:kyę̧   h-      ǫkweh'*
     this    3SGM-  man
     'It was lost to him, it is his wallet, this one, he is a man'
     [= 'The man lost his wallet.']

In fact, there are empirical differences which indicate that whatever the status of noun and verb is in these languages, not all lexical items are treated alike. For example, there is a tense-mood auxiliary in front of the nominal "verb" but not the other nominals in Tongan, and a tense prefix on the verb but absent from the verbal "nouns" in Cayuga, and Cayuga has a nominal suffix on one of the "nouns" (for a more detailed critique of Sasse's analysis of Cayuga, see Mithun to appear). However, even if these empirical differences were absent, thus strengthening Sasse's argument, there is still a logical flaw in Sasse's argument.

Let us say that Sasse is right, that all Tongan utterances are nominal phrases and all Cayuga words are verbal sentences, and that this reflects fundamentally different underlying conceptualizations of experience. How does Sasse arrive at this conclusion? By looking at the grammatical elements: the inflections and associated grammatical particles. But one can arrive at this conclusion only by assuming that the grammatical elements have the same meaning in Tongan and Cayuga that they do in familiar European languages. That is, we must assume that the semantics of the grammatical elements is universal, in order to demonstrate that the semantics (conceptualization) of the concepts denoted by the lexical items is radically relative.

But there is no a priori reason to assume that the grammatical elements always call the shots. It could be that the semantics of the lexical items is universal and the semantics of the grammatical elements is determined at least in part by that of the lexical items. That is, the so-called nominal grammatical element 'a in Tongan is polysemous between a (nominal) genitive meaning and a (verbal) absolutive argument meaning; and the Cayuga prefixes are polysemous between a (verbal) agreement function and a (nominal) gender function. This is the core hidden assumption in radical linguistic relativity arguments (Hidden Assumption #4 in Croft 1993), which I call the Semantic Uncertainty Principle:

(20) *Semantic Uncertainty Principle*: determining the relativity of the conceptualization given by one grammatical element can only be done by assuming the universality of the conceptualization given by an associated grammatical element.

How do we decide between these two options? In the following section, I offer an interpretation of linguistic relativity and conceptualization that comes naturally to a typologist, based on the dynamic nature of language.

### 3.3. The dynamic, fluctuating character of linguistic "relativity" and the form-function relation.

A solution to the iconicity-conceptualization puzzle emerges when we consider how patterns like those found in Tongan and Cayuga arise. The process of grammaticalization, well studied by typologists, gives an account (see for example Lehmann 1982, Heine, Claudi and Hünnemeyer 1991, Traugott and Heine 1991, Hopper and Traugott 1993). In grammaticalization, constructions acquire new semantic uses over time, and can diverge syntactically as well (through replacement, renewal or split). For example, a nominalized verb form plus its genitive dependent often grammaticalize to the main verb predication plus its core argument. This has happened in Polynesian, and has led to the genitive case also encoding the core argument of the main predication, which itself is identical to an action nominal. Also, pronouns often grammaticalize into argument indexing affixes ("agreement" affixes) on verbs, and into determiners and thence into gender markers on nouns. Both of these processes have happened in Iroquoian, with approximately the same original pronouns (in fact, the grammaticalization into verbal indexes and nominal gender markers occurred at separate stages in the history of Iroquoian; Mithun to appear).

The grammaticalization process can be seen to involve three steps at the micro-level. First, there is a construction with a basic meaning—one form, one function. Then it is extended to a new meaning. This extension is the first step in grammaticalization. It involves one form, but multiple functions (e.g., genitive and absolutive in Tongan). This is the stage at which Sasse and others claim that a radical rela-

tivistic interpretation applies, and where I am suggesting that a polysemy analysis is, a priori, equally plausible. Finally, there is divergence
in syntactic behavior and/or phonological form—two distinct forms,
two distinct functions.

The Tongan and Iroquoian examples apparently illustrate the
intermediate stage, where a single form with one original function is
extended to a new function. If we put these examples in the larger
dynamic context of the grammaticalization process, a more complex
interplay between language-specific conceptualization and "universal"
semantics reveals itself.

The first step in the process is that a construction is extended to a
new function, previously encoded by some other construction. This
initial step is a crucial one, because the old and new constructions
contrast in the function in question. It is widely accepted among
cognitive linguists and many other linguists that when there are two
different constructions for a single function in the same language, the
two contrasting constructions offer alternative conceptualizations of
the same experience, each highlighting different aspects of the function they are competing to express, to the extent that they can contrast in use. That is, the new construction imposes the conceptualization of its original structure and function.

In the next step, the old construction in the new function is eliminated, or (more likely) marginalized to the point that it no longer
significantly contrasts with the old one. At this point, the "new"
construction becomes conventionalized in the new function, which
has now become one of its normal functions. At this point too, the
highlighting of particular aspects of the function expressed by the new
construction fades, because of the absence of grammatical contrast.
The conceptualization of the experience encoded by the lexical items
occurring in the construction reasserts itself, so to speak, in the new
function.

At this point, the construction has become conventional in its new
function. It is completely polysemous with respect to its original
meaning. The independence of the construction in its new function

from the original construction in its original meaning is demonstrated by the last step in the grammaticalization process: the new construction undergoes shifts in grammatical structure and behavior in keeping with its new function. These shifts will manifest themselves as syntactic, morphological and phonological changes that occur only to the construction in its new function, thereby making it distinct from the old construction in its original meaning. In fact, these grammatical differences manifest themselves rapidly; I noted some differences in Tongan and Cayuga above (see also Mithun to appear, Croft 1998).

There is a complex interplay of conceptualizations offered by lexical items and grammatical constructions in any actual utterance. Every utterance, whether novel or conventional, involves the combination of a large number of grammatical units. The grammatical system is therefore always in a state of tension:

> ...the form-meaning relation is often in a state of flux because of the complex analogies and differences between conceptual structures, which can be reflected in syntactic structures. Variation and change in linguistic structures in a single language suggest that the conceptualizations underlying different structures are not only not incommensurable, but also simultaneously available to speakers of a language at any given time (Croft 1993: 177)

We may summarize the relation between syntax, semantics and conceptualization as follows. Syntactic structure reflects semantic structure. The semantic structure corresponding to a syntactic construction represents a conceptualization of experience. But what I am calling experience, which cognitive linguists treat as the raw material which is shaped by linguistic semantics, is itself not a single resolvable structure, but an experience in which alternative, conflicting conceptualizations are simultaneously immanent, and are rendered available by the different grammatical elements, from lexical items to grammatical constructions, that make up a speaker's utterance in context. The multidimensional character of experience can lead to a reconstrual of the semantic structure in the process that I have described in this section. The reconstrual of semantic structure leads in turn to the alteration of the formal syntactic structure. The two-way interplay between form, meaning, and experience is summarily illustrated in Figure 2:

SYNTACTIC STRUCTURE        [reflects, but can be altered by:]
   ⇓⇑
SEMANTIC STRUCTURE         [conceptualization of, but can be reconstrued by:]
   ⇓⇑
EXPERIENCE                 [immanent conflicting conceptualizations]

*Figure 2.* The interplay between form, meaning and experience

## 4. Conclusion

Thinking like a typologist about two fundamental questions in cognitive linguistics, the nature of grammatical knowledge and the relationship between form and meaning, has, I hope, offered a new perspective on these old problems. Cross-linguistic and intralinguistic variation reveals a flaw in assumptions about the relative priority of constructions and their syntactic components. It is the former that are basic and primitive—a very nonreductionist view, to appeal to another way that a cognitive linguist thinks—and the latter that are derived. A dynamic, diachronic perspective puts semantic relativity into a larger context where it finds its proper place in the process of grammaticalization and syntactic change. In both cases, cognitive linguistics has also informed typology, with the notions of prototypes, conceptual spaces, and conceptualization. May the interchange between typology and cognitive linguistics continue to bear fruit.

# References

Anderson, Lloyd. B.
1974    Distinct sources of fuzzy data: ways of integrating relatively discrete
        and gradient aspects of language, and explaining grammar on the basis
        of semantic fields. In: Roger W. Shuy and Charles-James N. Bailey
        (eds.), *Towards Tomorrow's Linguistics*, 50-64. Washington, DC:
        Georgetown University Press.
1982    The 'perfect' as a universal and as a language-particular category. In:
        Paul Hopper (ed.), *Tense-Aspect: Between Semantics and Pragmatics,*
        227-64. Amsterdam: John Benjamins.
1986    Evidentials, paths of change, and mental maps: typologically regular
        asymmetries. In: Wallace Chafe and Johanna Nichols (eds.), *Eviden-
        tiality: The Linguistic Encoding of Epistemology*, 273-312. Norwood:
        Ablex.
1987    Adjectival morphology and semantic space. In: Barbara Need, Eric
        Schiller and Ann Bosch, *Papers from the 23rd Annual Regional
        Meeting of the Chicago Linguistic Society, Part One: The General
        Session*, 1-17. Chicago: Chicago Linguistic Society.
Anderson, Stephen R.
1976    On the notion of subject in ergative languages. In: Charles Li (ed.),
        *Subject and Topic,* 1-24. New York: Academic Press.
Bloomfield, Leonard
1933    *Language.* New York: Holt, Rinehart and Winston.
Bybee, Joan L.
1985    *Morphology: A Study into the Relation between Meaning and Form.*
        Amsterdam: John Benjamins.
Bybee, Joan L. and Joanne Scheibman
1997    The effect of usage on degrees of constituency: the reduction of
        *don't* in English. Paper presented at the Workshop on Constituency
        and Discourse, Santa Barbara, California.
Croft, William
1990    *Typology and Universals.* Cambridge: Cambridge University Press.
1991    *Syntactic Categories and Grammatical Relations: The Cognitive Or-
        ganization of Information.* Chicago: University of Chicago Press.
1993    A noun is a noun is a noun—or is it? Some reflections on the univer-
        sality of semantics. In: Joshua S. Guenter, Barbara A. Kaiser and
        Cheryl C. Zoll (eds.), *Proceedings of the Nineteenth Annual Meeting
        of the Berkeley Linguistics Society*, 369-80. Berkeley: Berkeley Lin-
        guistics Society.

1995    Autonomy and functionalist linguistics. *Language* 71: 490-532.
1998    Linguistic evidence and mental representations. *Cognitive Linguistics* 9: 151-73.
in prep. *Radical Construction Grammar: Syntactic Theory from a Typological Perspective.* Oxford: Oxford University Press.

Croft, William, Hava Bat-Zeev Shyldkrot, and Suzanne Kemmer.
1987    Diachronic semantic processes in the middle voice. In: Anna Giaco-lone Ramat, Onofrio Carruba and Guiliano Bernini (eds.), *Papers from the 7th International Conference on Historical Linguistics,* 179-192. Amsterdam: John Benjamins.

Cruse, D. Alan
1992    Monosemy vs. polysemy (review article on Ruhl, *On monosemy*) *Linguistics* 30: 577-99.

Dahl, Östen
1987    Case grammar and prototypes. In: René Dirven and Günter Radden (eds.), *Concepts of Case*, 147-161. Tübingen: Gunter Narr. [Originally published in *Prague Bulletin of Mathematical Linguistics* 31: 3-24, 1979.]

Downing, Bruce T.
1978    Some universals of relative clause structure. In: Joseph H. Greenberg, Charles A. Ferguson and Edith A. Moravcsik (eds.), *Syntax*, 375-418. (Universals of Human Language 4.) Stanford: Stanford University Press.

Fillmore, Charles J. and Paul Kay
1993    *Construction Grammar Coursebook, Chapters 1 through 11 (Reading Materials for Ling. X20).* University of California, Berkeley.

Fillmore, Charles J., Paul Kay and Mary Kay O'Connor
1988    Regularity and idiomaticity in grammatical constructions: the case of *let alone. Language* 64: 501-538.

Givón, Talmy
1971    Historical syntax and synchronic morphology: an archaeologist's field trip. *Papers from the Seventh Regional Meeting, Chicago Linguistic Society*, 394-415. Chicago: Chicago Linguistic Society.
1979    *On Understanding Grammar.* New York: Academic Press.

Goldberg, Adele E.
1995    *Constructions: A Construction Grammar Approach to Argument Structure.* Chicago: University of Chicago Press.

Greenberg, Joseph H.
1966a    Synchronic and diachronic universals in phonology. *Language* 42: 508-517.

1966b    Some universals of grammar with particular reference to the order of meaningful elements. In: Joseph H. Greenberg (ed.), *Universals of Grammar*, 73-113. (2nd edition.) Cambridge, Mass: MIT Press.

1969    Some methods of dynamic comparison in linguistics. In: Jan Puhvel (ed.), *Substance and Structure of Language*, 147-203. Berkeley/Los Angeles: University of California Press.

Harris, Zellig S.

1946    From morpheme to utterance. *Language* 22: 161-83.

1951    *Methods in Structural Linguistics.* Chicago: University of Chicago Press.

Haspelmath, Martin

1997    *Indefinite Pronouns.* Oxford: Oxford University Press.

Heine, Bernd, Ulrike Claudi and Friederieke Hünnemeyer

1991    *Grammaticalization: A Conceptual Framework.* Chicago: University of Chicago Press.

Hengeveld, Kees

1992    *Non-verbal Predication: Theory, typology, diachrony.* Berlin: Mouton de Gruyter.

Hopper, Paul and Elizabeth Traugott

1993    *Grammaticalization.* Cambridge: Cambridge University Press.

Jacobsen, William H., Jr.

1979    Noun and verb in Nootkan. *The Victoria Conference on Northwestern Languages*, 83-155. (British Columbia Provincial Museum Heritage Record No. 4.) Victoria, B.C.: British Columbia Provincial Museum.

Keenan, Edward L and Bernard Comrie

1977    Noun phrase accessibility and universal grammar. *Linguistic Inquiry* 8.63-99.

Kemmer, Suzanne

1993    *The Middle Voice.* (Typological Studies in Language 23.) Amsterdam: John Benjamins.

Lakoff, George

1987    *Women, Fire and Dangerous Things: What Categories Reveal about the Mind.* Chicago: University of Chicago Press.

Langacker, Ronald W.

1987    *Foundations of Cognitive Grammar, Vol I: Theoretical Prerequisites.* Stanford: Stanford University Press.

1988    A view of linguistic semantics. In: Brygida Rudzka-Ostyn (ed.), *Topics in Cognitive Linguistics*, 49-90. Amsterdam: John Benjamins.

Lehmann, Christian
  1982    *Thoughts on Grammaticalization: A Programmatic Sketch, Vol. I.* (Arbeiten des Kölner Universalien-Projekts, 48.) Köln: Institut für Sprachwissenschaft.
  1984    *Der Relativsatz: Typologie seiner Strukturen, Theorie seiner Funktionen, Kompendium seiner Grammatik.* Tübingen: Gunter Narr.
Leopold, Aldo
  1949    Thinking like a mountain. *A Sand County Almanac,* 129-33. Oxford: Oxford University Press.
Merlan, Francesca
  1994    *A Grammar of Wardaman.* Berlin: Mouton de Gruyter.
Michaelis, Laura A. and Knud Lambrecht
  1996    Toward a construction-based theory of language functions: the case of nominal extraposition. *Language* 72: 215-47.
Mithun, Marianne
  in press Noun and verb in Iroquoian languages: multicategorization from multiple criteria. To appear in: Bernard Comrie and Petra M. Vogel (eds.), *An Anthology of Word Classes.* Berlin: Mouton de Gruyter.
Nida, Eugene A.
  1949    *Morphology.* Ann Arbor: University of Michigan Press.
Prince, Ellen F.
  1978    A comparison of WH-clefts and *it*-clefts in discourse. *Language* 54: 883-906.
  1981    Topicalization, Focus-movement and Yiddish-movement: a pragmatic differentiation. In: Danny K. Alford et al. (eds.), *Proceedings of the Seventh Annual Meeting of the Berkeley Linguistics Society,* 249-264. Berkeley, CA: Berkeley Linguistics Society.
Sasse, Hans-Jürgen
  1991    Predication and sentence constitution in universal perspective. In: Dietmar Zaefferer (ed.), *Semantic Universals and Universal Semantics* 75-95. (Groningen-Amsterdam Studies in Semantics 12.) Berlin: Foris.
Siewierska, Anna
  1985    *The Passive: A Comparative Linguistic Analysis.* London: Croom Helm.
Stassen, Leon
  1985    *Comparison and Universal Grammar.* Oxford: Basil Blackwell.
  1997    *Intransitive Predication.* Oxford: Oxford University Press.
Thompson, Laurence C.
  1965/87 *A Vietnamese Reference Grammar.* Honolulu: University of Hawaii Press.

Thompson, Sandra A.
  1985    Grammar and written discourse: initial vs. final purpose clauses in English. *Text* 5: 55-84.
Traugott, Elizabeth Closs and Bernd Heine
  1991    *Aspects of Grammaticalization* (2 vol.). Amsterdam: John Benjamins.
van der Auwera, Johan and Vladimir A. Plungian
  1998    Modality's semantic map. *Linguistic Typology* 2: 79-124.

# Methods and generalizations

## Gilles Fauconnier

### 1. Meaning, language, cognition

Linguists agree on one thing—that language is diabolically hard to study. They do not always agree, however, on the hows, the whys, and the what fors: how one should go about studying it and how speakers manage to do what they do; why it is so hard and why exactly we bother to study it; what language is for, and what linguistics is for. A mainstream view that has been popular in the last thirty years (but not necessarily before that) offers the following answers.

How linguists do it: they collect grammaticality judgments from natives and concurrently build and check hypotheses about the formal structure of particular languages and languages in general. How humans do it: they come equipped biologically with innate language-specific universals, that require only minimal fine-tuning when exposed to a particular specimen.

Why it's hard: easy for the child who has the innate universals already set up, hard for the linguist lost in a forest of idiosyncrasies that hide the deeper principles. Why bother? So that we can discover such principles.

What is language for?: The story here is that this question is not a priority for the scientist. We can worry later about function, communication, and meaning generally.

And what is linguistics for? Well, there is the platonic reward of discovering structure for the sake of structure itself. And then there is biology: Since the universals are in the brain, they must also be in the genes; linguistics is theoretical biology; geneticists and neuroscientists will fill in the messy details of its implementation in our bodies.

This strange and simple story contains its own methods and generalizations. The appropriate methods are in the "how to do it"—collecting grammaticality judgments and so on. What counts as generalizations are the formal principles that apply to wider ranges of phenomena and/or languages.

In contrast to this sharply autonomous view of language structure, cognitive linguistics has resurrected an older tradition. In that tradition, language is in the service of constructing and communicating meaning, and it is for the linguist and cognitive scientist a window into the mind. Seeing through that window, however, is not obvious. Deep features of our thinking, cognitive processes, and social communication need to be brought in, correlated, and associated with their linguistic manifestations.

The cognitive linguistics enterprise, we believe, has already been remarkably successful. It is not far-fetched to say that perhaps for the first time a genuine science of meaning construction and its dynamics has been launched. This has been achieved by intensively studying and modeling the cognition that lies behind language and goes far beyond it, but which language reflects in certain ways, and which in turn supports the dynamics of language use, language change, and language organization.

Echoing Erving Goffman, I have called this backstage cognition. Language is only the tip of a spectacular cognitive iceberg, and when we engage in any language activity, be it mundane or artistically creative, we draw unconsciously on vast cognitive resources, call up innumerable models and frames, set up multiple connections, coordinate large arrays of information, and engage in creative mappings, transfers, and elaborations. This is what language is about and what language is for.

Backstage cognition includes viewpoints and reference points, figure-ground/profile-base/landmark-trajector organization, metaphorical, analogical, and other mappings, idealized models, framing, construal, mental spaces, counterpart connections, roles, prototypes, metonymy, polysemy, conceptual blending, fictive motion, force dynamics.

Well, where does all this come from? Did it all just spring up in the fertile mind of cognitive linguists, giving them an unlimited supply of new notions to draw from in order to explain some linguistic facts that they wish to talk about? And if so, isn't all this a considerable weakening of linguistic theory, letting in so many flaky new gimmicks that virtually anything at all becomes easily but vacuously explainable?

*Mais pas du tout.* Rather remarkably, all the aspects of backstage cognition just alluded to receive ample justification on non-linguistic grounds from a variety of sources. Some have been extensively studied in psychology (e.g. prototypes, figure-ground, analogy), others in artificial intelligence and/or sociology (frames, roles, cultural models), literature and philosophy (metaphor). Metonymy, mental spaces, force dynamics, conceptual blending, initially studied primarily by linguists have been shown to apply to cognition generally. The notion of viewpoint and reference point is presumably even more general, given the nature of our visual systems and orientation.

Needless to say, all these features of backstage cognition deserve to be studied and understood in their own right, not just as a means of explaining linguistic distributions. To cognitive scientists who are not linguists, the linguistic distributions matter very little. And for cognitive linguists, there has been a major shift of interest. The cognitive constructs, operations, and dynamics, and the understanding of conceptual systems have become a central focus of analysis. The linguistic distributions are just one of many sources of relevant data.

This shift bears on the methods employed and the generalizations obtained. Methods must extend to contextual aspects of language use and to non-linguistic cognition. This means studying full discourse, language in context, inferences actually drawn by participants in an exchange, applicable frames, implicit assumptions and construal, to name just a few. It means being on the look-out for manifestations of conceptual thought in everyday life, movies, literature, and science. This is because introspection and intuition are woefully insufficient to tell us about general operations of meaning construction. When we volunteer a meaning for an isolated sentence, we do it typically on the basis of defaults and prototypes. It is only in rich contexts that we see the full force of creative on-line meaning construction.

As for generalizations, the most powerful ones are those which transcend specific cognitive domains. In our work on conceptual blending, we see as a strong generalization the discovery that the same principles apply to framing, metaphor, action and design, and grammatical constructions. This is not an internal generalization about language, it is an external one relating linguistic phenomena to non-linguistic ones. Such generalizations seem primordial to the understanding of how language relates to general cognition, but they are precluded in principle by the autonomous approach evoked above. It is no surprise, then, if that approach finds no connection between language and the rest of cognition, for that autonomy is built into the very method that serves to build up the field of inquiry and the theories that are its by-products.

Although cognitive linguistics espouses the age-old view that language is in the service of meaning, its methods and results have been quite novel. The results in fact have been somewhat surprising. At the most general level, here are three that I find striking. I will call them respectively Economy, Operational Uniformity, Cognitive Generalization.

## 1.1 Economy and the Eliza effect

By Economy, I mean the following: any language form in context has the potential to trigger massive cognitive constructions, including analogical mappings, mental space connections, reference point organization, blends, and simulation of complex scenes. When we try to spell out backstage cognition in detail, we are struck by the contrast between the extreme brevity of the linguistic form and the spectacular wealth of the corresponding meaning construction. Very sparse grammar guides us along the same rich mental paths, by prompting us to perform complex cognitive operations. What is remarkable is that, by and large, subjects engage in quite similar constructions on the basis of similar grammatical prompts, and thereby achieve a high degree of effective communication. The reason seems to be that the cultural, contextual, and cognitive substrate on which the language forms operate is sufficiently uniform across interlocutors to allow for a reasonable degree of consistency in the unfolding of the prompted meaning constructions. How this works remains in many ways mysterious. What is clear is that language is radically different from an information carrying and information preserving system, such as a code or telecommunications. Language forms carry very little information per se, but can latch on to rich preexistent networks in the subjects' brains and trigger massive sequential and parallel activations. Those activated networks are of course themselves in the appropriate state by virtue of general organization due to cognition and culture, and local organization due to physical and mental context. Crucially, we have no awareness of this amazing chain of cognitive events that takes place as we talk and listen, except for the external manifestation of language (sounds, words, sentences) and the internal manifestation of meaning: with lightning speed, we experience meaning. This is very similar to perception, which is also instantaneous and immediate with no awareness of the extraordinarily complex intervening neural events.

What we are conscious of determines our folk theories of what is going on. In the case of perception, the folk theory, an extremely useful one for us as living organisms, is that everything we perceive is indeed directly the very essence of the object perceived, out there in the world and independent of us. The effect is contained entirely in the cause. In the same way, our folk theory of language is that the meanings are contained directly in the words and their combinations, since that is all that we are ever consciously aware of. The effect (meaning) is attributed essentially to the visible cause (language). And again, this folk theory is extremely useful to us as human organisms in everyday life. It makes sense. At another level, the level of scientific inquiry, this folk theory, like other folk theories, is wrong, and the information processing model of language breaks down. This reveals that, as humans experiencing language, we are fooled by an interesting variant of the Eliza effect. The famous computer program Eliza produced what looked like a sensible interaction between a psychiatrist and a subject operating the program, but the rich meaning that seemed to emanate from the machine was in fact read in (constructed) by the subject. And strikingly, just like a perceptual illusion, this effect cannot easily be suspended by rational denial. In the case of Eliza, the illusion may be hard to block, but it is easy to see. The more general illusion that meaning is in the language forms is both hard to repress and hard to acknowledge. And for that reason, it has made its way into many scientific accounts of language. In such accounts, the notion that forms have meaning is unproblematic, and the "only" problem becomes to give a formal characterization of such meanings associated with forms. Clearly, if the presupposition that there are such meanings is in error, the very foundations of such accounts are in jeopardy. It has been, I believe, a major contribution of cognitive linguistics to dispel this very strong unquestioned assumption.

## 1.2 Operational uniformity

It is commonly thought that very different operations apply to the various levels of linguistic analysis. For example, syntax governs the sentence, and semantics provides it compositionally with a meaning. At a higher level, other quite different operations apply to produce implicatures, derived meaning, indirect speech acts. Then rhetorical and figurative devices may kick in, such as metaphor and metonymy.

Our findings suggest a very different picture. Backstage cognition operates in many ways uniformly at all levels. Figure-ground and viewpoint organization pervades the sentence (Talmy 1978, Langacker 1987/1991), the Tense system (Cutrer 1994), Narrative structure (Sanders and Redeker 1996), in signed and spoken languages, and of course many aspects of non-linguistic cognition. Metaphor builds up meaning all the way from the most basic levels to the most sophisticated and creative ones (Lakoff and Turner 1989, Grady 1997). And the same goes for metonymic pragmatic functions (Nunberg 1978) and mental space connections (Sweetser and Fauconnier 1996, Van Hoek 1996, Liddell 1996), which are governed by the same general Access principle. Frames, schemas and prototypes account for word level and sentence level syntactic/semantic properties in cognitive and construction grammar (Lakoff 1987, Fillmore 1985, Goldberg 1997, Langacker 1987/91), and of course they guide thought and action more generally (Bateson 1972, Goffman 1974). Conceptual blending and analogy play a key role in syntax and morphology (Mandelblit 1997), in word and sentence level semantics (Sweetser [this volume]), and at higher levels of reasoning and rhetoric (Robert 1998, Coulson 1997, Turner 1996). Similarly, we find force dynamics and fictive motion (Talmy 1985, 1996) operating at all levels (single words, entire systems, like the modals, and general framing).

This operational uniformity is unexpected, remarkable, and counter-intuitive. It has taken cognitive linguists a lot of hard work and theoretical conceptual rethinking to uncover this series of powerful generalizations. There are quite a few interesting reasons for the difficulty of thinking in this new way. One is that language does not come with its backstage cognition neatly displayed "on its sleeve". Everything that counts is deeply hidden from our consciousness, and masked by the "folk theory" effects mentioned earlier. Another difficulty has to do with the long tradition of apprehending limited aspects of language in a self-contained, language-specific, descriptive apparatus. The resulting specialized technical vocabulary has been immensely helpful in launching a coherent linguistic science, but regrettably it has also shielded linguistics from a more comprehensive cognitive framework in which the right questions could be asked.

## 1.3 Cognitive generalization

Operational uniformity, as outlined in the previous section, pertains essentially to language and reasoning. The uniformity is across linguistic levels, the word, the sentence, the sentence and its context, the whole discourse, and ultimately general reasoning. And yet, there are broader and even more interesting generalizations, those that transcend specific cognitive domains. Cognitive linguists have been especially attentive to this dimension of the new research, and they have argued persuasively for the cognitive generality of the mappings, correspondences, bindings, integration, perspectival organization, windows of attention, pragmatic functions, framing, force dynamics, prototype structures, and dynamic simulations that underlie the construction of meaning as reflected by language use. As a result, linguistics is no longer a self-contained account of the internal properties of languages; it is in its own right a powerful means of revealing and explaining general aspects of human cognition.

## 2. The case of conceptual integration

Any science is deeply dependent on the methods at its disposal and finds its essence in the types of generalizations that it seeks to attain. For this reason, changes of methods and shifts in the notion of what constitutes a generalization have a major impact on the evolution of scientific inquiry. The transitions from alchemy to chemistry, from classical thermodynamics to particle kinetics, from Euclid's geometry to Descartes', display the full force of such changes when we look back at them with hindsight. At the time of the transition itself, however, things are more fuzzy. It is not immediately clear in what respect methods have changed, and to what extent the generalizations have become different. Some of this may be true today, mutatis mutandis, in the shifts of emphasis that cognitive science has triggered with respect to the role and study of language within the scientific field of cognition in general.

In the present paper, I will use the work some of us have been doing on conceptual blending to illustrate the more general epistemological issues evoked above. Some familiarity with conceptual blending in general is assumed. The reader may consult Fauconnier and Turner (1996, 1998) or Coulson (1997) for general presentations of the framework.

### 2.1 General features and origins of our conceptual blending theory

Blending is a widely applicable cognitive operation. It matches two input spaces through a partial cross-space mapping and projects selectively from both inputs into a third space, the blend, which gets elaborated dynamically. The cross-space mapping exploits shared schematic structure in the inputs or develops additional shared schematic structure. This common structure is contained and elaborated in a fourth space, the generic space. The four spaces (inputs, generic, and blend) are connected through the projective links and constitute a "conceptual integration network" (henceforth CIN for short). A typical example is Seana Coulson's "trashcan basketball", a game that students in a dormitory might invent, consisting of throwing crumpled paper balls into a trashcan, and scoring points as in basketball (Coulson 1997). The inputs would be respectively the game of basketball itself and the dorm situation. The mapping would link the basket to the trashcan, the players to the students, the ball to the crumpled paper, with additional links developed for zones, out of bounds, and so forth. The initial generic space consists of an object being thrown into a container by someone. In the blend, the new game gets elaborated along with the physical constraints on this game specific to the dorm situation. This elaboration yields the emergent structure of the blended space.

We know at present that blending operates as part of many cognitive phenomena in action, design, science, language, art, and so forth. We also know that it can operate very quickly on-line in everyday thought and action, or very slowly over centuries as in scientific evolution and conceptual change generally, that it can be novel or entrenched to various degrees, highly noticeable or cognitively invisible, purely mental or materially and physically anchored. None of this was immediately apparent. Blending was first noticed in isolated phenomena where it seemed exceptional and even exotic.

In my own work, blends first became manifest in analogical counterfactuals such as *In France, Watergate would not have hurt Nixon*, which set up a blended situation with some features of France and others of the U.S. and the Watergate scandal. This blend is elaborated and used to reason and make points about the French and American political systems, mentalities, cultural models, and so forth. Mark Turner and I started developing a theory of blends on the basis of anomalies in metaphor theory and source-target projection. Len Talmy had noticed lexical and metaphorical blends in his work on "rubbersheet cognition". Doug Hofstadter and David Moser had pointed out cases of frame blends and before that Erving Goffman had noted the phenomenon of frame-mixing. Arthur Koestler recognized in the Buddhist monk puzzle an instance of creativity through blending. And no doubt one could find similar observations throughout the history of thought, as suggested in Turner (1996), who points out a similar example in Aristotle.

In the research on this topic that Mark Turner and I started in 1993, the initial motivation was internal to metaphor theory—what we called a refinement of the theory from the two-domain (source/target) model to a four space model in order to accommodate richer inferential schemes. But quickly, other examples showed that metaphor was only one of many cognitive phenomena involving blending. There were the analogical counterfactuals that we already knew about, and then what we later called frame networks (the *Regatta, Kant,* and *Buddhist monk* examples).[1] These conceptual phenomena were manifested through language, but non-linguistic cases were quick to follow. We found that number theory in mathematics had gone through many successive blends, typically involving inputs of space and inputs of number. And Jeff Lansing pointed out to us other fascinating cases in physics (Fourier and Maxwell's work) where scientific evolution and conceptual change had been achieved through the construction of elaborate CIN's. Dan Gruen made us aware that computer interfaces, such as the Macintosh desktop, were also cases of the same cognitive construction process, and we went on to find many other cases in action and design generally. Back to language, we were now able to see Langacker's entrenched integration processes in grammar and Goldberg's fusion of grammatical constructions as yet other manifestations of the same uniformly characterizable cognitive operation. Later work would provide many more generalizations in diverse areas such as morphology and syntax (Mandelblit 1997), literature (Oakley 1995, Freeman 1997), music (Zbikowski 1997), humor (Coulson 1997).

The point of briefly recapitulating this development of the research on conceptual integration networks is to get back to the issue of method and generalizations. In the landscape of autonomous mainstream linguistics evoked at the beginning of this paper, there is virtually no way to generalize cognitive operations in the manner just outlined and there is no method that would lead to this type of generalization. It is worth discussing a little more why this is so. There are several aspects that conspire to make it so.

## 2.2 Limitations of conventional linguistics

First, within the study of language itself in conventional linguistics, components are sharply divided in such a way that the descriptive and theoretical primitives of each component are so different that they are generally incommensurable. This makes it impossible not just to find the appropriate generalizations, but even to ask the type of questions that might lead to such generalizations. So for example, in studying CIN's we find a continuum of networks that share fundamental properties and differ along certain gradients (single-framing networks, frame networks, one-sided networks, two sided networks, ...). On this continuum we find Fregean logical forms, counterfactuals, analogies, metaphors of various sorts, and many intermediate cases that fall in between these prototypical cases. I return below to some of the distinctions along this continuum. The problem, if one grants that this is a powerful generalization, is that it is meaningless in the standard vocabulary of conventional linguistics and so-called formal semantics, in which logical forms, metaphors, and analogical counterfactuals are not even comparable at any level, theoretical or descriptive, let alone cognitive.

Second, the methods of conventional linguistics weigh heavily against the possibility of discovering regularities of the kind exemplified by CIN's. Grammaticality or acceptability judgments are not the appropriate observational data. Truth-conditional inferences or Gricean implicatures are not either. The point here is that a certain way to conceive the problem space of linguistics, or of semantics in philosophy, has determined methods and observational categories in such a way that central questions (of the form suggested by CIN's and many other constructs of cognitive semantics) cannot even be posed. As I see it, this is not only a great obstacle to scientific progress; it is also socially among the researchers in the field a source of deep misunderstandings. To the extent that the observational categories are accepted and commonly used uncritically, the new questions are not just peripheral, less important, and so on, for conventional linguistics. Rather, they make no sense at all. This is a serious concern, since generation after generation of linguists is trained according to such methods and observational distinctions. It is not a matter of different frameworks or different theories. It is, more seriously, a matter of apprehending the world of the data and the data in the world in ways that are so different that they may end up being incommensurable.

Within conventional linguistics and philosophy of language, then, we find a pretheoretical division of components and phenomena, and accepted methods for gathering data which stand in the way of making important connections and generalizations. But as regrettable as those two aspects may be, there is a third which is possibly even worse. This third aspect is the separation of matters pertaining to form and meaning in language from everything else outside of language. In the case of CIN's, the pertinent generalization is not just the one that lets us see a continuum from Fregean propositions to frames to counterfactuals and to metaphors. It is the broader generalization that links this continuum itself to a vast array of conceptual, cultural, physically and socially embodied cognitive phenomena, for example the ones cited above—evolution of the concept of number in mathematics, design of computer interfaces, emergence of new activities such as games or other cultural practices, blending with material anchors, and many more. The generalization does not consist in a reduction. All these phenomena are acknowledged to be very different from each other and to constitute rich and diverse instances of human experience. The generalization consists in being able to identify a common cognitive operation that plays a part in all of these cases. The unity and uniformity of such processes remains hidden as long as incommensurable frameworks, methods and terminologies remain attached to different areas of action and cognition.

## 2.3 Generalizations and limiting cases

Let me now go into a little more detail, using aspects of conceptual integration theory to illustrate the broader epistemological points. Most of the examples I will use are taken from joint work in progress by Mark Turner and myself.[2]

Science proceeds by means of a dialectical succession of differentiations and unifications. In the case of language and thought, it is undeniably useful to identify and distinguish fixed and novel meanings, predicate-argument structure, figurative vs. more literal expressions, conditionals of various sorts, and so on. At the same time, when fine distinctions are made along many dimensions, a contrary force invites us to look for unity behind the diversity.

Take a straightforward example from geometry. An hyperbola, an ellipse, a parabola, a circle are all clearly different shapes. At an intuitive level, they fall into different categories. Mathematically, they can be given different precise geometric characterizations, specific to each kind of curve. Even more different intuitively from such curves are the straight line, or a fortiori the geometric point. And yet, all these geometric shapes can be viewed as variations on a single theme—the two-dimensional planar section of a three-dimensional (quadric) cone. Keep the plane perpendicular to the axis of the cone, and you get all circles, tilt the plane to obtain ellipses, tilt a little more for parabolas, and tilt again for hyperbolas. Move the plane parallel to one of the sides of the cone until the parabola condenses into a straight line. Move the plane towards the vertex of the cone, until ellipses or circles shrink into a single point. All of these shapes are conic sections, and in spite of the sharp differences they display, fit on the same conceptual continuum. On this continuum, we find prototypes—the oval of an ellipse, the parabola of the cannonball shooting through the air, the circle of a beer coaster, the asymptotic hyperbola. And we find limiting cases—the straight line, the point, the circle itself relative to ellipses, or the parabola as a limiting case of ellipses stretched out to infinity.

A theory of conic sections offers a way to see a useful mathematical unity behind the obvious diversity of shapes and figures, without reducing this diversity to a single prototype (we do not say that because these shapes, when viewed from this perspective, belong to the same continuum on which the circle is a prototype, they are therefore all more or less prototypical circles). CIN's offer a similar way to see unity behind the obvious diversity of particular manifestations of meaning constructions. We start, as in the conic section case, by formulating the general characterization evoked above (cross-space mapping, projection into a blend, emergent structure by completion and elaboration, etc.). Then we look at specific variants of this general structured dynamic process.

Coulson's trashcan basketball, in spite of its simplicity, represents a fairly general kind of CIN. It is called a two-sided network, because there is frame projection from both inputs (basketball and throwing paper into baskets). There is emergent structure in the blend through mental elaboration and physical confrontation with the affordances of the real world in which the blend is run. Notice that the basketball blend does not fall into one of the particular more specific forms which I shall show are prototypes along the continuum of blending. It is not understood as a metaphor. It is not counterfactual; the new game really takes place. It is not a Fregean composition of basketball and paper-throwing. It is not an analogy between two preexisting domains (basketball and waste disposal)—the point of the blend is not to point out some analogy between those two domains, and exploit one (basketball) to make inferences about the other (paper disposal).

Now, as in the "point as conic section" example, let's look at some limiting cases of CIN's. A generic space has elements and relations. Take a limiting case where the number of relations is zero and the number of elements is two. Take Input 1 in the network to be a subpart with two role-elements and one relation of a more general frame, for example the *father-child* subframe of our more general kinship frame. And take Input 2 to consist only of two elements with no relation between them, for instance, *Paul* and *Sally*. A simple cross-space mapping can link the two inputs, with a minimal generic space, as in Figure 1.

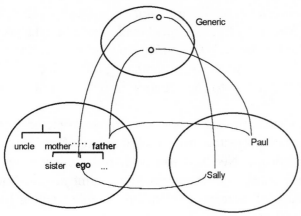

*Figure 1*

Now, project structure from both inputs into a blended space, with fused counterparts, as shown in Figure 2.

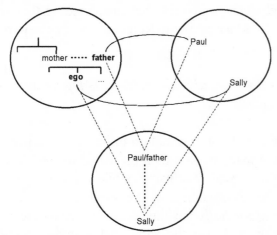

*Figure 2*

This is of course a very simple network, and the structure in the blend is almost entirely obtained by composition of the input structures. It is essentially equivalent to a Fregean composition, expressed in logical notation by something like

(1)  FATHER ( Paul, Sally )

It is also equivalent to filling in slots in a frame (father, ego) with fillers (Paul, Sally). In English, this blend would be triggered by sentences like *Paul is the father of Sally*. Another way to think about the resulting blend is to view it as instantiating the projection of the kinship frame in Input 1 onto the situation in Input 2, consisting of Paul and Sally.

We call a CIN with such properties (frame projected from one input, and content projected from the other input) a *Single-framing Integration Network*. Needless to say, if this were the only form of integration ever observed, there would be scant justification for setting up a theory of conceptual blending. Simple framing (or its Fregean equivalent) would suffice.

Still, in spite of the glaring simplicity of single-framing frameworks, it is worth looking just a little at the embryonic blending that they do contain, because it will turn out to have consequences for our continuum. First, there is some non purely compositional structure in the blend after all, since a new role has been created that was in neither input, the role *father of Sally*. Reference to this new role is possible after it has been created:

(2)    *Paul is the father of Sally. As such, he is legally responsible for this auto accident.*

Second, some structural information in Input 2 was used in setting up the cross-space mapping and then projected to the blended space: that *Sally* is a girl or woman's name, while *Paul* is a boy or man's name. Since *father* is specified in the kinship frame as "man", it matches *Paul* and not *Sally*. In the blend, we have the information that Paul is a man, and also the additional structure that Sally is a daughter, not a son. This is provided less trivially than it seems by automatic alternations in the kinship frames of Input 1 (female ego-father / daughter-ego). As a result, another role, *daughter of Paul*, is set up implicitly in the blend.

Now we can take another look at the Generic space. When a kinship frame is mapped onto two people, the generic is more than just any two elements. It has attribute structure; fathers and daughters are people; Paul and Sally are people. So the generic space in our example is the simple structure of "two people". This is a slightly abstract notion, since the kinship roles are people in an abstract sense. As the CIN gets elaborated dynamically, the Generic space itself gets elaborated. The two people are additionally a man and a woman/girl. The fact that all spaces, including the generic, get elaborated dynamically in the construction of a network is an important general property of CIN's. So after elaboration, the Single-framing CIN in our kinship example looks something like the configuration of Figure 3.

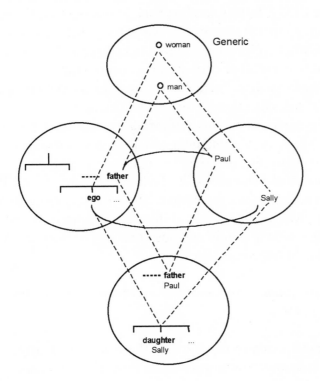

*Figure 3*

Recall that this kind of example would not by itself constitute strong evidence for blending. The point is different. If CIN's generally are part of our meaning construction capacity, then Single-framing CIN's are available as one particular type of CIN, and they account for the kind of meaning construction usually subsumed under framing or Fregean propositions. In other words, we do not need CIN's for one kind of phenomena, and Fregean propositions or framing for another. This is of course like saying that we do not need a theoretical framework for circles distinct from the framework used to study ellipses and hyperbolas. That in turn does not mean that we can't study the special properties of circles (as opposed to other conic sections). By the same token, we may want to study the special properties of Single-framing networks (as opposed to other CIN's), because such networks are common and constitute a prototype on the continuum of CIN's. In fact, looking back in this light on the Fregean (and Tarskian) approach to meaning, we can say that typical semantic theories took what we're calling here Single-framing CIN's to be the defining prototype for all of core meaning construction, and dismissed other phenomena such as metaphor or analogy as belonging to entirely different areas like rhetoric or general reasoning.

The above argument for understanding framing as a prototypical (and limiting) case on a continuum of CIN's is based on theoretical economy and generality of cognitive operations. But we can offer additional empirical evidence in its favor. If we are indeed dealing with a continuum, then we should find CIN's that are close to Single-framing, but that let in slightly different projections or emergent structure, not available purely compositionally. Consider first mythological variants of fatherhood such as:

(3)  *Zeus is the father of Athena. She was born out of his head, fully clad in armor.*

This example points to the fact that there was more pattern completion and projection from inputs in the *Paul* and *Sally* case than we had realized. We would have inferred naturally from that case the existence of a mother, biological birth, baby, and so on. All these inferences are cancelled in the *Zeus* and *Athena* case. But some more general schemas of human progeneration are maintained—the offspring comes out of the body of a parent. The key to this is selective projection from the inputs and particular elaborations in the blend. In

Input 2, the actors are deities with special dispensations with respect to ordinary biology. The second sentence (*She was born ...*) explicitly asserts a particular elaboration of the blend that prevents the usual projections from the kinship input 1. Fregean compositionality would fail to allow any of this. There would either be excessive projections from the kinship frame, which would make the Zeus case contradictory. Or else, there would be a stripped down minimal notion of fatherhood, which would then fail to account for the richness of inference in the ordinary case of Paul and Sally. Of course, the Zeus case cannot be attributed to figurative speech or analogy. In spite of the non-conventional birth methods employed, Zeus is still quite literally Athena's father. Family structure is inferred along with sentiments and emotions that come with it.

Now consider a neighbor who takes care of Sally for the day while Paul is away, carrying out fatherly duties like making her lunch, accompanying her to school, reading bedtime stories. That neighbor can say to Sally: *I'm your father for today.* A different blend than before is constructed. Family structure, genealogy, and progeneration are no longer projected, but many other typical aspects of the father-daughter relationship are projected (routines, taking care, responsibility, affection, protection, guidance, authority, etc.). Compositionality is no longer at all an option to account for this case. Too many properties felt as central are missing. We have moved along the CIN continuum from the pole of Single-framing networks. But clearly, we have not reached a point on the continuum that would be felt intuitively to be metaphorical. Fatherhood is not a metaphor for what the neighbor is doing. In fact, although some analogy has now contributed to the mapping, the function of this blend is stronger than just analogy between the neighbor's actions and a father's actions. The neighbor in this local context is really filling in the role of the father in relevant respects, not just doing something "similar" to what the father does. The flexibility of blending with selective projection and contextual elaboration allows for this intermediate kind of situation which doesn't fit a prototypical semantic or pragmatic characterization.

## 3. The continuum of C.I. networks

This brings me back to the epistemological issue of what constitutes a generalization. I am offering evidence for seeing apparently disparate notions like framing, metaphor, and so forth, as manifestations of a deeper unitary operation of integration. But that evidence, in addition to generalizing over the types of phenomena, suggests that we are not dealing with discrete types but rather with a continuum, on which certain CIN's stand out as prototypical of metaphor, or counterfactuality, or framing, and so forth. This predicts correctly that we will find a range of conceptual integration phenomena along this continuum, which do not fit neatly into the usual types. The analogy here could be made with numbers. It was a non-trivial extension of arithmetic to view integers and fractions ("proportions") as belonging to a common continuum of rational numbers, and the concept of that continuum in turn led to the consideration of other types of numbers that might lie among (and between) the others. Their empirical manifestation was found in "distances" (lengths), for instance, the Pythagorean hypotenuse of a right triangle.

Consider further examples linked to *father*:

(4)  a. *The Pope is the father of all catholics.*
     b. *The Pope is the father of the Catholic church.*
     c. *George Washington is the father of our country.*

They are farther along the continuum. The first still has people in the generic space. Selective projection has emphasized authority, size of the family, responsibility, leadership, social role (from the kinship input) and specific properties of religion, catholicism from the input with *the Pope* and *all catholics*. The second arguably projects the role of a child to a single social entity (*the Church*). The corresponding generic is more abstract. The blend reflects a type of socio-cultural model, in which a social entity (church, nation, community) is the "child" of its leader. Although *father* is no longer applied in anything like a literal sense, such examples are probably felt to be extensions of the use of *father* rather than clear metaphors. With the George

Washington sentence, we go a little bit further by highlighting the causality in time between the parent and child, and between the founder and the nation. This abstraction, forcing a generic schema at a higher level, increases the perceived difference between the two inputs and their domains. The impression of metaphor is undoubtedly stronger. And that subjective impression reaches a higher point when the two domains are even more explicitly distinguished, as in *Newton is the father of physics*. Physics, as opposed to church and country does not even stand in metonymic relation to people and groups of people. Yet, Newton and Washington as adult men, have all the criterial biological features of possible fathers plus some of the stereotypical social ones (authority, responsibility, ...). The CIN's are two-sided—they bring in frame structure from both inputs. Even more subjectively metaphorical are cases like Pound's *Fear, father of cruelty* (Turner 1987), where the two domains (emotions/qualities and people/kinship) have no literal overlap at all, and the projected shared schema is correspondingly abstract (causality). And finally, Wordsworth' acrobatic metaphor *The child is the father of the man* (Turner 1987) comes around almost full circle by using background knowledge (children grow into men) to create emergent structure in the blend giving a rich instantiation to the abstract generic causal structure which maps kinship to the human condition in an unorthodox way.

This gradient of the CIN continuum along the dimension of metaphoricity allows us to see the similarity between framing in prototypical metaphors and framing in logic. In the blend for *Fear, father of cruelty*, a new conception of fear and cruelty has been created. Fear and cruelty are endowed with a kinship structure which is much more than an abstract causal relation. This is the equivalent in CIN terms of what Lakoff and Johnson have often said about enriching the conceptualization of a target through metaphor. But it is also of the same cognitive nature as the much less spectacular process of projecting a kinship subframe onto Paul and Sally. Extension is possible in both cases. We can wonder who the mother, siblings or children of Sally might be. And we can wonder who the mother, siblings or children of cruelty might be. We can ask if Fear and Cruelty travel together like

Father and Son, or if the Son shows up only when the Father has prepared the ground for him. In other words, elaboration of the blend in a metaphorical CIN will rely heavily on rich aspects of the "source" input, not just on the abstract causal schema in the generic space. This is parallel to the elaborations of a blend in a Single-framing CIN on the basis of the frame projected from the framing input. It's once we know that Paul and Sally are father and daughter that we think of looking for the rest of their family or of asking what their father-daughter relationship is like. Blends lead to new conceptualizations which lead to new actions. For example, the notion of *computer virus* is a blend of biological and computational inputs. The conceptualiza-tion *computer virus* helps to lead the expert's thinking and action in a certain direction: the creation of *vaccines* and *disinfectants*.

I will return below to other noteworthy aspects of the CIN contin-uum, in particular along other dimensions than the metaphorical. But first, let us recapitulate the arguments for generalization and see if there is or is not available evidence from other sources. The first argument is one of structural and dynamic generality. Previously sharply distinguished processes like framing and metaphor can be viewed as instances of the more general (and independently needed) notion of CIN. The second argument is one of continuity. Between a Single-framing CIN based on *father* and a metaphorical one also based on *father*, we find many intermediate cases, which are not prototypically Fregean or prototypically metaphorical. Such CIN's can differ from each other in their one-sidedness (entire frame from one input) or two-sidedness (frame projection from both inputs), in the type of selective projection, in the similarity or dissimilarity of the domains for the inputs, in the abstractness of the generic space, and other factors not yet mentioned.

The kinds of blends we have been talking about can be constructed using language. The evidence we have invoked is semantic. Can we find syntactic evidence for the generalizations defended here? One kind of evidence would be very strong: if the phenomena considered here are indeed instances of the same kind of meaning construction (through CIN's), then this might be reflected syntactically by the use of a single syntactic form to prompt their construction. In fact, English, almost too good to be true in this regard, has a construction which is specialized in exactly this way. The construction is the apparently harmless but actually immensely powerful construction "$NP_x$ is $NP_y$ of $NP_z$". Turner (1991) has explained how this construction can systematically prompt metaphorical and analogical mappings. $NP_x$ and $NP_z$ identify elements x and z in a target space. NP identifies element y in a source space. The copula *is* indicates that x and y are counterparts. And the understander must identify the two relevant domains and set up an implicit element w to be the counterpart of y. Turner gives examples like *Vanity is the quicksand of reason*. The target is concerned with human traits like reason and vanity, the source has to do with travelling and falling into quicksand. The missing element w is the traveler. The structure in the source is one of a traveler falling into quicksand, and therefore failing in his enterprise (perhaps to the point of dying). In the target we understand that reason is similarly seriously impeded by vanity. The blend corresponding to the grammatical construction "$NP_x$ is $NP_y$ of $NP_z$" is thus:

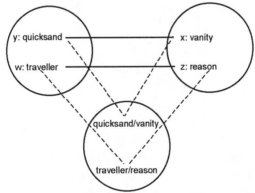

*Figure 4*

But now, quite interestingly from the point of view of our generalization along the CIN continuum, we see that the same construction also provides Single-framing blends, when the mapping is not a metaphor, but a simple framing. *Paul is the father of Sally* has the very same syntactic form as *Vanity is the quicksand of reason*, and as argued above yields the blend of Figure 2, mapping the kinship sub-frame "father-ego" onto the two people Paul and Sally, and integrating the two inputs into a more richly structured blend. The mapping scheme is exactly the same as in the metaphorical case: x and z in one space are Paul and Sally. y in the other space is the role "father", and it is the counterpart of x (Paul). The missing element w is the "ego" of the kinship frame. This is shown in Figure 5, identical to Figure 2 plus the x, y, z, w labels:

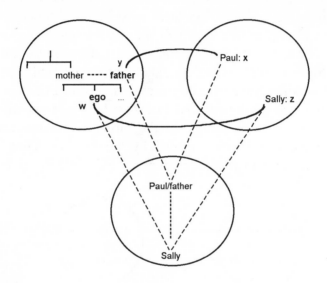

*Figure 5*

We can therefore take the construction "NP *be* NP *of* NP" in English to be a general prompt to construct an XYZ blend (a CIN). The construction will cover not only single framing and metaphor, but also all the intermediate CIN's mentioned above (*Zeus is the father of Athena, I'm the father of Sally for today, The Pope is the father of the Church*, and so on).

But doesn't *of* have a prototypical meaning linking part and whole, as in *the door of the car* or *the top of the building*? Of course, and this is precisely the point of our generalization and an illustration that prototypes are found all along the continuum. The word *top* does not in itself denote a part of a building. It is part of a more general frame—roughly things that have vertical orientations and are bound in space. So when we point to a location in the building and say *This is the top of the building*, we are constructing a Single-framing XYZ blend, just as in the other cases. *"this"* identifies location x in Input 2 (the building); *"the top"* identifies a vertical extremity y in the "top-bottom" frame of Input 1, *"the building"* identifies element z in Input 1. The missing element w is the general notion of vertically oriented thing in the frame of Input 1. This is shown in Figure 6.

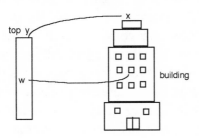

*Figure 6*

In this Single-framing CIN, the relevant generic relation common to the two inputs is indeed "part-whole": y is a part of w, and x is a part of z. So we see that because we have more general vs. more specific frames, one effect of Single-framing can be to set up a part-whole relationship. The same is true for *"door of the car"*. *door* identifies quite generally something that opens into a container. That general frame of a container with a "door" is projected onto the more specific frame of "car", and the XYZ mapping scheme plus construction of the Single-framing CIN identifies a part of a car with specific properties of the "container with an opening" frame.

So the picture that emerges is something like the following. *"x is the y of z"* is a syntactic construction that prompts the conceptual construction of a CIN with the general properties outlined above—x and z in one input, mapped to y and w in another input, and integration into a blend from those two inputs. The kind of CIN will depend on the kinds of inputs we build based on the linguistic characterizations of x, y, z, and background and contextual information. Words like *father*, *top*, *door*, will evoke certain frames easily, and may prompt Single-framing (a simple default strategy that yields what we perceive to be a more literal meaning). But discrepancy between the two inputs (as in *father of cruelty*) will lead to more elaborate CIN's and subjective feelings of increased non-literality and metaphoricity along the continuum.

Notice that when an entrenched metaphor is the appropriate conventional way to frame an input, as for example with TIME AS SPACE (*Christmas is not far*) the corresponding CIN will constitute the default, and there will be no feeling at all of metaphoricity. For example with our XYZ construction, expressions like *the end of the week, the middle of the month* construct a CIN based on the cross-space mapping of space (middle of an object, end of an object or path) onto time. Because this cross-space mapping is the conventional metaphor TIME AS SPACE, it is directly available and the expression is "felt" to be literal. Subjective feelings of metaphoricity or non-literality have more to do with distance from entrenched defaults and basic mappings, than with whether metaphor is actually involved or not. Another way to say this is that conventional blends based on basic and general metaphors are not felt subjectively to be different from many kinds of conventional single framing, although they are technically in different positions on our continuum of CIN's. Cognitive effort and specificity of domains interact in this respect with the continuum. This can be taken as an additional argument for the fundamental unity of the processes at work.

The fact that syntactic constructions may characterize CIN's in this way allows us to look at issues of composition and compositionality in a more revealing way. There has often been a tension in linguistic theories between the formal compositionality of syntactic forms and the non-compositionality of the corresponding meanings. But we can now see syntactic forms as prompting mapping schemes rather than conveying static truth conditions. And those mapping schemes (as opposed to static truth conditions) can be composed in a way that follows the overt syntactic composition.

In Fauconnier and Turner (in preparation), we show in some detail how this works for the "*x is the y of z*" construction discussed above.

We show that the successive blends systematically triggered by sentences like:

(5)  a.  *Elizabeth is the roommate of the daughter of Paul.*
     b.  *Prayer is the echo of the darkness of the soul.*

are exactly the same, in spite of the fact that the first composes two Single-framing networks (and is therefore equivalent to an ordinary Fregean composition), while the second composes two highly metaphorical CIN's and is not truth-compositional.

I will not give the technical derivation here, but the idea is fairly simple. *"Elizabeth is the roommate of z"* sets up a CIN linking an initial space with people to a frame of housing (input space APARTMENT). A blend is created in which Elizabeth has the role roommate with respect to a second element z, constructed by a second *of*-construction which links z to another space containing the kinship frame ego-daughter. *"the daughter of Paul"* links z to *daughter* and *Paul* to ego, and blends again, giving the configuration of Figure 7:

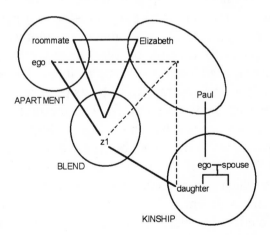

*Figure 7*

Applying the very same instructions to the formally identical sentence, *Prayer is the echo of the darkness of the soul,* yields exactly the same blending configuration, as shown in Figure 8.

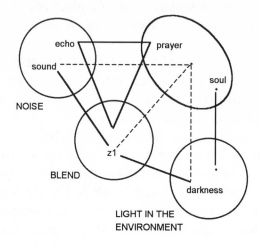

*Figure 8*

In Figure 7, we have a composite frame, and the links in the CIN allow us to access the appropriate inputs—the two people Paul and Elizabeth in one space, the role roommate in another, and the role daughter in a third. As a result of this successive blending, a third person has now been added to the "people" input. The space element for that person is entirely characterized by its position in the blend and links to the spaces containing frames. The meaning in this case is created by successive Single-framing CIN's. In Figure 8, the ultimate mapping configuration is the same, but the cross-space mappings are metaphorical. The blend is intuitively more complex, because it contains elements which belong simultaneously to the domain of sound and to the domain of light. The understander presumably expands more cognitive effort because the overall integration is none-standard and because the CIN's are highly two-sided.

It is also interesting to see in these examples that the composition of the mapping schemes can follow the linear order of the English sentence: *Elizabeth* to *roommate* starts the cross-space mapping; *of* signals the integration and the blended space; *daughter* moves us to a kinship space with a second projection; *of* signals the second integration; *Paul* provides the last missing element for this integration, from the initial input space. The same would be true in the composite metaphorical blend: the metaphor of *prayer* as an *echo* starts the process, and sets up a space of sound. *darkness* links the first blend to a new space of light, and *soul* provides the last missing element to complete the second integration and the multiple metaphor.

The mapping schemes could also be composed in the reverse order, "daughter of Paul" first, and then "roommate of". The resulting configuration (Figure 7) does not reflect any ordering. This seems desirable since we might be processing the sentence from scratch and be introducing the frames in the order in which they appear linguistically, or we might have already set up the integration "daughter of Paul" before building the composite blend.

Fregean composition does not apply for the metaphorical case, and for the single-framing one, it would have to follow the reverse order, building the compositional meaning bottom up, right to left.

Our view of compositionality, only sketched out here, would generalize a fundamental process of meaning construction over the entire continuum of CIN's. It would retain the insights of truth-conditional composition for strict single-framing networks, while accounting for the many cases which are not compositional in the sense of truth-conditional semantics.

## 4. Conclusion

I have attempted in this paper to discuss some general methodological issues pertaining to the study of language in the framework of modern cognitive science, and to illustrate some of the points with examples from current work on conceptual integration.

One emphasis from this perspective is that explaining linguistic distributions is not an end in itself. Rather, it is one of the many facets of an overall understanding of cognition and language. A second point, *economy*, is that language forms carry very little information per se, but derive their power by activating preexistent networks in a way that creates emergent structure. A third point is the *operational uniformity* of much backstage cognition, hidden from consciousness, counterintuitive, and masked by our folk theories. From uniformity follows *cognitive generalization*. Linguistics becomes more than a self-contained study of language; it contributes to revealing and explaining general aspects of human cognition.

## Notes

1. Here are brief descriptions of the three cases of frame networks mentioned in the text:

   **The debate with Kant** *[philosophy teacher expressing his/her opinion]*
   I claim that reason is a self-developing capacity. Kant disagrees with me on this point. He says it's innate, but I answer that that's begging the question, to which he counters, in *Critique of Pure Reason,* that only innate ideas have power. But I say to that, what about neuronal group selection? And he gives no answer.

   **The Buddhist monk**
   Riddle of the Buddhist monk and the mountain: A Buddhist monk begins at dawn one day walking up a mountain, reaches the top at sunset, mediates at the top for several days until one dawn when he begins to walk back to the foot of the mountain, which he reaches at sunset. Making no assumptions about his starting or stopping or about his pace during the trips, prove that there is a place on the path which he occupies at the same hour of the day on the two separate journeys.

   **The boat race** *[excerpt from a sailing magazine]*
   As we went to press, Rich Wilson and Bill Biewenga were barely maintaining a 4.5 day lead over the ghost of the clipper *Northern Light*, whose record run from San Francisco to Boston they're trying to beat. In 1853, the clipper made the passage in 76 days, 8 hours. —"Great America II" *Latitude* 38, volume 190, April 1993, page 100.

   (They are analyzed in Fauconnier and Turner 1996, 1998)

2. I thank Mark Turner for permission to include examples from our joint work to illustrate the methodological issues of the present article.

# References

Bateson, Gregory
1972    *Steps to an Ecology of the Mind.* New York: Ballantine Books.
Coulson, Seana
1997    Semantic leaps: Frame-shifting and conceptual blending. Ph.D. dissertation, University of California, San Diego.
Cutrer, Michelle
1994    Time and tense in narratives and everyday language. Ph.D. dissertation, University of California, San Diego.
Dinsmore, John
1991    *Partitioned Representations.* Dordrecht: Kluwer.
Fauconnier, Gilles
1994    *Mental Spaces.* New York: Cambridge University Press. [Originally published (1985) Cambridge: MIT Press.]
1997    *Mappings in Thought and Language.* Cambridge: Cambridge University Press.
Fauconnier, Gilles and Eve Sweetser (eds.)
1996    *Spaces, Worlds, and Grammar.* Chicago: University of Chicago Press.
Fauconnier, Gilles, and Mark Turner
1996    Blending as a central process of grammar. In: Adele Goldberg (ed.), *Conceptual Structure, Discourse, and Language*, 113-130. Stanford: Center for the Study of Language and Information [distributed by Cambridge University Press].
1998    Conceptual Integration Networks. *Cognitive Science* 22(2): 133-187.
in prep. Making Sense.
Fillmore, Charles
1985    Frames and the semantics of understanding. *Quaderni di Semantica* 6(2): 222-253.
Freeman, Margaret
1997    Grounded spaces: Deictic -self anaphors in the poetry of Emily Dickinson. *Language and Literature* 6(1): 7-28.
Goffman, Erving
1974    *Frame Analysis.* New York: Harper and Row.
Goldberg, Adele
1994    *Constructions.* Chicago: University of Chicago Press.
Hofstadter, Douglas
1995a   *Fluid Concepts and Creative Analogies.* New York: Basic Books.
Koestler, Arthur
1964    *The Act of Creation.* New York: Macmillan.

126    Gilles Fauconnier

Lakoff, George
   1987    *Women, Fire, and Dangerous Things*, case study 1, 380-415. Chicago: University of Chicago Press
Lakoff, George, and Mark Johnson
   1998    *Philosophy in the Flesh: The Embodied Mind and its Challenge to Western Thought.* New York: Basic Books.
Lakoff, George, and Mark Turner
   1989    *More than Cool Reason: A Field Guide to Poetic Metaphor.* Chicago: University of Chicago Press.
Langacker, Ronald W.
   1987/91 *Foundations of Cognitive Grammar. Vol. I, II.* Stanford: Stanford University Press.
Liddell, Scott K.
   1996    Spatial representations in discourse: Comparing spoken and signed language. *Lingua* 98: 145-167.
Mandelblit, Nili
   1997    Grammatical blending: Creative and schematic aspects in sentence processing and translation. Ph.D. dissertation, University of California, San Diego.
Moser, David, and Douglas Hofstadter
   (undated ms.) Errors: A royal road to the mind. *Center for Research on Concepts and Cognition.* Indiana University.
Nunberg, Geoffrey
   1978    *The Pragmatics of Reference.* Bloomington, Ind.: Indiana University Linguistics Club.
Oakley, Todd
   1995    Presence: the conceptual basis of rhetorical effect. Ph.D. dissertation, University of Maryland.
Robert, Adrian
   1998    Blending in the interpretation of mathematical proofs. In: Jean-Pierre Koenig (ed.). *Discourse and Cognition: Bridging the Gap,* 337-350. Stanford: Center for the Study of Language and Information (CSLI) [distributed by Cambridge University Press].
Sanders, José, and Gisela Redeker
   1996    Perspective and the representation of speech and thought in narrative discourse. In: Fauconnier, Gilles and Eve Sweetser (eds.), *Spaces, Worlds, and Grammar,* 290-317. Chicago: University of Chicago Press.
Sweetser, Eve
   1990    *From Etymology to Pragmatics: Metaphorical and Cultural Aspects of Semantic Structure.* (Cambridge Studies in Linguistics 54.) Cambridge: Cambridge University Press.

Talmy, Leonard

1977    Rubber-sheet cognition in language. *Papers from the 13th Regional Meeting of the Chicago Linguistic Society* 13: 612-628.

1978    Figure and ground in complex sentences. In: Joseph H. Greenberg (ed.), *Universals of Human Language: Syntax,* Vol. 4, 625-649. Stanford: Stanford University Press.

1985    Force dynamics in language and thought. In: William H. Eilfort *et al.* (eds.) *Papers from the Parasession on Causatives and Agentivity,* 293-337. Chicago: Chicago Linguistic Society.

1996    Fictive motion in language and "ception". In: Paul Bloom, Mary A. Peterson, Lynn Nadel, and Merrill F. Garrett (eds.), *Language and Space,* 211-276. Cambridge, MA: MIT Press.

Turner, Mark

1987    *Death is the Mother of Beauty.* Chicago: The University of Chicago Press.

1991    *Reading Minds: The Study of English in the Age of Cognitive Science.* Princeton: Princeton University Press.

1996    *The Literary Mind.* New York: Oxford University Press.

Van Hoek, Karen

1997    *Anaphora and Conceptual Structure.* Chicago: The University of Chicago Press.

Zbikowski, Lawrence

1997    Conceptual blending and song. Manuscript, University of Chicago.

# Compositionality and blending: semantic composition in a cognitively realistic framework

## Eve Sweetser

Compositionality is a central fact of language, and one which has been given inadequate treatment in formal semantic models. Cognitive linguistics has been sensitive to the need for complex and diverse treatments of the structure of linguistic categories, as required by the complexity of actual cognitive categorization and linguistic usage. Attendant on a more complex theory of meaning, however, are the problems of describing compositional combinations of these complex semantic entities.

This paper uses Fauconnier and Turner's (1995, 1996, 1998) theory of Mental Space Blending to describe the mechanisms of linguistic compositionality involved specifically in the English Adjective-Noun modification construction. An analysis in terms of blended spaces allows us to give a simple and effective treatment of apparently intractable cases such as *likely candidate* or *usual suspect*. Among the entities accessible for blending must be the speaker's epistemic and speech-act spaces (*cf.* Sweetser 1990, Dancygier and Sweetser 1996). A blended spaces treatment also, as it turns out, permits us to unpack a host of unacknowledged but genuine possibilities for interpretation of supposedly more tractable examples such as *red apple*. Since even these "simple" cases turn out to require a broad range of cognitive mechanisms (including metaphor, metonymy, frames, mental spaces, active zones and profiling, and implicit evocation of the speaker's epistemic and communicative spaces), we have surely lost no economy in making reference to these same mechanisms in an account of *likely*. What we stand to gain is a more satisfying and unified treatment of adjectival modification, and potentially of compositionality in general.

## 1. Introduction. Hunting for *likely candidates* for an analysis of *fake gun* in a theory with *rampant polysemy:* the *usual suspects* won't do.

What do we do when we put together a "simple" pairing of semantic elements like the senses of a modifying adjective and a noun? We know that even *red pencil* and *red apple* do not refer to the simple intersection of pencils or apples with red things. We know that *fake guns* may well be real objects, and hence are not the intersection of guns and fake things (*cf.* Vendler 1967); *good parents* may be bad accountants or bad swimmers, and thus are not plausibly the intersection of independently-determined sets of parents and good things (*cf.* Austin 1964). To bring more complex and less-discussed examples to the fore, combinations such as *likely candidate, rampant polysemy, usual suspect* or *professional suicide* pose problems that are perhaps even more severe than some of the ones previously mentioned. Examining such cases has eliminated the plausibility of a simple set-intersection theory of the semantic relationship of noun with modifying adjective. This result in itself is not any particular surprise, since the last twenty years of cognitive semantic research as a whole has argued strongly against the plausibility of individual word-meanings referring to membership in classical sets.[1] But the process of understanding the combination of these non-classical categories into non-truth-functional larger semantic units is a serious challenge for the cognitive linguist. My goal here is not to pretend to offer a complete and correct theory of semantic compositionality, but to show how far we have come towards meeting some parts of that challenge, and make some suggestions as to how we can go further.

First, I shall lay out examples showing that we need (at least) all of the major semantic mechanisms proposed in recent cognitive linguistic theories, merely to account for the combinatorial semantics of English Adjective-Noun (henceforth A-N) modification. Such a complexity is a problem for any theory which does not have equivalent mechanisms available to give an account of the relevant data. And my claim may gain some initial plausibility from the fact that there has so far been little agreement among linguists as to any general treatment of the semantics of such basic constructions as A-N modifications (whether "compounds" or "free") or Noun-Noun compounds;[2] the variability and complexity of these constructions' interpretation suggests that a variety of mechanisms may be involved in their semantic composition. (The same is surely true of any number of other "simple" constructions, but we will focus for the moment on these.) Further, "easy" cases such as *red N* require so much complex interpretation that there is no tidy division to be drawn between them and the "tough" cases like *fake N, likely N,* or *proverbial N.*

Next, I shall present some more complex cases, such as *safe N,* and demonstrate that the mechanisms postulated for *red N* are also sufficient to account for these. The frames involved in the meaning of *safe* will be used as an example of the ways in which compositionality involves flexible matching between frame-evoked roles and individuals referred to.

Then I shall try to lay out a general compositional formula for the interpretation of A-N constructions in English, drawing on the work of a number of cognitive linguists. My formula will be based on Fauconnier and Turner's (1995, 1996, 1998) idea of Blended Spaces, and I put forward this case study as a rich example of the ways in which mental space structures, inter-space mappings and counterpart relationships interact with frames, metonymic and categorial relationships, active zone phenomena, profiling, viewpoint, and speech-act interactional context. It is no secret that such interaction exists—but it has perhaps been most fully discussed in the context of structures which are recognized as involving clausal (or higher-level) interpretation: conjunction, modals, anaphora, sentential modifiers, verb tense and aspect, and so on. However, it seems very clear that the semantics of nominal determiners are closely tied to mental space structure; the negotiation of mental space structure seems in fact to be the central function of definite and indefinite articles (Fauconnier 1985; Epstein 1994, 1996). Indeed, all of the forms involved in nominal grounding (in Langacker's [1987, 1990, 1991] sense) seem to be involved in representing aspects of viewpoint and mental space location. But articles and demonstratives have been recognized in most theories as linked to the broader discourse context, and therefore not interpretable exclusively on the basis of purely local linguistic content—while adjectival modification has not been clearly recognized as being directly linked to such broader structure.

Finally, my analysis of A-N constructions will turn out to require as background an understanding of multiple, implicitly available mental spaces, including a space representing the current speech interaction and a space representing the speaker's ongoing epistemic processes. I have argued extensively elsewhere for the necessity of incorporating such spaces into our semantic analyses (*cf.* Sweetser 1990, Dancygier and Sweetser 1996).[3] Other work outside the framework of Mental Spaces theory has given us compelling evidence of the need to bring the speaker's mental processes and the speech interaction: for example, Traugott (1982, 1988, 1989, 1995; Hopper and Traugott 1993) treats grammaticalization as centrally involving subjectification (defined as the integration of the speaker and the speech setting into the meaning); and Langacker's (1991a) treatment of subjectivity crucially involves a cline between implicit and explicit reference to the speech-interactional context and to the speaker's viewpoint, as a pervasive aspect of lexical and grammatical semantics as well as of contextual interpretation. And work within Mental Spaces theory has of course been based from the start on the need to bring a speaker's "base" space into any space-building process, as well as to map the negotiation between that space and others.[4] There can be no loss of economy in adding the A-N construction to the list of those whose interpretation may require implicit reference to this complex of speaker-related spaces; and this addition strengthens the impression that such implicit reference pervades the interpretive processes of English speakers, with respect to the most basic constructions of their grammar.

## 2. What is compositional depends on what semantics is

I do not know any linguists who see semantics as intrinsically non-compositional, although there may possibly be philosophers or literary critics who hold such a view. Linguists all agree, and so does the average lay person, that the reason *The cat stole the hat* means something different from *The cat ate the hat* is that *stole* and *ate* make different contributions to the interpretation of the whole, and that those contributions are systematically related to the usual conventional ranges of interpretations of *eat* and *steal* in other possible uses by English speakers. We may disagree about major related issues: for example, the extent to which idioms are processed compositionally (whether as well as, or instead of, being processed as units); the extent to which it is important to talk about meanings of syntactic constructions; the relationship between "semantic" and "pragmatic" components of a linguistically conveyed message; the relationship between linguistic interpretation and general reasoning processes of context-based inference; or the assessment of what proportion of everyday utterance-content is produced and processed by accessing already-present routines, as opposed to by brand-new composition of elements. But the basic fact of compositionality remains, and remains also for more apparently complicated cases than those involving cats, hats, and mats.

All of the last two decades of work in cognitive linguistics has radically changed our understanding of semantics. What has emerged is a semantics which is attempting to be cognitively realistic—it takes seriously the need for semantic categories to be humanly accessible and learnable, and for them to be processed against the kinds of frameworks genuinely involved in the process of understanding. As a result, there is now a community of semanticists who no longer think that meaning is a set of binary features, corresponding to objective truth-conditional relationships between form and real world. We still take seriously, as any linguist must, the need to account for the compositional nature of linguistic meaning. But we recognize that the task is a far more difficult and complex one than we might once have thought, since the meanings being put together are so much richer and less rigid than we might have imagined twenty-five years ago. The work of researchers such as Langacker (1987, 1990, 1991), Lakoff (1987), Goldberg (1995, 1997), Fillmore, Kay, and O'Connor (1988), and Kay and Fillmore (1999) on the semantics of constructions has explored new issues in the relationship between the meaning of a larger construction as a whole and the meanings of the parts of the construction. Langacker has insightfully set out other complexities of the composition of meaning, giving us concepts such as *active zone* and *elaboration*. Fauconnier's theory of Mental Spaces (Fauconnier 1985, 1997; Fauconnier and Sweetser 1996) has given us a language to talk about how linguistic forms may refer to counterparts of the primary described referent, as well as functioning to instruct the hearer about space-construction.

I shall not here be primarily concerned with the problem of assigning meaning to larger constructions as wholes, rather than to words or morphemes: I shall be working instead on the complexity of constructing compositional meaning. Some very brief examples will show how important frames, active zones, and mental spaces are in such construction. Frames (see Fillmore 1982, 1985; Fillmore and Atkins 1992) are schematic relational structures which represent the connected roles and relations that constitute the background to some semantic or conceptual category; *buy, sell, goods*, and *price* all evoke the same "commercial event" frame, but highlight or refer to different pieces of that frame. Frame structure is a powerful cognitive mechanism which underlies many instances of meaning extension: A metonymic usage such as *the pen is mightier than the sword* relies on the tight connection between certain action frames and the instruments used in those frames, which enables *pen* and *sword* to refer to those action frames and not only to the physical objects.

Like frames, active-zone phenomena are pervasive in language. As an example, let us take Langacker's (1991) discussion of the word *pencil*. When I say *I put the pencil on the desk*, my hearer is likely to understand that the whole pencil was put on top of the desk; but when I say *I put the pencil in the pencil-sharpener*, the hearer will probably understand me to mean that I inserted only the sharpenable writing end of the pencil into the sharpener. In this second case, the writing end of the pencil is the contextually relevant *active zone*, and is taken as the referent of the phrase *the pencil*.

Mental spaces, the third major theoretical construct I shall be using in my account of compositionality, are an extremely general mechanism for describing the interconnections between parts of complex conceptual structures. Although mental spaces may correspond to the sorts of structures which might in other theories be analyzed as possible worlds (for example, conditional "spaces" might be so treated), in other instances a mental space corresponds to a belief state, or to a visual representation, or to something more like a semantic domain. The crucial characteristic of a mental space is that there can be systematic cognitive mappings between it and other mental spaces, with consequences for (inter alia) reference. For example, because of the mappings between our understanding of reality and our understanding of paintings and photographs and plays, it is normal to use the name of a person to refer to the representation of that person in a painting or photograph or play. Mental spaces have internal structure which includes frame and active-zone structure; one could view Fillmore's commercial event frame as a rather schematic (partially-filled) and conventional mental space, or as a possible internal structural component of more filled-out mental spaces.[5]

Recently, Fauconnier and Turner (1995, 1996, 1998) have suggested that Noun-Noun compounds in English can best be accounted for as involving *Blended Spaces*; that is, each noun evokes a space structured by some appropriate frame, and the meaning of the whole is a successful blending of the two spaces involved. For example, in *land yacht* (used to refer to a large expensive car), the blending results in a new space wherein we imagine a land vehicle (inheriting various features from our normal framing of land transportation) which is in some ways the counterpart of a yacht (in our framing of water transportation): personally owned, expensive, luxurious, status-marking, not primarily functioning for practical transportation, and so on. Crucially a *land yacht* is not a kind of *yacht*. Fauconnier and Turner's work should be particularly welcome, since the best and most honest efforts of past linguistic analysts have vividly laid out the unpredictability and apparently unlimited semantic flexibility of the English Noun-Noun compound, without making much progress at general mechanisms for the modelling of that flexibility; an exception to this is Ryder (1994), who makes use of frames in setting up her flexible templates for Noun-Noun compound meaning, and who might well see Fauconnier and Turner as proposing an analysis which is compatible with her basic approach.[6] Coulson and Fauconnier (in press) have further suggested that in the semantics of an adjective like *fake*, there are automatically two mental spaces involved, before even blending it with any other semantics (such as that of a noun): the mental space of a dupe who sees the object as a member of some class (e.g., a gun), and that of the trickster or some more knowledgeable person who knows it is not a gun but is passing it off as one.

All of this is in evident contrast with traditional "building-block" ideas of semantic compositionality. Instead of each word or morpheme always representing the same rigid and stable semantic chunk or building-block, the same word can represent very different complex meaning structures in different contexts, and may alter flexibly depending on the meanings surrounding it: *Shakespeare* can refer to a book rather than to the author, *pencil* can refer to an active zone of the pencil, and *yacht* may not refer to a boat if preceded by *land*. Instead of making only complementary contributions to the larger compositional meaning (as blocks cannot overlap in a larger physical structure), meanings of constituents can and do overlap extensively. And instead of being separate from the builders, as blocks are, meaning structures frequently incorporate models of aspects of the meaning-constructors' interaction and viewpoints; sometimes, as we shall see, they do this without any explicit mention of the speaker and hearer.

Evidently, many analysts who see semantics and pragmatics as more separate from each other would see many of the aspects of interpretation which I have been discussing as pragmatic, not semantic. But it seems impossible to maintain this viewpoint, while giving a non-circular definition of semantics. First of all, in the A-N construction, neither the meaning of the Adjective nor that of the Noun is independent of the other's meaning. (Recall that *red hair* is not the color which *red* evokes in non-hair-related contexts, and a *stone lion* is not a lion, just as—to give a N-N example as well—a *land yacht* is not a *yacht*.) One possibility, then, is that special semantic processes apply in these cases, which replicate the pragmatically based interpretive processes seen elsewhere (e.g., the apparently contextually prompted non-focal-red reading given to the word *red* in the utterance "It's red," said on examining a new baby's hair color.) Another possibility is that the interpretation of all modification constructions is pragmatic rather than semantic—which opens the door to further questions, so that in the end one would have to say that all meaning-composition is pragmatic.[7]

My own feeling is that there is little point to insistence on modularity at the cost of generalization. Inasmuch as we make use of grammatical and lexical conventions in interpreting meaning compositionally (e.g., our knowledge about the semantics of *red*, and about the A-N construction), we are using information not dependent specifically on one context of interpretation. On the other hand, interpretation is never truly context-free; because form only very partially specifies ("prompts") meaning construction,[8] we can only actually interpret complex linguistic forms by constructing some possible use or uses of those forms to convey meaning. "Neutral-context" interpretations are simply those which are so accessible from our entrenched conceptual structures that their construction requires very little help from a specific context in the outside world. Whether we call it semantics or pragmatics, such construction is part of the basic linguistic capacity to deal with compositional meaning in a systematic way.

## 3. Blending, overlap and redundancy

Let us examine a so-called simple case of A-N compositional semantics, *red ball*. One particular interpretation seems, without context, to spring to mind: a ball whose surface material is red. Of course, this is illusory: In the right context, the phrase can easily be imagined to mean a ball (from among a group of balls which are all painted blue on the surface) whose interior constituent material is red. Or a ball which is distinguished from other balls by the fact that it is filled with red paint instead of some other color of paint; or the ball which has a red mark on it, instead of otherwise similar balls marked with different colors. Or the ball belonging to the team which wears red uniforms. As Langacker (1987, 1990, 1991) has made clear to us, all semantic elaboration relationships depend on the identification of an appropriate *active zone* of the elaborated concept. The active zone of the ball may be its exterior surface—indeed, that is one highly conventionalized usage, which therefore springs readily to speakers' minds without much extra help. But it can also readily be any other relevant part of the frame associated with the ball, whatever frame has been set up in the context—so long as one can imagine that part of the frame as being the active zone which the speaker intends to elaborate by labelling it *red*.

Our prototypes and frames for *ball* and *red* are also relevant to the senses available for the phrase *red ball*. First of all, we are likely (unless otherwise informed) to imagine an object which is close to a prototypical "ball" shape (i.e., spherical), and close to the central or focal shade of red.[9] Knowing that balls are human-made objects which can be artificially colored is what influences us to readily access a sense of *red* that may be close to focal red, rather than the senses we might have accessed most immediately for *red hair* or *red apple*. (Indeed, so strong is this framing effect that it is quite difficult to imagine calling a ball *red* rather than *brown*, if it were in the color range of auburn hair.) And one might suppose further that many hearers would begin by imagining a ball used for some child's game or adult sport, rather than other ball-shaped objects such as a glass ball hung on a Christmas tree, or a candy ball.

What makes us initially feel that the red-surface sense of *red ball* is "simple" and regular and objective—that we access it without needing to engage in choosing a perspective or an active zone, or in flexibly negotiating meaning between the two word senses and between senses and context—is not merely the existence of an already conventionalized sense for the phrase, or the guidance we are given by prototypes and frames. It is also the fact that there is considerable overlap between the frames involved in the semantics of *red* and of *ball*. Even if we have to choose an active zone, balls are already physical objects, have surfaces, are made up of constituent material, and so on—and the color red can be imagined as applying to some part of them or to some related object in their physical environment. Active zones are not far to seek. Figure 1 gives a partial blended-spaces analysis of the interpretation of *red ball* as meaning a ball (perhaps a rubber ball, or other game ball) whose exterior surface is red. Compositional interpretation of the phrase requires blending of the two input spaces, one contributed by *red* and the other by *ball*, to create a coherent blended space. At first glance, the two spaces are relatively non-overlapping in structure: One refers to a color, the other to a three-dimensional solid object. But colors, of course, are conceptualized (conceptually framed) as being colors of visually perceived surfaces of objects; thus one obvious mapping between the two spaces is to map the ball onto the object whose surface is visually perceived as exhibiting the color red.

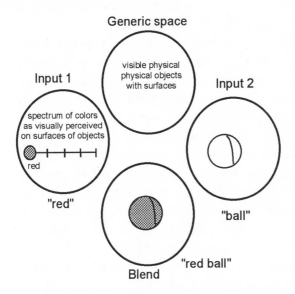

*Figure 1.* "red ball" interpreted as meaning a ball with a red surface

Yet the very fact that *red* may also refer metonymically to the identifying mark on the surface of the ball, or to the uniforms of the team who own and use the ball—or even metaphorically serve as a slur on the politics of the government of the country where the ball was manufactured—makes us already aware that the connection between the referent noun and the concept actually elaborated by *red* may go far beyond the amount of frame structure which is necessarily conventionally evoked by the word *ball*'s value as a linguistic sign. Linguists have, however, treated the most direct cases (red surface of the ball, for instance,) as the central examples, and the others as the deviations or extensions—a fact to which we shall return.

We have already said that overlap or redundancy is often preferred, rather than outlawed, in linguistic structure. But much traditional semantic analysis has been based on the opposite assumption. With some salient exceptions (Langacker's [1991] treatment of the English passive stands out as a good example here), it has been common for semanticists to say that, if a constituent morpheme of a construction apparently adds no meaning beyond that expressed by the other morphemes in the construction (contributes no added meaning as its unique contribution), it is "meaningless."

A case study in point is the treatment of *then* in English conditional constructions. Analysts have treated *then* as a meaningless formal marker of conditional consequent status, a status already sufficiently marked by the presence of *if* on the protasis, and often by clause order as well. Dancygier and Sweetser (1997) argue instead that conditional *then* is closely semantically related to temporal *then*; both are deictic to mental spaces presumably accessible to the addressee, with the difference that temporal *then* refers to a temporal space, while conditional *then* refers to a conditional one.[10] This account has the advantage of predicting some salient gaps in the use of conditional *then*, which are unmotivated by an analysis of *then* as a meaningless grammatical marker. Dancygier and Sweetser note that *then* is not possible in *even if* conditionals, for example, and that (given a deictic semantics for *then*) this fact would be predicted on the grounds that *even if* conditionals do not define a unique mental space within which the consequent holds: Indeed, their whole point is that the consequent holds in a range of mental spaces, including the one described in the consequent clause.

For example, although (1) can readily be interpreted as meaning that we'll go out to dinner only in the space wherein she arrives in time, (2) presupposes a range of spaces or situations wherein people might vote for a candidate, and includes the consequent space as an unlikely addition to this range. In (2), therefore, there is no unique referent space for *then* to refer back to.

(1)  If she arrives in time, (then) we'll go out to dinner.
(2)  Even if he commits a crime, (#then) they'll vote for him.[11]

Why did so many analysts think they could (and should) get by with a meaningless treatment of conditional *then*? The reason for this blindness was largely that the meaning of conditional *then* overlaps to a very significant extent with the meaning relations expressed by the *if P, Q* construction, *when that construction is being used predictively.* A predictive conditional such as *If she arrives on time, we'll go out to dinner* is used precisely to mean that the speaker predicts the possibility of going out based on the arrival time of the relevant participant. As Dancygier and Sweetser point out (1996, 1997), the interpretation of such a prediction as relevant is often based on the assumption that there is a two-way correlation between the two parameters P and Q— that P is being used as a predictor of Q because not only will Q occur if P, but Q is only likely to occur if P (the classic "conditional perfection" or "IFF implicature"). Under such circumstances, P is the unique space under consideration wherein Q will occur. This is true whether or not conditional *then* refers back to that unique space. And so, in such cases, conditional *then* adds little to the meaning constructed (in context) by a hearer from a simple *If P, Q*, although we might say that it formally and explicitly marks some aspects of meaning which the *If P, Q* form itself does not conventionally denote.

In general, meaning-composition is easy when there is appropriate overlap between the conceptual structures to be combined in a blend. However, either conventional lexical meaning or context may contribute that overlap. In a context where we know that there are teams of ball-players with uniforms of different colors, *red ball* can access the broader frame for *ball*, which includes the teams and their uniforms; and *red* may then apply to the color of the ball-owning team's uniforms, making use of the same mapping and blending principles which allowed us to interpret *red* as describing the external surface of the ball itself.

## 4. More obviously extended cases: safe distances, usual suspects, and intellectual sleeping pills.

Let us examine some of the more problematic cases of A-N modification for a simpleminded theory of semantic compositionality based on traditional logical semantic categorization and combination. In the case of *safe distance*, we might initially say (as objectivist semanticists) that a distance itself cannot be safe. But *safe* involves a frame of risk or danger, i.e. a possibility of harm happening to some endangered entity (here I draw on the analysis of RISK in Fillmore and Atkins 1992). The frame includes some potential cause of harm which is the source of the danger, and the knowledge that keeping endangered entities physically separate from possible sources of physical harm may prevent harm from happening, thus keeping the entities "safe." The question is how this frame is to be mapped to the frame of the noun modified by *safe*. A use like *safe baby* might encourage us to identify the baby with the endangered object (as in Figure 2), since we consider babies to be harmless, vulnerable, and deserving of cherishing and protection from harm.

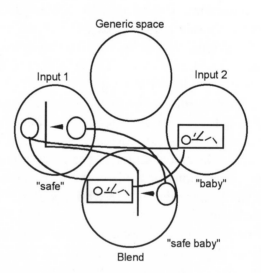

*Figure 2.* "safe baby" interpreted as meaning that the baby is the potentially endangered object

On the other hand, *safe dog (for the baby to play with)* or *safe beach (for the baby to play on)* might encourage us to identify the dog or the beach with the possible source of danger (as in Figure 3). All of this is of course contextually shaped: A *safe dog* could also mean a dog which is unlikely to be caught by a bear.

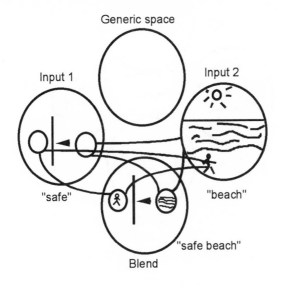

*Figure 3.* "safe beach" interpreted as meaning that the physical beach is the potential source of danger, and a human visitor is the potentially endangered object

By this analysis, a *safe house* might be a house which is not itself endangered (by an earthquake, for example), a house which is not a source of danger (to children playing in it), or a house wherein potentially endangered people are not accessible to some other source of danger (e.g., discovery by the police). Figure 4 portrays these different possible mappings between the input space defined by *safe* and that defined by *house*. A *safe distance*, on the other hand, seems most readily to mean a distance between endangered object and source of harm, which is sufficient to keep the source from harming the endangered object. Unlike *house*, which can readily fill many different slots in the frame of *safe* (since a house is commonly conceptualized variously as a valued object, a potentially dangerous environment, and a protective location), *distance* is conceptually much easier to fit into one particular slot in the *safe* frame than into others.

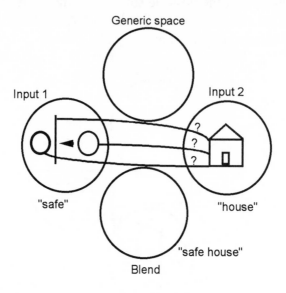

*Figure 4.* Some possible ways of interpreting "safe house"

Sometimes only metaphorical structuring will allow us to access a reading for an A-N phrase. *Intellectual sleeping pills*, as a label for sermons, is an example of this. Ignoring the composition of *sleeping pills* (itself an interesting phrasal compound), we might say that *intellectual* is typical of a class of adjectives which we might call domain adjectives (after Ernst's [1984] treatment of "domain adverbs"). It specifies a range of mental spaces, structured by frames involving intellectual activity, as opposed to physical entities and activities, or even religious or political entities and activities. The hearer's job, in finding a reading for the phrase, will therefore be to blend the space involving sleeping pills with some space involving the intellect rather than the body. Metaphoric blending achieves this: The pills, which map onto the sermons, cause physical inactivity or unconsciousness, which maps onto mental inactivity or unawareness caused by the sermons. The humor of this phrase derives from the fact that sleeping pills are intended to cause sleep, and people normally take a sleeping pill only when they need sleep and welcome the sleep which they intend it to cause; while sermons, although intended by the preacher to intellectually benefit the listeners, are not actually causing a welcome effect (or fulfilling anyone's intention) by boring the listeners to a state of mental stupor as in this scenario.

It is important to notice that within a semantics structured by mental spaces, and within a treatment of metaphor as involving a specialized variety of space blending,[12] we get metaphorical reference "for free". That is to say, we need construct no special mechanism whereby the phrase *sleeping pills* is allowed to profile not actual sleeping pills, but their "counterpart" in the intellectual domain (see Figure 5).

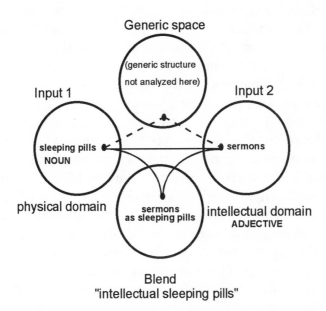

*Figure 5.*

As Fauconnier (1985) noticed, there is pervasive use of nominal forms to refer not to their direct referent but to the counterpart of that referent in another mental space. For example, an author's name can refer to a work by that author; a real person's name can refer to a picture of that person; an actor's name can refer to the character performed by that actor, and vice versa. Metaphorical reference is a unidirectional counterpart mapping relationship between spaces, which permits the use of source-space descriptions to refer to their counterparts in the target space, but not vice versa. Hence *sleeping pill* can refer to a sermon (as construed via this unidirectional blending process), but *sermon* would be unlikely to refer to a sleeping pill, via this set of metaphorical mappings. This means that, with the right contextual help from space-blending, an accessible conceptual active zone of *sleeping pill* is sermons, an entity indeed appropriately elaborated by *intellectual*.

Now, a metaphor analyst who believes that metaphorical readings are obtained by rejection of literal ones[13] might say we have just discussed such an example: *intellectual* clashes with *sleeping pills*, a coherent literal meaning is hard to find, and the hearer eventually has recourse to the metaphorical one. But notice that cross-space links are part of referent-location in any case (*cf.* Fauconnier 1985, 1997; Turner 1991;[14] Fauconnier and Sweetser 1996). A hearer of phrases like *a gentler, kinder Maggie Thatcher, the painted* (as opposed to *flesh-and-blood*) *Sandy*, or for that matter *my Berkeley roommate*, has to figure out that the speaker is not referring to Sandy but to Sandy's portrait; recognize that the relevant domain of search for the roommate is the speaker's Berkeley student life (which may not be the current situation); and either decide that Maggie Thatcher at a later date is being referred to as an entity contrasting with Maggie Thatcher at an earlier date, or decide alternatively that some other person is being referred to as a counterpart of Maggie Thatcher in another domain (*cf. Our new mayor is sort of a gentler, kinder Maggie Thatcher*). Are all of these accomplished via rejection of an original basic reading? If so, then not only metaphor but much of English modification is so accomplished. But there is nothing in what we know about the processing of adjectival modification at large to suggest to us that it generally requires garden-path styles of interpretation.

## 5. Generalizations about Adjective-Noun interpretation in English

What are the general rules about how to put together A-N meanings in English? Following Langacker's (1987, 1991a,b) treatment of modification as elaboration of active zones, we can say that the noun referentially *profiles* some entity as a member of the appropriate (non-classical) category, while the adjective *elaborates* some *active zone* of the entity profiled by the noun. In the red-surface reading of *red ball*, the noun *ball* profiles the concept of a ball, and the adjective *red* elaborates the color of the surface of the ball.

But "active zone" in my expanded sense may include things not mentioned in most previous work: not only parts or aspects of the entity itself, but parts or aspects of the frames associated with it in the complex context of the particular utterance, and even counterparts of the entity in another mental space (whether via metaphorical mappings, or by other inter-domain counterpart relationships such as depiction, belief, time, and so on). The reading of *red ball* as the ball used by the team with the red uniforms takes the team's uniforms (linked to the ball by a cognitive frame of competitive ball-playing) as an accessible active zone of the ball. An *intellectual sleeping pill* is the *counterpart* of a sleeping pill (the Noun's referent in the source-domain mental space of physical bodily causal forces and reactions) in the target-domain mental space of intellectual and psychological causal forces and reactions. Here, the adjective *intellectual* elaborates the relevant active zone by specifying in what mental space the ultimate referent of the phrase is located: the "active zone" of *sleeping pill* becomes the metaphorical cross-domain counterpart of the direct referent.

It should by now be clear how some other basic problems are to be solved. A *fake gun* is not a gun in the base space, but its counterpart in the mental space of some deceived person (evoked by the frame of *fake*, as Coulson and Fauconnier [in press] argue) is correctly described as a gun. The speaker's base space (not portrayed in Figure 6 below) is like that of the trickster, not like that of the dupe, since the use of the word *fake* involves the speaker's necessarily knowledgeable assessment of contrast between a knowledgeable trickster and an unaware dupe. Temporal modifiers such as *former* operate in a similar manner, so that a *former president* or an *ex-husband* does not fill the slot of a president or a husband in the relevant frame in the base mental space, but is the counterpart of an entity in a past mental space who fills such a slot in that space. *Former* depends on the speaker's present assessment of a contrast between the past and present mental spaces. *Fake* and *former* thus elaborate the referents of *gun* and *president* by (1) specifying a configuration of spaces, including a contrast between a space where the relevant description or property does hold and one where it does not hold, and (2) profiling the "deviant" space (the one which contrasts with the knowledgeable base space) which is therefore taken as the space within which the description *gun* or the role-value mapping *president* is taken as holding (see Figure 6).

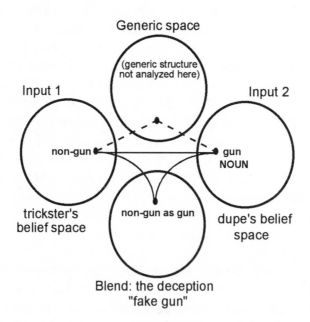

*Figure 6.* The ADJECTIVE, "fake", refers to the entire mental space structure, including the *contrast* between Inputs 1 and 2. It *profiles* Input 2.

The interaction of frame-structured spaces with interspace map-pings and active-zone phenomena thus automatically gives us the varied interpretations of A-N constructions involving an adjective such as *safe* or *intellectual* or *fake*. This is under the assumption that connected mental space configurations themselves constitute complex wholes subject to Langacker's active-zone principle.

Crucially, just as metaphoric readings do not seem to need previ-ous processing of and rejection of a literal sense (*cf.* Gibbs 1994), likewise most of these A-N examples do not seem intuitively to in-volve "garden-path" interpretation structures. What they do involve is a lot of flexibility, but not mostly in revising or rejecting structural connections in these cases—rather, in fitting appropriate aspects of each word's meaning to appropriate aspects of the cognitive structure at hand (*cf.* Turner 1991, Coulson 1997). This is what humans are apparently virtuosi in accomplishing: the finding of cognitive "affor-dances" to connect aspects of cognitive structure to each other, espe-cially when we are given material which is assumed to represent some coherent structure accessed by the speaker. Part of what makes that affordance-finding and affordance-developing easy is that cross-domain reference-location is not a difficult task but a normal one: We constantly access multiple spaces, and context and the ongoing dy-namic process of meaning-building will determine whether the "sim-plest" reading of some word is the literal (or "direct") reading or one demanding interspace connections.

We know that speakers' access to readings is not determined simply by a decontextualized metric of directness of form-meaning fit, but also by contextual evocation of one reading or another as rele-vant. "Indirect" interpretations, involving Gricean reasoning for ex-ample, seem often to be more accessible in context than the so-called "direct" interpretation would be. In Coleman and Kay's (1981) ques-tionnaire research about the use of the verb *lie*, they gave each re-spondent a list of brief stories to read, and then asked whether the protagonist of each story had lied. One story involved John and Mary, who had recently begun dating; John asks Mary whether she has seen her old boyfriend, Valentino, lately, and she responds that Valentino's been sick with mononucleosis for the last month. The narrator informs us that Valentino has indeed been sick, but that Mary also had a date with him the night before. Some respondents went so far as to say not only that Mary had lied, but that "Mary said no, she hadn't seen Valentino." It seems harder for speakers to remove the conversational inferences from their interpretation of this utterance than it is for them to perform the inferences.

Similarly, Gibbs (1994) shows that metaphorical interpretations need not be accessed more slowly than literal ones, in contexts where the metaphorical reading is the relevant one. Sperber and Wilson's (1986) general claim that the most relevant reading is always the one most readily accessed needs more precision to become non-circular and testable, but it seems relatively clear how to compare pairs of readings such as those dealt with by Gibbs. Priming effects are of course the most general evidence for contextually differential access of meaning; and Coulson (1997) provides an insightful examination of some aspects of on-line mental space construction, leading the way in applying psycholinguistic methodology to the analysis of mental space constructs.

So the flexible affordance-finding cognitive strategies which char-acterize A-N interpretation are only the same strategies used in all our space-building and meaning-construction. And the work of such affordance-finding is often not much work for the processor, although it may present significant difficulties for the analyst trying to "unpack" the results.

## 6. Inter-level blends: what's so likely about a candidate, or so possible about a textbook?

An example such as *likely candidate* or *possible textbook* is in one sense a simple case: We do not have much tendency for the two components to contradict each other, so we won't have much prob-lem with altering the central range of readings of either. But it's also less obvious than with *red ball* what to think of as a prototypical range of readings. *Red* centrally refers to physical color, and *ball* to a class of physical objects, so there is automatically some overlap in their central space-structuring frames. In the case of *likely* or *possible*, we might want to say that the primary referential range is that of epistemic evaluation of a theory or hypothesis about a present or future event (how *likely* does the evaluator feel it is that the hypothetical or described mental space matches reality, or will match future reality.) *His arrival is likely but not certain* means that the evaluator is not certain that the hypothetical event of arrival will match reality, but thinks there is a good chance it will. A *likely story*, by metonymy, is one which expresses a theory that is plausible to someone. Since the frame for *story* inherently involves an expressed content, which is something in the teller and hearer's epistemic spaces, it is fairly easy to see how to blend this frame with that of *likely*; we assume that what is linked to *likely*'s "plausible theory" slot is the *content* slot from the story frame. What about *candidate* or *textbook*? The frames for these words do not seem to automatically evoke a slot involving a hypothesis about some state of affairs.

The answer seems to be that the speaker's and hearer's epistemic spaces are generally accessible parts of the frame of speech interaction. *Likely candidate* therefore asks the hearer to build a mental space wherein there is some hypothesis which the speaker could evaluate as likely, and wherein the candidate can also find a slot. Among the obvious hypotheses are ones about the sequential structure of the frame for candidacy: It may be likely that someone will become a candidate, or that someone (once a candidate) will succeed as a candidate by winning the election for which candidacy was declared. These frame structures of candidacy initiation and of success in the goal of candidacy are automatically evoked by the use of the category *candidate*. And indeed, *likely candidate* can mean someone likely to be or become a candidate or to succeed as a candidate. In Figure 7, I give a partial blended-spaces analysis of the reading of *likely candidate* which takes it to mean that the person is likely to be a candidate. The scenario which is being evaluated (within the speaker's mental space) as to its likelihood of matching reality is a scenario wherein a particular individual is the filler for the role of candidate in the conceptual frame of an election.

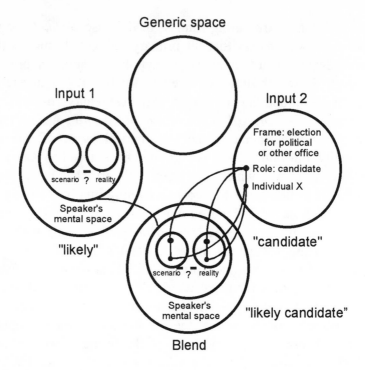

*Figure 7.* *"likely candidate"* interpreted as meaning a person likely to become or be a candidate

But *likely candidate* can also mean plenty of other things: the candidate whom a reporter sees as more likely to grant an interview than other candidates, the candidate who would be likely to cave in under the pressure of negative advertising which the speaker is planning, the candidate who is likely to care about some particular issue, the candidate who would be likely to be home on Friday night to answer an urgent query, and so on. So long as we can think up a scenario relative to the candidate in question, and evaluate that scenario for likelihood, *likely candidate* can mean the candidate who figures in the scenario we have labelled as likely. Only context will tell us what scenario that is; and it may or may not be a scenario which is itself part of the conventional frame of candidacy. Either the word *candidate* itself may evoke the scenario (as in the readings where it is declaration of candidacy or election which are likely), or context may provide the scenario, relative to some particular candidate (as in the "home on Friday night" reading—which could just as well apply to *likely colleague*, for example).

*Possible textbook* functions similarly. Assuming again that speakers evaluate primarily event-scenarios as possible or impossible, the hearer is here invited to find a scenario relevant to the textbook which can be evaluated in this way. For a faculty member, scenarios of textbook choice and textbook use in a class may be readily accessible; readings of "a textbook which one could adopt" or "a textbook which one could (effectively) use for teaching" are therefore unsurprisingly accessible readings of the phrase. But of course, given the right contextually evoked scenario, the phrase might get understood as meaning "the textbook which one could use to prop up the overhead projector to the right angle."

Adjectives like *possible* and *likely*, along with epistemic modal verbs and other such markers, refer to frames of epistemic structure and epistemic behavior (reasoning, plausibility-evaluation, comparison of mental spaces with a "reality"-space, and so on). They therefore generally demand a different kind of space-blending than that which is involved in *red ball*.

The important point here is that in order to account for these nominal modification constructions, we need all the apparatus required to deal with sentence-level phenomena such as modals and domain adverbs. Because the semantics of *likely* evokes a frame of epistemic evaluation, when it is used without explicit reference to such a frame in the content of the utterance, it is interpreted by reference to the implicit presence of the speaker's epistemic processes. This is just what is necessary for other examples such as sentential *probably*, in the epistemic domain, or for speech-act modifiers like *frankly*.

(3)  *Frankly and honestly*, Rhett told Scarlett what he thought of her.
     (Content-level interpretation:[15] *frankly and honestly* modifies the described activity of telling, and frankness and honesty are attributed to its agent, Rhett.)

(4)  *Frankly and honestly*, my dear, I do not give a damn.
     (Speech-act level interpretation: *Frankly and honestly* modifies
     the current speech act, and frankness and honesty are attributed
     to the speaker.)

The semantics of *frankly* evokes a frame of speech interaction and
speaker sincerity. When used without explicit content reference to
such a frame, it can be interpreted by reference to the implicit presence of the present speech interaction; word order and intonation
must allow "sentential" level of modification, for this option to be
available. Although it does not seem as though *frank* and *honest* as
modifying adjectives can be given this kind of implicitly speaker-based
interpretation, adnominal modifier uses such as *bona fide* (as in *a
bona fide antique*) or *honest-to-God* (as in *an honest-to-God best-
seller*) are certainly interpretable as referring to the speaker's honesty
in this way.[16]

## 7. What kind of theory do we need?

A genuinely plausible theory of semantic compositionality cannot be
based on a few cases which logicians find convenient, with the assumption that it can be extended some day to handle the rest of the
data. It has to deal with the immense combinatorial complexity of
everyday constructions in real languages, as used by speakers engaged
in the linguistic construction of mental space structure within a rich
context. And to any linguist it is clear that the linguistic constructions
discussed in this paper represent a microscopic fraction of the possibilities out there in the world. This doesn't mean our theory has to be
uneconomical. It will surely be a richer and more complex theory of
semantic categorization and combination than many formal semantic
ones, but this added complexity will involve cognitive structures and
processes which are necessarily part of any plausible theory of cognition in general: fuzzy and prototype-structured categorization, salient
instances, metaphorical and metonymic links, frames, active zones,
roles and values, mental spaces and so on. There is of course no

global parsimony to the exclusion of these factors from linguistic semantics, if they are real aspects of the cognition underlying language. Our theory can certainly still follow Occam's razor, in the sense that we should not posit unmotivated structure for its own sake, but rather do so as needed to account for data.

None of these claims are completely new; I have cited a broad spectrum of semantics work within and outside of the cognitive linguistics community, which has all tended in the same direction. What I have tried to do in this paper is to show how fully the need for a richer semantics is manifested in a single, very "simple" English construction which formal semantics continues to treat as essentially combinatorial despite extensive scholarly examination of the problems with such a treatment. A cognitive semantics allows us to give a treatment of Adjective-Noun modification which is genuinely unified, and genuinely compositional, and at the same time is flexible enough to account for the actual data. Without invoking mechanisms such as metaphor or frames, we would either have to give up on the claim that there is any general principle about combining the semantics of adjectives and nouns in a modification construction, or give up on compositionality itself. If formal semantics can claim to be the heir of the generative tradition in placing a high value on minimal theoretical apparatus, it cannot (on actual inspection of the data) simultaneously claim to maintain a principle of regular semantic compositionality. While there are plenty of non-compositional, or incompletely compositional, aspects to linguistic semantics—no linguist would want to treat all idioms as fully compositional—nonetheless compositionality is a basic and pervasive aspect of linguistic semantics, and cannot be adequately described without adequate description of the categories to be combined.   These issues have been obscured to some extent, for many linguists, by the traditional quality of linguistic examples. But as Langacker has long been telling us, it suffices to examine *purple potato* (is it the interior flesh or the exterior skin which is purple?) instead of *red apple*, to see how much linguists' interpretation of the former has depended on already-conventional construction of active zones and pre-definition of the overlap between the meanings of the noun and the adjective. Here I have tried to show that by taking our responsibilities for *red apples* and *purple potatoes* seriously, linguists get almost for free a reasonable account of supposedly deviant or problematic cases such as *safe distances, likely candidates*, and *fake guns*. I argue that mechanisms such as the implicit evocation of the speaker's epistemic or speech-act space are not required only to account for conjunctions and discourse markers (*cf.* Sweetser 1990, Dancygier and Sweetser 1996), but also within the compositional semantics of the Adjective-Noun construction; this is added evidence of their basic status in linguistic cognition.

Speakers are engaged in prompting shared mental space construction by linguistic use. Linguistic compositionality must be described in a way flexible enough to reflect the facts that forms may be adding structure to any one of many accessible mental spaces; crucially, besides multiple content spaces (the picture, "reality", various conditional and temporal and locational spaces, and so on—*cf.* Fauconnier 1985, 1997), forms may be adding structure to the epistemic space, the speech-act space, the metalinguistic or metatextual space. Speakers know what aspects of form are flexible in this way: English appears, for example, to be unusually flexible in its use of the basic conditional construction. Crucially, composition is not just a matter of putting together pieces of the "same kind" of content into a single homogeneous structure. Compositionality looks more homogeneous, or at least more unified, if we recognize the range and diversity of the units to be combined.

As a final observation, I would like to add that it seems to me almost impossible to construct an adequate theory of meaning which is simultaneously objectivist and regularly compositional. Less flexible meaning units will simply not produce the range of actual compositional meanings, by regular composition. Since all the contrasts in compositionally constructed meaning discussed in this paper are relevant to truth conditions,[17] and yet cannot be accounted for without recourse to a wide range of non-objectivist semantic and conceptual constructs, we presumably need to accept accounts of "truth", as well as of semantic compositionality, which take conceptual structure into account.

# Notes

1. *Cf.* Rosch (1977), Mervis and Rosch (1981), Kay and McDaniel (1978), Coleman and Kay (1981), Sweetser (1987), Fillmore (1982, 1985).
2. *Cf.* Downing's (1977) treatment of N-N compounds. Ryder (1994) suggests a variety of inter-related templates for N-N compounds, with frame-structuring as part of the semantics to be composed; this approach is clearly in many ways consistent with Fauconnier and Turner's (1995, 1996, 1998) recent blended-spaces approach to N-N compounds.
3. Sweetser (1990) postulates the potential accessibility of the speech-interactional context and of the speaker's mental processes, as a general background to interpretation of utterances; I also argue specifically for the need to attach such interpretive possibilities by convention to the semantics of particular forms (e.g, the English modal *may* has a speech-act reading, but most other English modals do not).
4. See the papers in Fauconnier and Sweetser (1996), in particular Sanders and Redeker (1996).
5. For the basic literature on Mental Spaces theory, see Fauconnier (1985, 1997); a number of papers developing different aspects of the theory can be found in Fauconnier and Sweetser (1996), which contains an introductory chapter laying out central aspects of Mental Spaces theory.
6. A related frame-based approach to modifying relative clauses in Japanese can be found in Matsumoto (1997).
7. *Cf.* Searle's (1979) discussion of the different interpretations of the verb *open*, in *open the door, open the book, open your eyes*, and so forth. Once again, one cannot know which interpretation to give to the verb until one negotiates between the meaning of *open* and that of the object NP. An insightful treatment of this issue can be found in van der Leek (1996).
8. See the particularly useful discussion of this in Fauconnier's preface to the 1994 Cambridge University Press reprint of Fauconnier (1985).
9. See Kay and McDaniel (1978).
10. Schiffrin (1992), in a study of the uses of *then* in a spoken corpus, comments that almost all of the conditional *then* uses in her corpus also had some clear temporal referent frame attached to the condition.
11. The editors have commented to me that examples like (2) seem more acceptable with an *even* in each clause: (3) *Even if he commits a crime, even then they'll vote for him.* Note that in (3), *then* must be stressed and contrastive, *forcing* a unique-referent reading for the space in which the voting occurs. The unstressed and non-contrastive *then* in (2) seems to need to presuppose a unique referent space to refer back to; it cannot impose its unique-referent reading on the scalar reading of *even*.

12. Specifically, a one-sided network (cf. Fauconnier and Turner 1998), with the asymmetry between source and target domains which characterizes metaphorical structure (cf. Lakoff and Johnson 1980, Lakoff 1993).
13. *E.g,* Searle (1979).
14. Note particularly Turner's pp. 209 ff.
15. *Cf.* Sweetser 1990, Dancygier and Sweetser 1996, for discussion of the distinction between content, epistemic, speech-act, and metalinguistic readings.
16. It should be noted that gesture is of special interest in understanding how the speaker's own cognitive and interactional spaces are blended with the content space (Kendon 1995 and Sweetser 1997 address some gestural uses which seem to call for this kind of analysis). The same is of course true of signed languages; Liddell (1998) treats ASL as creating blended spaces grounded in the speaker's physical space).
17. See Kittay's (1987) argument about the status.

# References

Austin, J. L.
    1964    On 'real'. Chapter 7 of S*ense and Sensibilia.* Oxford University Press.
Coleman, Linda and Paul Kay
    1981    Prototype semantics: the English verb *lie. Language 57:1*, 26-44.
Coulson, Seana
    1997    Semantic leaps: Frame-shifting and conceptual blending in meaning construction. Ph.D. dissertation, University of California, San Diego.
Coulson, Seana and Gilles Fauconnier
    in press Fake guns and stone lions: Conceptual blending and privative adjectives. In: Barbara Fox, Daniel Jurafsky and Laura Michaelis (eds.), *Cognition and Function in Language,.* Stanford CA: CSLI Publications.
Dancygier, Barbara and Eve Sweetser
    1996    Conditionals, distancing and alternative spaces. In: Adele Goldberg (ed.), *Conceptual Structure, Discourse and Language*, 83-98. Stanford CA: CSLI Publications.
    1997    *Then* in conditionals. *Cognitive Linguistics* 8:2, 1-28.
Downing, Pamela
    1977    On the creation and use of English compound nouns. *Language* 53, 810-843.
Epstein, Richard
    1994    Discourse and definiteness: synchronic and diachronic perspectives. Ph.D. dissertation, Department of Linguistics, UCSD.

1996    Viewpoint and the definite article. In: Adele Goldberg (ed.), *Conceptual Structure, Discourse and Language*, 99-112. Stanford, CA: CSLI Publications.

Ernst, Thomas Boyden
1984    *Towards an Integrated Theory of Adverb Position in English.* Bloomington, IN: Indiana University Linguistics Club.

Fauconnier, Gilles
1985    *Mental Spaces.* Cambridge MA: MIT Press. (Reprinted 1994, Cambridge: Cambridge University Press).
1997    *Cognitive Mappings for Language and Thought.* Cambridge: Cambridge University Press.

Fauconnier, Gilles and E. Sweetser (eds.)
1996    *Spaces, Worlds and Grammars.* Chicago: University of Chicago Press.

Fauconnier, Gilles and Mark Turner
1996    Blending as a central process of grammar. In: Adele Goldberg (ed.), *Conceptual Structure, Discourse and Language*, 113-130. Stanford, CA: CSLI Publications.
1998    Conceptual integration networks. *Cognitive Science 22:2*, 133-188.

Fillmore, Charles J.
1982    Frame semantics. In: The Linguistic Society of Korea (ed.), *Linguistics in the Morning Calm*, 111-138. Seoul: Hanshin.
1985    Frames and the semantics of understanding. *Quaderni di semantica* 6:2, 222-253.

Fillmore, Charles J. and Beryl T. Atkins
1992    Toward a frame-based lexicon: the semantics of RISK and its neighbors. In: Adrienne Lehrer and Eva Feder Kittay (eds.), *Frames, Fields and Contrasts: New Essays in Semantic and Lexical Organization*, 75-102. Hillsdale, NJ: Lawrence Erlbaum Associates.

Fillmore, Charles J., Paul Kay, and Mary Catherine O'Connor
1988    Regularity and idiomaticity in grammatical constructions: the case of LET ALONE. *Language* 64:3, 501-538.

Gibbs, Raymond
1994    *The Poetics of Mind.* Cambridge: Cambridge University Press.

Goldberg, Adele
1995    *Constructions: A Construction Grammar Approach to Argument Structure.* Chicago: University of Chicago Press.
1997    The relationships between verbs and constructions. In: Marjolijn Verspoor, Kee Dong Lee, and Eve Sweetser (eds.), *Lexical and Syntactical Constructions and the Construction of Meaning*, 383-398. Amsterdam: John Benjamins.

Hopper, Paul and Elizabeth Closs Traugott
1993    *Grammaticalization.* Cambridge: Cambridge University Press.

Kay, Paul and Chad K. McDaniel
  1978    The Linguistic significance of the meanings of the basic color terms. *Language* 54:3, 610-646.
Kay, Paul and Charles J. Fillmore
  1999    Grammatical constructions and linguistic generalizations: the *What's X doing Y?* construction. *Language* 75:1, 1-33.
Kendon, Adam
  1995    Gestures as illocutionary and discourse markers in Southern Italian conversation. *Journal of Pragmatics* 23, 247-279.
Kittay, Eva Feder
  1987    *Metaphor: Its Cognitive Force and Linguistic Structure.* Oxford: Oxford University Press.
Kyratzis, Amy, Jiansheng Guo and Susan Ervin-Tripp
  1990    Pragmatic conventions influencing children's use of causal conjunctions in natural discourse. In: Kira Hall et al. (eds.), *Proceedings of the sixteenth annual meeting of the Berkeley Linguistics Society*, 205-214. Berkeley, CA: Berkeley Linguistics Society.
Lakoff, George
  1987    *Women, Fire and Dangerous Things: What Categories Reveal about the Mind.* Chicago: University of Chicago Press.
  1993    The contemporary theory of metaphor. In: Andrew Ortony (ed.), *Metaphor and Thought*, 202-251. Cambridge: Cambridge University Press.
Lakoff, George and Mark Johnson
  1980    *Metaphors we Live by.* Chicago: University of Chicago Press.
Langacker, Ronald W.
  1987    *Foundations of Cognitive Grammar I: Theoretical Prerequisites.* Stanford CA: Stanford University Press.
  1991a   *Foundations of Cognitive Grammar II: Descriptive Application.* Stanford CA: Stanford University Press.
  1991b   *Concept, Image and Symbol: The Cognitive Basis of Grammar.* Berlin: Mouton de Gruyter.
van der Leek, Frederike
  1996    Rigid syntax and flexible meaning: the case of the English ditransitive. In: Adele Goldberg (ed.), *Conceptual Structure, Discourse and Language*, 321-332. Stanford, CA: CSLI Publications.
Liddell, Scott K.
  1998    Grounded blends, gestures, and conceptual shifts. *Cognitive Linguistics* 9:3, 283-314.
Matsumoto, Yoshiko
  1997    *Noun-modifying constructions in Japanese: a frame-semantic approach.* Amsterdam: John Benjamins.

Mervis, Carolyn and Eleanor Rosch
   1981    Categorization of natural objects. *Annual Review of Psychology* 32, 89-
           115.
Rosch, Eleanor
   1977    Human categorization. In: N. Warren (ed.), *Studies in Cross-Cultural
           Psychology*, 1-49. London: Academic Press.
Ryder, Mary Ellen
   1994    *Ordered Chaos: The Interpretation of English Noun-Noun Com-
           pounds*. Berkeley, CA: University of California Press.
Sanders, José and Gisela Redeker
   1996    Perspective and the representation of speech and thought in narrative
           discourse. In: Fauconnier and Sweetser (1996), pp. 290-317.
Schiffrin, Deborah
   1992    Anaphoric *then*: aspectual, textual, and epistemic meaning. *Linguistics*
           30, 753-792.
Searle, John
   1979    *Expression and Meaning*. Cambridge: Cambridge University Press.
Sperber, Dan and Deirdre Wilson
   1986    *Relevance: Communication and Cognition*. Oxford: Basil Blackwell.
Sweetser, Eve
   1987    The definition of lie: an examination of the folk models underlying a
           semantic prototype. In: Dorothy Holland and Naomi Quinn (eds.),
           *Cultural Models in Language and Thought*, 43-66. Cambridge: Cam-
           bridge University Press.
   1990    *From Etymology to Pragmatics*. Cambridge: Cambridge University
           Press.
   1997    Regular metaphoricity in gesture: bodily-based models of speech inter-
           action. In *Actes du 16ᵉ Congrès International des Linguistes* (CD-
           ROM), Elsevier (1997).
Traugott, Elizabeth Closs
   1982    From propositional to textual and expressive meanings. In: Winfred
           Lehmann and Yakov Malkiel (eds.), *Perspectives on Historical Lin-
           guistics*, 245-271. Amsterdam: John Benjamins.
   1988    Pragmatic strengthening and grammaticalization. In: S. Axmaker, A.
           Jaisser and H. Singmaster (eds.), *Proceedings of the Fourteenth An-
           nual Meeting of the Berkeley Linguistics Society*, 406-416. Berkeley,
           CA: Berkeley Linguistics Society.
   1989    On the rise of epistemic meanings in English: An example of subjecti-
           fication in semantic change. *Language* 65, 31-55.
   1995    Subjectification in grammaticalisation. In: Dieter Stein and Susan
           Wright (eds.), *Subjectivity and Subjectivisation*, 31-54. Cambridge:
           Cambridge University Press.

Traugott, Elizabeth Closs, Alice ter Meulen, Judy Snitzer Reilly and Charles A. Ferguson (eds.)
    1986    *On Conditionals.* Cambridge: Cambridge University Press.
Turner, Mark
    1991    *Reading Minds: The Study of English in the Age of Cognitive Science.* Princeton, NJ: Princeton University Press.
Turner, Mark and Gilles Fauconnier
    1995    Conceptual integration and formal expression. *Journal of Metaphor and Symbolic Activity* 10:3, 183-204.
Vendler, Zeno
    1967    The grammar of goodness. In: *Linguistics in Philosophy.* Ithaca, NY: Cornell University Press.

# Idealist and empiricist tendencies in cognitive semantics

## Dirk Geeraerts

### Prologue

The methodological situation in present-day Cognitive Linguistics is characterized by the existence of two methodological extremes. On the one hand, there is the idealistic approach most conspicuously advocated by Anna Wierzbicka in her numerous publications (among which 1985, 1992, 1996). On the other hand, there exist various tendencies to objectivize the methods used in Cognitive Linguistics. Roughly, there are three main tendencies at this end of the methodological opposition: psycholinguistic research (as in Sandra and Rice 1995 or Gibbs 1994), neurophysiological modeling (as in Regier 1995), and quantitative corpus-based analysis (as in Geeraerts, Grondelaers and Bakema 1994). Most actual work in Cognitive Linguistics is probably situated somewhere in-between both extremes, or rather, the practical methodology used is more often introspective rather than data-driven, but without the outspoken idealistic commitments that Anna Wierzbicka explicitly describes. Whence the title of the following dialogue (taken from Machado de Assis' *Quincas Borba*): even those cognitive linguists who have never reflected on the epistemological underpinnings of their practical work, are implicitly caught up in the debate between the idealistic and the more empiristically minded approaches. My own position in the debate is clearly not on the idealist side, but the following dialogue (which suitably takes a platonic form) tries to establish why that choice is less self-evident than it may appear once one has made it.

## The cat, though it has not read Kant, may well be a metaphysical animal: A Philosophical Dialogue

Dramatis Personae:

DUODECIMUS EMPIRICUS, a cognitive linguist specializing in corpus-based techniques of analysis and experimental methods; author of the book *Quantitative Methods in Cognitive Semantics*.

ANTIPODA PROLIPHICA, a cognitive linguist of a platonic persuasion; author of the book *Universal Fundaments of Meaning*.

HISTRIO POLYMORPHUS, teacher and friend to Duodecimus and Antipoda, a perpetual source of knowledge, inspiration, and academic tolerance to both of them.

The scene is set in the garden of Histrio's villa, where the three of them meet regularly to discuss on a theme set by Histrio.

*D:* Well, master, the lavishness of last week's feast has more than soothed the hunger of our stomachs, but our minds are as thirsty for knowledge as ever. What then will be the topic for today's meeting? To what surprising views will your argumentation lead us, as unexpected as the vistas opening from your garden's paths?

*H:* Gardening, my young friend, is a matter of patience. Before the bushes and lawns, flowerbeds and trees acquire their ultimate architectural form, years of preparatory work are necessary. The wilderness has to be conquered, the grounds have to be laid out, and the plants have to be guided and protected year after year before the global pattern finally emerges. Allow me, therefore, to introduce you indirectly, with some sort of a detour, to the theme that I have in mind.

*A:* Most certainly so, master, but do allow us to drink to your health first. Such a long journey as you promise us should not be undertaken without invigorating the body first.

*D:* Right you are, Antipoda: may Histrio's thoughts continue to flower like a cherry tree in spring!

*H:* Your are too kind to a man in the autumn of his life. But let us take the first step—a step that brings us to physics rather than metaphysics. Do you know the story of the ether?

*A:* We know ether is a colorless liquid used as a solvent, or as an anaesthetic. Are you referring to the way it was discovered?

*H:* The word *ether* actually has yet another meaning, not well known nowadays, but extremely important in the physical theories of the 19th century. By the end of the 19th century, the majority of physicists was convinced of the existence of an ether: an odorless, colorless and tasteless substance that filled the universe and that functioned as the material bearer of waves of light. If light is a wave, it indeed requires a medium through which its waves are transported, just like the waves of the sea move through the material medium that is water.

*D:* So the ether was supposed to be a medium that filled the gaps between particles of matter? This sounds like a physical kind of *horror vacui*!

*H:* Exactly. But the analogy with a better known medium like water led to further refinements of the concept. A body like the earth, then, that moved through the ether would inevitably cause an ether wind: the ether particles in front of the body would be pressed together, while behind it an area with lowered pressure, so to speak, would be formed.

*D:* I can see that, but if this ether is odorless, colorless and tasteless, how could its presence be detected? As you know, such methodological questions particularly interest me.

*H:* Scientists tried to experimentally measure the ether wind: a light wave moving in the same direction as the earth would travel more slowly than a light wave that went along with the ether wind, because the former would have to overcome the resistance of the tightly packed ether particles in front of the moving earth. In 1881, this hypothesis was put to an experimental test by Michelson and Morley. Unfortunately, it appeared that the beam of light that was sent out in the same direction as the earth did not go faster than the one that shone in the opposite direction.

*D:* Perhaps the experimental equipment used had not been sophisticated enough?

*H:* I can see you have some experience with experimental research, dear Duodecimus: your suggestion is precisely what Michelson and

Morley thought. So the experiment was repeated in 1887 with more accurate instruments and with a truly ingenious design (which I will not describe, not to tax your patience). This new design did not bring the expected results either, however.

*A:* I can very well imagine the reason why not, master: don't we all know that the speed of light is invariable?

*H:* Certainly. But at the time of the experiments, science was not sufficiently advanced yet to have realized this: we all know *now* that the speed of light is constant, but that assumption as such is neither self-evident nor empirically obvious. Only in 1905, in fact, did Einstein proclaim the inexistence of the ether wind together with the invariability of the speed of light.

*D:* I am rather surprised that you say that Einstein 'proclaimed' the inexistence of the ether wind. Should we not rather say that he *discovered* its inexistence?

*H:* From our point of view, we can certainly say so—because *we* no longer believe in the ether either. But for Michelson and Morley things were not that obvious: they actually continued to believe in the existence of the ether a long time after Einstein described his alternative view, and they tried out ever more refined experiments—without much success, as you can imagine.

*A:* So were they not just being stubborn?

*H:* Not necessarily. The interesting thing about the story, in fact, is its methodological structure. When an experiment fails, two courses can be followed: either you assume that there is something wrong with the observational apparatus with which the experiment was carried out, or you assume that the theoretical assumptions of the experiment should be subjected to severe criticism. In the former case there is uncertainty concerning the actual result of the experiment. The experiment is considered undecided, and it is assumed that the uncertainty can be ironed out by using more refined experimental techniques. In the latter case the experiment is recognized as an actual rejection of an hypothesis. Michelson and Morley, by their repeated endeavors to make the experimental environment better fit to measure the existence of an ether and the presence of an ether wind, followed the first tack. Einstein, on the other, took the opposite course, by taking Michelson and Morley's experimental failure as a straightforward rejection of the hypothesis that there existed an ether.

*D:* I must confess that the first surprise in your story comes earlier than expected. Are you trying to tell us that falsification of scientific hypotheses is not a straightforward matter? That there are cases where it is difficult to disprove a hypothesis directly?

*H:* Well, try to look at it in this way. The existence of alternative ways of dealing with negative experimental results implies that, at least to some extent, theoretical presuppositions define what is a theoretically relevant fact: if one sticks to the existence of an ether wind, then the experiment simply does not yield an acceptable observation; due to the presumed problems with the experimental design, no theoretically interpretable fact at all is observed. If, on the other hand, one starts from the presupposition that there is no ether wind at all, the experiment produces a clear result.

*D:* But surely, one could not go on indefinitely ignoring the failure of the experiments?

*H:* I would like to leave open the question how long the first position can be maintained after repeated failures: the crucial point to see is that observational results do not exist in isolation, but that 'the facts' depend at least partly on the intensity with which one cherishes certain theoretical concepts—or conversely, on the degree to which one may be ready to give up such concepts. Of the utmost importance here is the notion of a 'theory of interpretation' as the embodiment of the view that there are no bare facts: facts only become facts through the intervention of background assumptions and interpretative principles.

*A:* When I let my initial surprise subside, I think I see a relationship with what we, cognitive linguists, know as 'internal realism'. Following ideas from Hilary Putnam, George Lakoff (1987) has characterized the epistemological position of cognitive linguistics as a rejection of both hard-core objectivism and radical idealism: there is no doubt about the existence of the outside world, but at the same time, the world as we know it is shaped by the concepts we impose upon it. Well, I need not repeat this to you, of course. As I see it now, the ideas that you just introduced define a kind of internal realism on the level of scientific methodology. Facts do not exist as such, but only *within* a particular framework?

*H:* I knew you would be clever enough to see that yourself, Antipoda.

*A:* But that does not mean I believe in it, yet.

*H:* Knowing your independence of mind, I had not expected otherwise. Before we start discussing alternatives, however, I have to say something about the status of such a position of internal realism within the philosophy of science. There is, in fact, a particular conception of the philosophy of science that embodies such an internal-realistic view, viz. the paradigmatic theory of science as represented by Thomas Kuhn, Imre Lakatos, and Paul Feyerabend. Internal realism is present in Kuhn's conception of scientific paradigms in the following way. Apparent counterevidence with regard to a paradigmatic theory is not simply accepted as such, but may merely be considered an indication of a problem that will be solved when the theory is developed further. Rather than occasioning an immediate rejection of the existing theory, counterevidence (if it is not simply disregarded as based on irrelevant experiments) leads to the attempt to explain away or solve the problems in the framework of the existing paradigm. Paradigmatic theories are given credit, they are given time to solve puzzles that arise.

*D:* That suggests to me that the structure and the epistemological role of scientific paradigms (seen as a set of theories clustered round a number of central assumptions) are similar to those of natural language categories (seen as clusters of conceptual applications concentrated round a prototypical center). Since both have a formative influence with regard to, respectively, new theories and new concepts, prototypical categories may be seen as a reflection, on the microstructural level of individual natural language concepts, of the same "paradigmatic" principles that govern the development of science on the macrostructural level of scientific theories.

*H:* I would say so, yes. But notice that the similarity between both positions should not be thought of in a simplistic way. Cognitive linguistics characterizes the relationship between natural language (and natural thinking, if you like) and the world in terms of internal realism. But cognitive linguistics itself is a scientific theory that may be characterized by internal realism.

*D:* So there are two epistemological levels involved: the level of thinking about the world (the level of folk knowledge, so to speak), and the level of scientifically thinking about thinking. And you suggest that there is a homology between both levels: the relationship between thinking and its object is the same on both levels, even if the object on the second level is thinking itself. Where is the problem with that?

*H:* As you will remember from the times when we discussed the concept of self-reference, interactions between different epistemological levels may yield remarkable results. In our case, questions about the objectivity of semantics arise. If not only our thinking as such, but also our thinking about thinking is influenced by pre-existing conceptualizations that function as interpretational schemata, what kind of a scientific enterprise is semantics? If it does not only deal with the way in which the speakers of a language construct interpretations for the expressions they encounter, but if semantics itself imposes interpretations on its subject matter, what claims to objectivity can it make? It's like the Liar's paradox, is it not? If you are Cretan and claim that all Cretans are liars, you undermine your own statement. In the same way, if you claim that all human knowledge is a non-objectivist construction, you inevitably undermine your own position, to the extent that you suggest that your own general statement is something of a construction.

*A:* I get the impression we are reaching the central topic for today. Makes me thirsty, actually. Shall I fill your glasses?

*H:* Please do.

*A:* Here you are. To be honest, I am less convinced there is a problem than you are. After all, you should not forget that there is a crucial difference between the two levels. On the first level, there is an ontological distinction between the object and the subject of the epistemological relationship: the known object is the outside world, and the knowing subject is a human person (a mind, if you wish). But on the second level, subject and object coincide. The object is the way we humans conceptualize the world, that is to say, the way in which the world is known to us in our knowing minds. At the same time, it is that very same mind that investigates its own knowledge of the outside world. On the first level, we deal with consciousness, but on the second level, the discussion is about self-consciousness. And because subject and object coincide in the case of self-consciousness, there is a transparent relationship between them.

*D:* So you believe in the unmitigated powers of introspection, the full epistemological presence of the mind to itself, the ultimate transparency of self-knowledge?!

*A:* There is no reason to be ironical. You know my methodological starting-point perfectly well. I am convinced that the best guide to and the ultimate ground in semantic analysis is an examination of one's own consciousness—what one *knows* of the concepts to be analyzed. "Chasing the phantom of 'objectivity' through supposedly scientific methods one loses the only firm ground there is in semantics: the terra firma of one's own deep intuitions" (Wierzbicka 1985: 43).

*D:* That makes me an objectivist phantom-chaser, then. *You* know perfectly well that I practice semantics in the opposite way: not by denying the importance of intuition, to be sure, but by supplementing and supporting any reliance on introspection with corpus analysis or experimentation. When I make a claim about a word's meaning, for instance, I want to check that claim against the way in which people actually use the word. Or rather the other way round: if I try to define a word's meaning, I need evidence about the way the word is being used first. For instance, a definition should fit the referential range of application of a word: if you do not know what objects a word can refer to, how can you define the word?

*A:* But if you know the word, you know how to use it, do you not? So you will not have to look any further for evidence about how it is to be used: just consult your own knowledge.

*D:* No, that will not do, because there is sufficient evidence that an introspective analysis of how people actually use words does not necessarily conform to what people actually do. I could give you several examples, but let us maybe just restrict the discussion to a single case that both of us have already done research on. At one point (Wierzbicka 1985: 382), you defined *dress* in the following way:

> a kind of thing made by people for women and girls to wear; imagining things of this kind people could say these things about them:
> - they are made to be worn on the body, below the head, to cover most of the body,
> - so that all the parts of a woman's body which people think should not normally be seen are covered with that one thing,
> - and to protect most of the body from undesirable contact with the environment,
> - and to cause the woman wearing it to look good,
> - they are made in such a way that when they are on the body the lower half surrounds the lower half of the woman's body from all sides,
> - so that the legs are not separated from one another,
> - and so that the genital area of the woman's body seems to be hidden,
> - and so that women wearing things of this kind look different from men,
> - things of this kind are thought of as something suitable for women to wear in most kinds of places and in most kinds of circumstances.

Now, as you know, I did a corpus-based study with my collaborators exploring the actual referential use of clothing terms in Dutch. When we have a look at the actual garments that occur in our database as instances of *jurk* (the Dutch equivalent of *dress*), we find cases in our material that do not conform to the description. If, for instance, "covering most of the body" is interpreted as "covering more than 50% of the body", then a number of very short summer dresses with open backs and low necklines do not display the feature in question. And if "the parts of a woman's body which people think should not normally be seen" include the upper part of the thighs, then dresses with long side slits contradict the image. Furthermore, some dresses have such wide armholes and such a plunging décolletage that they could not normally be worn without exposure of the breasts (unless they are worn with an additional t-shirt or blouse underneath). The comparison shows, in other words, that the description you propose may well be adequate for the majority of cases in the range of dress, but does far from cover all possible instances.

*A:* This is irrelevant. What my definition describes is not the objective features of the things that might be called dresses, but the conceptual knowledge that people have of dresses. Not an extension, if you like, but rather an intension. In fact, by introducing the phrase "imagining things of this kind people could say these things about them" in the definition, the perspective is shifted from the objective features of the things that are being called dresses to the subjective knowledge that people know they have about dresses when they examine their own consciousness.

*D:* So you define *dress* by referring to what people think dresses are?

*A:* Yes. Is that not a natural thing to do for a so-called 'cognitive' analysis? What I try to define is the concept "dress" that people have, not actual dresses. Let us maybe look at another example. You once made similar remarks about my analysis of the category *fruit*. In my definition of the category, I included the feature that people, "wanting to imagine such things [fruits], would imagine them as growing on trees". You then commented that this feature does not apply to all fruit: raspberries, for example, are fruit, and yet they do not grow on trees. "In my view, however, this indisputable fact does not disprove the existence of a conceptual link between 'fruit' and 'trees' (just as the fact that ostriches do not fly does not disprove the existence of a conceptual link between 'birds' and 'flying'). ... From the fact that people think of ostriches as birds, and of birds as flying, it doesn't follow that they think of ostriches as flying" (Wierzbicka 1996: 164). And from the fact that people think of fruit as growing on trees, and of raspberries as fruit, it does not follow that they think of raspberries as growing on trees.

*D:* That amounts to saying that a definition should not necessarily cover the entire range of the category to be defined. But such a position contradicts what you once said, namely that "a valid definition must be empirically adequate, that is, it must be phrased in such a way that it covers the entire range of use of a given word, expression, or construction. It is not good enough if it only fits the more common or more typical cases" (Wierzbicka 1989: 738).

*A:* But again, do not forget that the features in my definition refer to mental states, so to speak, not to objective features of dresses or fruit or birds. What I claim is that people think of trees any time they think of fruit.

*D:* I am afraid I cannot follow you there. Even if we think of the features in your definition as truly conceptual features, they still do not have the required generality. For instance, if a definition such as that of *dress* is to be applicable to all the things that may be called by that name, people should be able to assert all the characteristics mentioned in the definition any time they see a dress. But surely, when imagining a less typical kind of dress than the kind whose features are included in the definition, people will not imagine it as a typical case. Or would they? What people could say about dresses changes when peripheral members of the category are at stake: default dresses, for instance, may well cover most of the body, but I would say that that feature is suppressed when a fancy type of summer dress is involved. Or, in the case of fruit, what would be the semantics of a sentence like *A raspberry is a fruit*? If you paraphrase it as "a raspberry is one of those things we think about (among other things) as growing on trees", you do imply that raspberries are thought of as growing on trees, and that is obviously not the case. And similarly for ostriches and birds: if *An ostrich is a bird* reads "an ostrich is one of those living beings thinking about which we would imagine them as being able to fly", then the sentence would be false. Which amounts to saying that the type of definition you use is incapable of accounting for categorization judgements. The definition of *fruit* that you suggest is unable to explain why a raspberry belongs to the category in question.

*A:* Do not jump to conclusions, dear Duodecimus. I would say there are two aspects to your remark. First, how is it we can say that raspberries are fruit, if our concept of *fruit* does not allow us to decide? Second, is a sentence like *Raspberries are fruit* contradictory? To tackle the first point first, the referential range of a category like *fruit* might be settled in a conventional way, more or less in the same way in which Hilary Putnam (1973) describes the semantics of natural kind terms. Whether a particular thing is to be called *tiger* is one thing, and the knowledge that people have of tigers is quite something else. On the one hand, there is a social convention about the names of things, on the other, there is a social convention about the knowledge (called 'stereotypical' by Putnam) that the speakers of a language are supposed to have of the category. Crucially, it is not what you know about jade that allows you to determine whether something is jade or not. According to Putnam, ordinary language users possess no more than 'stereotypical' knowledge about natural kinds, that is to say, they are aware of a number of salient characteristics, such as the fact that water is a transparent, thirst-quenching, tasteless liquid. The technical definition of water as $H_2O$, on the other hand, is to be located primarily with scientific experts. It is the experts' knowledge that ultimately determines how natural kind terms are to be used. On the one hand, a 'division of linguistic labor' ensures that there are societal experts who know that water is $H_2O$, that there is a distinction between elms and beeches, how to recognize gold from pyrites, and so on. On the other hand, laymen attune their own linguistic usage to that of the expert scientists, technicians, and so forth. The members of the non-specialized group are not required to have expert knowledge, but if they wish to be considered full-fledged members of the linguistic community, they are supposed to know the 'stereotype' connected with a category. A stereotype is, thus, a socially determined minimum set of data with regard to the extension of a category.

D: Well, I am fairly familiar with Putnam's theory, and I do not think that his particular model of the division of linguistic labor is empirically adequate. Also, his model is restricted to the semantics of natural kind terms, so we should be careful with generalizing it. But I admit that that is less relevant for what you are trying to say: if you assume that naming is a conventional act that need not be backed up by conceptual knowledge, then yes, you need not adapt your definition of *fruit* to allow for raspberries. But what about the

other objection? Is a sentence like *Raspberries are fruit* contradictory?

*A:* Let me ask you a question in return. Do you think that the semantic knowledge that we possess at one particular moment is always
sufficient to categorize the entities, situations, events, processes or
whatever that we encounter in reality?

*D:* I do not see yet where this is leading to, but no, I do not think so.
One of the crucial aspects of human cognition is the way in which
it can adapt itself to changing circumstances in the outside world.
The knowledge that we have has to be applied in flexible ways to
new experiences. Incidentally, that is precisely the reason why
prototype-theoretical models of semantic structures exert such an
appeal on cognitive linguists. At least to some extent, the peripheral, slightly deviant cases of a category are precisely those that result from the application of an existing category to cases that are
similar enough to be included, but that may differ in subtle ways
from the existing concept.

*A:* So you accept that there is a distinction between stored knowledge
and actualized knowledge? Between the semantic knowledge that
is mentally stored and the meanings that appear in actual utterances?

*D:* Absolutely. This is, to be sure, intimately connected with the 'cognitive' nature of Cognitive Linguistics itself. Cognitive Linguistics
is cognitive in the same way that cognitive psychology is: by assuming that our interaction with the world is mediated through in-
formational structures in the mind.

*A:* Now if you accept that, *Raspberries are fruit* is not contradictory
once you realize that my definition of *fruit* describes the knowledge that we have of the concept "fruit" on the deep-seated level
of stored meanings. It tells you what we know about fruit out of
context, so to speak. Conversely, *Raspberries are fruit* is an actu-
alization of that knowledge on the surface level, where the conceptual interaction between what we know about raspberries and
what we know about fruit may lead to a contextual attunement of
the underlying concept.

*D:* So you have a semantic deep structure, and a semantic surface structure, and semantic transformations that change deep structure into surface structure?

*A:* Your terminology has unfortunate historical connotations, but okay, let us accept this way of putting it as a convenient figure of speech. An alternative terminology could be to distinguish a level of 'deep semantics' from a level of 'contextual' semantics.

*D:* Ah yes, but then I do not quite understand why you concentrate your powers of analysis and description (which are considerable, let me be quite clear about that) on the deep-structural, deep-semantic level. The surface level, after all, is the level where most of the semantic action is to be found; I mean, most of the phenomena that a semanticist could be interested in are surface level phenomena. It follows from your own analysis of *Raspberries are fruit*, for instance, that truth conditions are to be investigated on the surface level. And the same holds for polysemy. Standard tests for polysemy, like the zeugma test, or Quine's *p and not p*-test, can only be properly applied to the utterance level.

*A:* Really? But if you define polysemy in terms of definability (two meanings are different if you cannot define them as being identical), and if definition refers to the deep-structural, stored readings, then clearly polysemy questions can be answered on the basis of an introspective methodology.

*D:* Still, it remains a matter to be settled empirically whether the lexical knowledge that people have in their minds conforms to the definition that you retrieve introspectively. It is not a priori given that the idea of a category that people may introspectively retrieve from memory is an adequate reflection of the extent of that person's actual knowledge of the category. On the contrary, if it is part of his knowledge to produce or accept an application of *dress* or *fruit* to cases that do not conform to the stored concept as introspectively defined, then he "knows" more about the category than would be included in his introspectively retrieved idea of the category. That knowledge, to be sure, is not necessarily conscious knowledge; it is less "knowledge that (lexical item x may refer to entities with such and such characteristics)" but rather "knowledge how (lexical item x may be successfully used)". In order, then, to get a better grasp on the lexical "knowledge how", usage-based investigations of the type illustrated by my own studies are vital, precisely if it is suspected that conscious knowledge may only partially cover the full extent of a person's "knowledge how". So I really believe that your position will only remain defensible if you provide us with an explicit model that describes how stored meanings are transformed into contextual readings at the utterance level.

A: I am sorry to disappoint you, but it may take some time before I come up with such a model. After all, why should I? The crucial phenomenon is the underlying concept, and the only proper way to investigate it is by introspection. So why should I spend my energy on what is (from my point of view) a secondary phenomenon?

D: One reason could be that your approach implies that your position becomes practically immune to criticism if you do not provide a full model of what happens when stored conceptual knowledge is contextualized. If an introspective examination of your own consciousness is the ultimate basis of semantics, how can your analyses be falsified at all? Is not your introspective methodology a gigantic immunization strategy? To put it slightly differently, how can you ensure that what you come up with in the analysis has anything to do at all with the knowledge of the language that we share, as speakers of the same language?

A: "My own experience in lexicographical analysis carried out over many years in seminars and group discussions has led me to the conclusion that the problem of objectively identifying the 'shared knowledge' and the shared notions may in fact be more apparent than real [...] Certainly if you ask a group of people what a cup or a skirt is, they will at first come up with overlapping rather than identical responses. If, however, each of them is induced to investigate his or her own concepts in depth, investing in the task a large amount of time and effort, then the differences in their responses will gradually diminish. If they are given a chance to discuss their differences the agreement will grow even further and the residual differences will often disappear. In the process, it will become clear that the underlying concept is the same for all the participants and that the initial differences in their responses were due to the fact that they had not yet explored sufficiently their own consciousness" (Wierzbicka 1985: 42-43).

D: I doubt whether the results of such a discussion will always be as uniform as you pretend, but I can see that, within your framework, intersubjectivity would indeed be a way of avoiding excessive .... Master?! Are you feeling alright? Quickly, pour him something to drink!

H: Thank you, thank you children, but I am perfectly okay. I was actually just closing my eyes to get a better view of your argumentation. Quite a nice pattern is emerging from your lively conversation, I must say.

A: Surely not as well-balanced as the pattern of your pleasant garden, I dare say.

H: Oh yes, there is symmetry in what you have said. If you have not been carried off entirely by your ardent interchanges, you will remember that your discussion was triggered by my little story about the ether wind. Recall that the essential point about the story was this: ontological assumptions, i.e. assumptions about what is, need not be subject to straightforward falsification. Now, in what both of you have said so far, I discern two different 'paradigms' in the Kuhnian sense; two different ways of considering cognitive phenomena that start from more or less opposing ontological assumptions. Your position, dear Antipoda, is idealistic in a double sense: an ontological sense and a methodological one. Ontologically, you believe in the existence of well-defined, deep-seated meanings that are the true essence of our conceptual knowledge—a platonic realm of ideas, really, but with a psychological rather than a metaphysical status. Methodologically, your position is an idealist one to the extent that you believe in the transparency of the mind to itself—in the epistemological primacy of introspection, in other words.

A: That is a fair picture of my position. What about Duodecimus?

H: I would say that his position is the opposite of yours. He believes in the epistemological primacy of utterance meaning. Ontologically speaking, I think he would say that meaning is to be situated pri-

marily at the level of performance. Meanings exist primarily as realized meanings, that is to say, as meanings inherent in utterances,
in actual events of using language. Methodologically, this view
correlates with the idea that utterances are the place where meanings are closest to us, where they are so to speak most palpable.

D: Precisely. Corpus-based studies and experimental psycholinguistic
research are important to see what actually happens when people
use the language. It has sometimes been said that Cognitive Linguistics is a usage-based model, but I feel cognitive linguists
sometimes neglect to draw the methodological consequences of
that recognition—viz. that actual language use is the methodological basis of Cognitive Linguistics.

A: But since you do believe in the importance of stored meanings (as
you explained earlier), what is the status of such stored meanings?

D: That is an interesting point, and I must confess that I have not yet
arrived at an entirely satisfactory picture of what is going on.
Methodologically speaking, the matter is quite clear: stored semantic knowledge is inferred; it can hardly be observed directly,
but it functions as a hidden entity that helps one to explain the actual behavior that one finds reflected in the usage data. There is
nothing extraordinary about that, surely: making reference to hidden entities as hypothetical constructs is common practice to quite
a number of sciences. Ontologically speaking, however, things are
less straightforward. Traditionally, cognitive scientists have conceived of such stored meanings in a symbolic fashion, as information encoded in some form of mental language or 'Mentalese'. But
that is a far-reaching assumption that should be handled with great
care. Connectionism in particular has made it clear that we had
better be careful with thinking about stored knowledge as something encoded in a symbolic fashion. So, to be on the safe side, I
would not want to go any further at this point than simply say that
the stored knowledge is the mental apparatus that enables us to
understand and produce meanings (where 'meanings' are to be
found on the level of usage). As far as I am concerned, it is not
even certain that it is useful to speak of 'meanings' as a specific
kind of entity on this level at all. At least as far as I can see, we

have only a very rudimentary view of how to think about mental meaning, which gives me one more motivation to start from the other end—that is, the level of utterances, performance, usage.

*A:* I can see clearly now how our views mirror each other. But I am not yet convinced that the ether wind story is applicable to our situation. Master, how exactly did you see the link?

*H:* Let us look back at the conversation the two of you had a moment ago, and reconstruct it along the lines of my earlier story. Antipoda started from the initial assumption that, for instance, the word *dress* had a specific unitary meaning. You, Duodecimus, formulated an experiment that could prove Antipoda wrong. The "experiment" (an empirical investigation into real language use, actually) did not establish the correctness of Antipoda's view, just like Michelson and Morley's experiment did not establish the existence of the ether. But instead of accepting your experiment as a straightforward rejection, Antipoda used different possibilities to salvage her original position: either to claim that your methodology was not the most appropriate one (meaning can only be grasped by an introspective methodology), or to make slight theoretical adjustments (the meaning to be defined is a "deep-structural", "deep-semantic" phenomenon). Michelson and Morley, as I mentioned, took the road of methodological adjustment, but in the case of the ether just as in the case of Antipoda's meanings, some people took the road of theoretical adjustments. (One such approach involved so-called 'Lorentz Fitzgerald contraction'—the idea that the effect of the ether wind could not be measured because the moving objects underwent a contraction.) And the ironical thing, Duodecimus, is that you cannot even blame Antipoda for doing so, because her strategy is a legitimate one, if you are willing to extrapolate your position of internal realism from the theoretical to the metatheoretical level.

*D:* Good. You have established that deciding between the two models is not self-evident. But a decision should be possible, should it not? After all, the debate about the ether was decided eventually. I mean, ontological assumptions cannot be selected at random: if I start from the ontological assumption that the earth has two moons, the world itself will prove me wrong. You have made the point that the extrapolation of the notion of internal realism to the methodological level creates a broad margin for theoretical and methodological differences; quite different assumptions may make it more difficult to assess competing theories in a straightforward way. But there clearly are limits to that flexibility, are there not? If you have a theory that produces a model that systematically describes how surface readings are related to stored semantic knowledge, then surely the pure scope of such a theory would be a reason for preferring it over a model that restricts itself to stored meanings only!

*A:* The point is rather too hypothetical for my taste: you will have to admit that at this point, neither of the two approaches has developed such an encompassing model yet. So it is rather irrelevant to compare them on this point. There is another thing, however, that the two of you seem to forget. The relationship between both approaches, in fact, is not as symmetrical as Histrio's picture suggests. I am convinced, dear Duodecimus, that you are somewhat of a closet introspectivist.

*D:* Again a surprise! What do you mean?

*A:* Let us consider the clothing terms project that you referred to earlier. The methodological starting-point of the project was to investigate to which actual referents specific terms referred. Right?

*D:* Most certainly so. By choosing clothing terms as the field of investigation, we could get independent access to the referents of the terms in question, for instance by examining the photographs that the clothing terms refer to in fashion magazines and the like. Then we described the various features of the referents of any specific clothing term, and on the basis of this featural description, described the structure of the semasiological range of application of the different garment names.

A. Now notice that your approach is not completely free of intuitive aspects, in the sense that your own understanding of the instances of language use under investigation is entirely ignored or suppressed. More precisely, the referential approach does not entail that the investigation proceeds in a purely objective fashion, without any recourse to interpretative activities on the part of the investigator. The point may be illustrated by considering the initial selection of the descriptive features included in the componential system. The choice of those features cannot be dictated automatically by the referents of the words themselves. In principle, an infinite number of characteristics could possibly be included in the descriptive framework. In the case of trousers, for instance, it would be possible to refer to the presence of lining in the legs, to whether the hip pockets have a flap or not, or to the number of nooses in the waist intended to hold a belt. The fact that, in actual practice, you decided not to include these features in the componential system is undoubtedly determined by assumptions about their relevance for the description. Ultimately, I would say that it is your own pre-existent knowledge of the field of Dutch clothing terms, and your own intuitions about what would be pertinent features for describing that field, that have played their role in the choice of a particular componential system.

*D:* Oh, but I have no wish to deny that any semantic analysis has to rely at least to some extent on an intuitive understanding of linguistic expressions. But we opt for a referentially enriched corpus (as we prefer to call it) precisely to guide our intuitions, and to restrict the possibilities of an uncritical or unmitigated reliance on intuitive judgements.

*A:* But if you accept that meanings are only realized mentally, and that you need intuition anyway to grasp them at all, why not just accept introspection as the basic method of research? After all ...

*H:* Excuse me for interrupting you, but I feel we are reaching the heart of the matter here, and I would like you both to see quite clearly what is at stake here.

*D:* Master, we are eminently interruptible when you summon us. Pray explain the stakes to us.

*H:* It will be a pleasure. But shall we perhaps leave our seats and stroll around the garden for a while? I feel we could use a little exercise.

*A:* We certainly can. Could we perhaps walk to the sundial down yonder? I have never had a chance to take a good look at it.

*H:* Certainly. But I suggest not to follow the path that leads directly to it; we could take the path through the orchard instead. In fact, just as I introduced the topic of our conversation by making a detour, I would now like to follow another side-path, to see whether another excursion can help us to bring the discussion to a close.

*D:* Fine. Let us go peripatetic then.

*H:* What Antipoda's last remarks make clear, is the fact that semantics is basically a *hermeneutic* enterprise. Lexical description, for instance, does not simply consist of recording referents, but of trying to determine what features of the referents motivate or license the use of a particular item, in short, of *understanding* expressions. I would now like to show to you that the opposition between both of you is not uncommon in the hermeneutic sciences.

*D:* 'The hermeneutic sciences'—what do you understand by that?

*H:* From a very general point of view, hermeneutics is the 'theory of interpretation', a methodological reflection on the principles underlying interpretative activities concerned with literary products, works of art, juridical texts, and so on. It is, in fact, from the sources of biblical exegesis and philological scholarship that hermeneutics as a theoretical enterprise came into being in the course of the 19th century. More specifically, hermeneutics is a philosophical tradition, inaugurated by Wilhelm Dilthey at the end of the previous century, that takes interpretation to be the basic methodological concept of the human sciences (*Geisteswissenschaften*). Dilthey's explicit aim was to provide the human sciences with a philosophical understanding of their methodological basis that could be set off against the positivist self-understanding of the natural sciences.

*D:* So the hermeneutic sciences coincide with the human sciences, because they use an interpretative methodology?

*H:* More accurately, Dilthey's views consist of a characterization of the subject-matter of the human sciences, and of a characterization of their method. The products of the human mind that constitute the subject-matter of the human sciences are the expression of an inner experience, an understanding of life in terms of the intellect, the will, and the emotions that all human beings possess. The

method of the human sciences, in return, consists of an interpretative attempt to recover the original experience behind the expressions. In this sense, the logic of the human sciences is fundamentally different from that of the natural sciences: whereas the latter are based on 'Erklärung' (positivistic explanation in terms of the immutable laws of nature), the former are based on 'Verstehen' (understanding of lived experience through its expressions).

*A:* This emphasis on experience must imply a natural affinity between Cognitive Linguistics and Diltheyan hermeneutics, then.

*H:* All the more so because Dilthey thinks of that experience in terms that will sound familiar to cognitive linguists. I think you will also be happy to note, for instance, that Dilthey mentions the study of language as the epitome of the hermeneutic enterprise. And because experience is a mental phenomenon, there is a link between hermeneutics and psychology. This is not to say that the experiences that are being expressed are always and only highly personal phenomena. Rather, human experience is also a cultural and historical phenomenon, and products of human life such as systems of laws, rituals, and everyday conventions clearly embody the historically transmitted experience of cultures rather than just individuals—but even then, the cultural message would cease to exist if it were not incorporated into the personal experience of individuals. At the same time, the hermeneutic methodology is just as encyclopedic as human experience itself. While the experience that is being expressed is an encompassing phenomenon in which feelings, thoughts, memories, expectations and so forth, come together, the interpretative methodology of the human sciences will ideally be an interdisciplinary fusion of historical, psychological, anthropological, and linguistic research.

*D:* I understand there is an affinity with Cognitive Linguistics, but we have had many conversations before in which you revealed that Cognitive Linguistics has many predecessors, both in philosophy and linguistics. What makes Dilthey special?

*H:* You are absolutely right. If we restrict the perspective to philosophy, Dilthey is but one representative of a larger number of theoreticians who worked round the turn of the century and who discussed epistemological problems that are quite relevant to us to-day. Think of all those, like Brentano and Husserl, who explored the concept of intentionality. But Dilthey is special in the context of our present discussion, because he has explicitly drawn the attention to the methodological importance of interpretation for the human sciences. Moreover, and this is the reason that I mentioned his name at all, both his own work and the further development of philosophical hermeneutics foreshadow the debate between the two of you.

*A:* Neither of us ever had the intention of being absolutely original, I am sure.

*H:* Please do not feel diminished—I would be the last to overestimate historical originality. But I think I had better explain to you where the tension in Dilthey's work may be situated. If the method of the human sciences is based on interpretation (that is, on recovering the experience behind the expressions), can this process of recovery be concluded in an objective fashion? Does it lead to certainty? Can we be sure that our interpretations are correct? Can we truthfully determine the original experience and the authentic intention behind the expressions? At this point, a particular tension within Dilthey's work becomes apparent. On the one hand, Dilthey's attempt to place the human sciences on as secure and as respectable a footing as the natural sciences induces him to stress the objectivity of the human sciences. In his text 'Die Entstehung der Hermeneutik' (1961, originally 1913), for instance, he reacts against the danger of 'romantic arbitrariness' in the conception of the hermeneutical enterprise. If the hermeneutic act is basically an empathic subjective re-enactment of an original creative act, objective standards for assessing the success of an interpretation may be hard to come by. Conversely, if hermeneutics is modeled on the example provided by biblical (and generally, philological) textual exegesis, interpretative rules might indeed be found. At this point, Dilthey is quite outspoken that the latter course is the one to take. He emphasizes the importance of subjecting the hermeneutical, interpretative enterprise to critical scrutiny, and stresses that the task of hermeneutics should be to develop a general theory of interpretation, a universally applicable interpretative methodology that specifies the criteria for correct interpretations.

*A:* You spoke of a tension in his work, so there must be other tendencies at work as well.

*H:* In fact, Dilthey's emphasis on the historicity of human experience also introduces a note of relativism into his views. While nature is governed by the necessity of natural laws, human life is governed by purposive action and conscious effort; the realm par excellence of human life is the unfolding of history. As such, can there be a general interpretative method that universally spans the entire range of the history of mankind, disregarding the historical differences between the objects of its interpretative activities? Can all historical products be interpreted on the same basis? More importantly still, if man in general is caught in history, can interpreters free themselves from their own historical background when confronting products from the past?

*A:* I can see the tension quite clearly now, but did he find a solution for it in any way?

*H:* In Dilthey's own work, the tension between the claim to universality implied by the search for objectivity, and the relativist tendency suggested by the emphasis on historicity is far from resolved. In the later development of hermeneutics, however, the non-universalist, non-objectivist tendency becomes most prominent, most clearly so in the developmental line leading from Martin Heidegger to Hans-Georg Gadamer on the one hand, and to Jacques Derrida on the other.

*D:* If I understand you correctly, you are making the point that the differences of opinion that Antipoda and I have do not involve a choice between an idealist and an objectivist conception of linguistic semantics, but rather between two ways of thinking about the interpretative, or if you wish 'hermeneutic' aspects of linguistics?

*H:* Indeed. In your discussion of a few moments ago, Duodecimus tried to find hard and fast evidence that Antipoda's view is straightforwardly wrong, in the way in which it would be indubitably wrong to claim that the earth has two natural satellites. But at least as long as we do not have two full-fledged models to com-

pare, such a straightforward falsification may be difficult to attain
at this stage in the development of Cognitive Linguistics. Also, the
methodological extrapolation of the concept of internal realism
teaches us that theoretical comparison need not be self-evident. So,
perhaps, it may be useful to think of your conflicting views from a
different angle, viz. as different ways of dealing with the interpretative nature of semantics. Specifically, while Antipoda basically
*trusts* intuitive interpretation, the position taken by Duodecimus is
a prolongation of the critical approach that I mentioned in connection with Dilthey.

D: I have no objections to thinking about my point of view in this
way. When I insist on the importance of corpus-linguistic (or for
that matter, psycho-experimental or neurophysiological) data as
the backdrop for semantic research, I basically try to achieve a semantic analysis that is consonant with as many factors as possible:
the way words are actually applied to things in the world, the way
in which language is actually processed, the material embodiment
of our linguistic skills, but also all contextual information we have
about the historical and cultural background of the speakers of the
language—everything, in a sense, in which language may be said to
be *grounded*. Indeed, grounding may well be the essential concept
in a Cognitive Linguistic theory of interpretation.

A: That would seem to put me in the corner of 'romantic arbitrariness', or even worse, postmodern license à la Derrida. I really have
to protest against that impression! There are at least two aspects of
my approach that counteract any tendencies towards subjective arbitrariness. First, there is the importance of intersubjectivity which
I drew your attention to a few minutes ago already.

D: And second?

A: Second, I firmly believe that semantic description should be
couched in a vocabulary of universal concepts—a set of innate indefinables that is common to all languages of the world and that
constitutes the core of their vocabulary. If definitions are required
to be formulated in terms of such a natural set of primitive semantic elements, that will sufficiently restrict the process of interpretation, will it not?

*D:* Again a very platonic idea, this universal set of innate ideas. But is it indeed introspectively clear what those innate ideas are? Is it part of our intuitive knowledge that we can identify the universal set of primitive semantic elements?

*A:* I do not think so, actually. The set of universal concepts rather emerges from the definitional analyses themselves. Carefully defining yields a set of indefinables.

*D:* How is that? I would say such an idea contradicts the idea that this set of indefinables has restrictive power. On the one hand, the set of primitives is supposed to restrict the set of possible definitions. On the other hand, the definitional analysis itself is supposed to yield the set of innate concepts. Is that not circular: the definitional analysis yields the set of restrictions to which it is supposed to conform?!

*A:* I may have expressed myself inaccurately. The actual criterion for the definitions is their cross-linguistic transparency, their understandability, if you like. A superior definition, you will agree, is one that can be understood without prior knowledge of the language to be defined. In actual practice, this is achieved by couching the definition in terms that are cross-linguistically unambiguous, such as SEE and HEAR, THIS, I, YOU, WHERE, GOOD and BAD, SAME and OTHER, or THINK. So the ultimate restriction is not the innateness of the defining terms, but the cross-linguistic transparency of the definitions.

*D:* I sometimes doubt whether transparency is exactly what you achieve with your type of definitions, but anyway, what strikes me as particularly odd in this conversation as a whole, is the affinity that now becomes apparent between Cognitive Linguistics and formal semantics.

*A:* Now it is my turn to be surprised—flabbergasted, rather. A likeness between Cognitive Linguistics and formal semantics? What in Jove's name are we to understand by that?

*D:* You may remember that Histrio once tried to convince us that formal semantics was (originally at least) a normative enterprise, a method of stipulating requirements for how to describe meanings.

But perhaps, master, you had better tell us about that yourself. Am I overlooking something?

*H:* You are absolutely right from a historical point of view, Duodecimus. Formal semantics, as it was developed by applying formal logic to natural language, was explicitly intended by at least some of its founding fathers (like the members of the Vienna Circle) as a tool for separating metaphysical speculation from empirically viable statements. Logic is concerned with the validity of arguments, and the merits of formalization in logic consist in restricting possible propositions to ones whose validity may be tested, in contrast with mere speculation. And so formal semantics, like Antipoda's approach, tries to solve Dilthey's problem (if we may call it that—I mean the problem of controlling the process of interpretation lest it slide off towards 'romantic arbitrariness') by imposing restrictions on *how* possible interpretations might be expressed. The clarity of the logical language is a way of ensuring the epistemological viability of statements. *What* can be legitimately expressed as an interpretation of utterances in a natural language, is restricted by *how* it can be expressed in the language of formal logic.

*D:* In the same way in which Antipoda wishes to restrict the boundless freedom of interpretation by imposing requirements on how the interpretations are expressed. *My* approach to finding restrictions, by contrast, is not *representational*, but rather *empirical*: I want suggested interpretations to be empirically grounded in what we know of the cultural background, the actual behavior of the language users, the physiology of the human conceptual apparatus.

*A:* All that is very fine, but I do not exactly feel like a formal semanticist. I think you have an obligation to explain the differences between my position and the formalists. But master, what are you scribbling there in the sand? I hope we are not boring you.

*H:* On the contrary. I was thinking about a way to answer your question. Perhaps you would care to have a look at my little sketch here. If we make a distinction between the restrictive principles applied by the various approaches on the one hand, and their major aim on the other, the difference between Antipoda's approach and the formalists' is to a large extent that the latter are hardly interested in cognitive relevance, in the psychological sense in which Cognitive Semantics tends to conceive of that term. Cognitive Semantics is interested in the full range of semantic phenomena that seem to play a role in actual language use—including those that cannot be formally described within the framework of logical semantics. Formalists, by contrast, seem willing to accept the restriction of the description to the truth-functional properties of language alone, given that those may well be (they feel) the only ones that can be described according to the high demands of formalizability that they wish to impose on linguistics.

| RESTRICTIVE PRINCIPLE | METHODOLOGY | MAJOR AIM |
|---|---|---|
| empirical restrictions | "empiricist" cognitive linguistics | cognitive relevance |
| representational restrictions | "idealist" cognitive linguistics | |
| | formal semantics | logical validity |

A: You take the words right out of my mouth, master. "Despite its name, 'formal semantics' [...] doesn't seek to reveal and describe the meanings encoded in natural language, or to compare meanings across languages and cultures. Rather, it sees its goal as that of translating certain carefully selected types of sentences into a logical calculus. It is interested not in meaning (in the sense of conceptual structures encoded in language) but in the logical properties of sentences such as entailment, contradiction, or logical equivalence" (Wierzbicka 1996:8).

*D:* Very illuminating indeed—but I notice the sundial is just on the other side of this hedge. What a beautiful object! How should one read it?

*H:* Let me show you. See that shadow here? The number that it falls on along this circular band indicates the hour of the day: what you see is not time itself, but a sign of time.

*D:* And just so, linguistic behavior is not the conceptualization as such, but only a sign to be interpreted.

*A:* Hmm, if you interpret this shadowy sign correctly, you will notice that the tables are now likely to be being laid out; the hour of dinner is approaching. Shall we perhaps walk back to the house?

*H:* Yes, we should: a happy hour is awaiting us.


**Epilogue**

In the foregoing philosophical dialogue, I have compared an empiricist and an idealist conception of the methodology of Cognitive Semantics. Against the background of my previous research, this comparison continues the confrontation of Cognitive Semantics with philosophical epistemology that I began in Geeraerts (1985), where the possible 'backfiring' of Cognitive Semantics' adherence to internal realism was first described. Other work along this line of thought includes Geeraerts (1993), and the final chapter of Geeraerts (1997), which includes a discussion of Diltheyan hermeneutics. At the same time, the dialogue is a methodological reflection on the type of work presented in Geeraerts, Grondelaers and Bakema (1994), which takes a heavily empiricist attitude.

The dialogue proceeded in eight steps. First, the notion of internal realism was introduced on the basis of an example taken from the natural sciences, involving the interpretation of Michelson and Morley's experiments. Second, it was recalled that internal realism characterizes the epistemological conception that Cognitive Semantics has of the relationship between language and the world. Third, the adherence to internal realism was shown to raise a methodological problem: can it be extrapolated to the relationship between language and the linguistic description of language? And if so, what safeguards are there against a lapse into radical subjectivism? Empiricist and idealist approaches in Cognitive Semantics were presented as different answers with regard to these questions. Fourth, the initial discussion between the proponents of both approaches remained an open-ended one. Although it was shown that an introspective, idealist methodology does not always yield an adequate description of the way in which words are actually being used, there were at least two possibilities for the idealist to escape from the consequences of this discrepancy and to keep the debate open: to dissociate judgements about category membership from conceptual knowledge (in a way linking up with Putnam's theory of natural kind terms), or by imposing a radical distinction between semantic structure and surface structure. Fifth, the open-ended discussion was placed in a wider framework, by interpreting it against the philosophical background of Wilhelm Dilthey's notion of hermeneutics. It was shown that the Diltheyan conception of language fits Cognitive Semantics very well. Sixth, starting from this recognition, it was suggested that the debate involves a choice between two ways of thinking about the interpretative aspects of linguistic semantics, rather than a straightforward choice between empiricist objectivism and idealist subjectivism in any crude form. More specifically, the two competing approaches were seen as representing alternative ways of avoiding the danger of 'romantic arbitrariness' as formulated by Dilthey. Whereas the 'empiricist' approach tries to achieve maximal empirical grounding for posited interpretations, the 'idealist' approach tries to restrict the set of possible interpretations by couching it in a vocabulary of allegedly universal concepts. Seventh, without enforcing a final decision, I suggested that the grounding approach represents the more radical safeguard against arbitrariness. Finally, the two approaches within Cognitive Semantics were compared with formal semantics as yet another answer to Dilthey's problem. Relying on a vocabulary of universal primitives, the idealist approach within Cognitive Semantics shares with formal semantics a 'representational' strategy for imposing restrictions on linguistic descriptions. At the same time, it shares with the empiricist approach in Cognitive Semantics a desire to describe the full range of semantic phenomena that play a role in natural language use, rather than restricting the domain of inquiry to the 'logical', truth-functional properties of language.

What emerges from the discussion, then, is not exactly a straightforward answer with regard to the initial question—although I do feel that an empiricist approach imposes stronger demands on the semantic enterprise than the idealist one, and as such, provides a more outspoken answer to Dilthey's problem. The picture emerging from the discussion does, on the other hand, provide an illuminating view of the present-day situation in linguistic semantics. Perhaps surprisingly, the major conceptions of linguistic semantics appear to pattern together as different answers with regard to Dilthey's problem, that is, the problem of what constitutes a legitimate interpretation of natural language expressions. I would like to suggest that this is a good reason for putting the interpretative nature of linguistic semantics in the forefront of theoretical attention.

# References

Dilthey, Wilhelm
  1961    Die Entstehung der Hermeneutik. In W. Dilthey (Hrsg.), *Gesammelte Schriften,* Band V, 317-331. Leipzig: Teubner. Originally 1913.
Geeraerts, Dirk
  1985    *Paradigm and Paradox. Explorations into a Paradigmatic Theory of Meaning and its Epistemological Background.* Leuven: Universitaire Pers.
  1993    Cognitive semantics and the history of philosophical epistemology. In: R. Geiger and B. Rudzka-Ostyn (eds.), *Conceptualizations and Mental Processing in Language,* 53-80. Berlin: Mouton de Gruyter.
  1997    *Diachronic Prototype Semantics. A Contribution to Historical Lexicology.* Oxford: The Clarendon Press.
Geeraerts, Dirk, Stefan Grondelaers and Peter Bakema
  1994    *The Structure of Lexical Variation. Meaning, Naming, and Context.* Berlin: Mouton de Gruyter.
Gibbs, Raymond W., Jr.
  1994    *The Poetics of Mind. Figurative Thought, Language, and Understanding.* Cambridge: Cambridge University Press.

Lakoff, George
    1987    *Women, Fire, and Dangerous Things. What Categories Reveal about the Mind.* Chicago: University of Chicago Press.

Putnam, Hilary
    1975    The meaning of 'meaning'. In H. Putnam, *Mind, Language and Reality. Philosophical Papers II.* Cambridge: Cambridge University Press.

Regier, Terry
    1995    A model of the human capacity for categorizing spatial relations. *Cognitive Linguistics* 6: 63-88.

Sandra, Dominiek and Sally Rice
    1995    Network analyses of prepositional meaning: Mirroring whose mind—the linguist's or the language user's? *Cognitive Linguistics* 6: 89-130.

Wierzbicka, Anna
    1985    *Lexicography and Conceptual Analysis.* Ann Arbor: Karoma.
    1989    Prototypes in semantics and pragmatics. *Linguistics* 27: 731-769.
    1992    *Semantics, Culture, and Cognition. Universal Human Concepts in Culture-Specific Configurations.* Oxford: Oxford University Press.
    1996    *Semantics. Primes and Universals.* Oxford: Oxford University Press.

# Partial Autonomy. Ontology and methodology in cognitive linguistics

## Peter Harder

## 1. Introduction[1]

### 1.1. 'Continuism' as a methodological bias

For a long time ontological questions were banned from scientific discourse, because they were believed to be non-scientific. In the heyday of positivism and unified science, scientific statements were thought to be defined by their form, while the issue of what the world was really made of was out of bounds to serious scientists. With the demise of positivist foundations of science, it became legitimate to raise this issue once again, and to argue that scientific methods must be suited to the types of objects you are looking at. This does not imply that we are free to postulate weird types of entities and then go on to devise even weirder methodologies to investigate them. However, it does mean that there is no royal road to knowledge and understanding based on methodology alone. Ontology therefore necessarily comes in as a source of critical evaluation of actual methods and results.

There are several reasons why I think there is a point in looking at the issue of what kind of things there are in the world in the context of cognitive linguistics. The more specific reason lies in what has been called the 'continuism' of cognitive linguistics (cf. Stjernfelt 1995). This continuism, which is motivated by opposition to the pointed separation within mainstream generative linguistics between linguistic structure and everything else, is associated with many of the design features of cognitive linguistics: instead of a sharp distinction between competence and performance, a usage-based model in which the difference between language and usage is taken not to be terribly important; no sharp distinction between language on the one hand and human experience generally, because the concern of cognitive linguistics has been to assert the embeddedness of language in a wider cognitive and experiential context; no sharp distinction between cognitive and biological phenomena, because language is grounded in the human body, and because all skills can be seen as mediated by neurological patterns (which can be modeled by increasingly sophisticated connectionist simulations).

The continuism also goes with the fact that cognitive linguistics is explicitly concerned to use language as a window on cognitive structures generally, so that one can move freely and gradually from facts about language to facts about human cognition and further on to facts about human life generally, including politics, as in Lakoff's (1995) analysis of the organization of politically central value systems in terms of two cognitive models of the family.

Let me repeat that I think that this emphasis on continuity in itself is valuable; in the opening words of Searle (1995), we live in exactly one world, not two or three or seventeen. I also think that cognitive linguistics has achieved impressive results in showing the wealth of implications that continuity has for the proper understanding of linguistic facts down to minute details in the fabric of meaning and structure, as demonstrated in the central works of Langacker, Talmy, Lakoff and others. What I want to do now is not to deny this continuity, but to turn around and look at those differences that are backgrounded when the continuity is emphasized.

The key phrase for this endeavor will be 'partial autonomy', understood as a central fact about the relationship between related domains: cognitive facts are partially autonomous of brute facts; linguistic facts are partially autonomous of experiential facts; syntactic facts are partially autonomous of facts about the meaning of elements and social facts are partially autonomous of mental facts. This phrase implies also that the domains in question are partially non-autonomous: in other words, they are grounded rather than self-contained. The adjective *partial* thus implies rejection of 'computational functionalism', according to which higher-level patterns are totally independent of their 'implementation'.

## 1.2. The ontology of levels: two types of differentiation

The notion of partial autonomy must be understood in connection with an assumption according to which there are irreducible differences between entities at different ontological levels: some things are true of particles, some of atoms, some of molecules, some of living cells, some of organisms, some of minds, and some of societies, and so forth. This division into levels means that even if the world consists wholly of particles in fields of force (cf. Searle 1995), you cannot reduce all statements to statements about particles.

This way of thinking is familiar in the context of natural science (cf. also Køppe 1990); in the linguistic context it has been used by Fodor and Pylyshyn (1988) in defense of an autonomous level of pure syntax. However, one of the merits of partial autonomy (cf. below, section 3.2) is that one can accept the necessity of a separate level of analysis for syntax (as they rightly insist one should), without accepting the conclusions that they see as following from it—because partial autonomy places the difference of levels within the context of an overall continuity.

But the problem in the Fodor-Pylyshyn position is not only the missing account of the continuity within which the partial autonomy belongs. The other equally fundamental problem is that the difference of levels that is necessary in order to understand syntax is not of the kind that goes from particles up to galaxies. Rather, it is based on a more complex type of difference of levels based on functional differentiation, which is central in understanding language.

Physical levels are built bottom-up. Molecules consist of atoms, and atoms consist of particles; you can have particles without atoms, and atoms without molecules, but not vice versa. Functional levels, however, are constructed top-down: you must have the larger whole before functional differentiation can arise. An example is the functional differentiation between organs in a biological organism: certain animals have legs and claws and hearts and stomachs, etc - but these parts presuppose the larger whole to which they belong. Atoms and particles can drift around on their own, and may become parts of molecules when conditions allow it; but you cannot have hearts and legs and stomachs drifting around, occasionally combining into a whole animal. This means that you can only understand a leg properly by looking outside the leg itself, to what it is attached to. With some caution, this can be understood as reflecting a developmental order that is reflected in the history of evolution: organisms (as the higher level that organs such as legs presuppose) existed before legs did; legs arose as part of a process whereby organisms became more complex and developed a more subtle internal division of labor.

The same point applies to the division of labor between syntactic elements in an utterance. We cannot have subjects and predicates drifting around at a proto-stage before they get combined into whole utterances. Rather, as exemplified in animal languages, we can have whole utterances with little internal structure before we have a language with a systematic internal division of labor between constituents.

The two directions of level-formation simultaneously create two forms of grounding, if (as I suggest) the relation of grounding is understood as linking an entity with its ontological foundations. Physical phenomena are grounded in facts about their constituents; functional roles are grounded in patterns of interaction between the object that has the functional role and its context; more on this below (section 2.2). In the context of cognitive linguistics, one implication of the emphasis on partial autonomy within an ontology that includes functional relations, is that cognitive facts should not be understood as autonomous, any more than linguistic facts should. Like legs and teeth, brains are organs, functionally hooked up with the organism as a whole in its interaction with the environment, and partially shaped by their functional role.

Partial autonomy is a difficult concept, but one that it is essential to come to terms with, not only in linguistics and cognitive science, but in scientific description generally. The concept should not be understood merely as a wishy-washy compromise solution, giving both parties a little of what they want, but as a hard fact about the way the world works. To support this contention, before I go into language and cognition, I am going to offer a different scientific field as an illustration case, namely economics.

## 1.3. Economics: an analogy

Economics is an attractive illustration from a linguistic point of view: in addition to the analogy itself, the comparison is motivated by the fact that when structural linguistics arose, it was inspired by the theoretical apparatus of economic theory. The notion of 'value' (*valeur*) was imported from economics into semantics by de Saussure as indicating something totally distinct from the 'natural' properties of an object. Just as the exchange value, i.e. the market price of an object, cannot be inferred from any pre-economic properties of the object in question, but arises only within an economic system with a market shaped by forces of supply and demand, and so forth—so the role of a word in the language is totally severed from the nature of the word's links with the non-linguistic world. Thus, autonomy in linguistics and in economics have the same intellectual roots.

The issue of autonomy as applied to economics can be boiled down to the question of the relation between exchange value and use value. The basic issue is the following: is the economic system, which is built on exchange value (= money value) and operates in terms of concepts like turnover, profit and gross national product, autonomous of the natural, non-monetary world? To be specific, is the world of human needs, grounded in the human body, and the capacity of objects in the real world to satisfy those needs irrelevant to an economist?

The discussion below is based on the assumption that the natural reply for any cognitive linguist should be emphatically negative. But if that is so, it becomes interesting to look at the sort of facts that underpin the autonomy assumption in economics: if we understand the relative sense in which economics does indeed have a life of its own it may throw light on both the relative autonomy of syntax within the overall life of human languages, and on the relative autonomy of individual cognition within the overall theory of human life.

As a natural starting point, it should be emphasized that the consequences of overestimating autonomy in economics are even more serious than they are in linguistics. This is so because the autonomy assumption is built into the whole rationale of economic decision-making, driving the effort to maximize economic growth regardless of the drain on natural resources and of the satisfaction of real human needs (cf. Daly 1996). In economic calculations, the value of an object arises only the moment it comes inside the economic system of exchange of goods and services, cf. above. Therefore, the proceeds of exhausting a mineral deposit counts as income—whereas the fact that the deposit is now gone appears nowhere as cost! The explanation is (I remember how this was explained to me when I did two years of undergraduate economics back in the sixties) that there is no good way to translate 'pre-economic' properties into anything that would interact with the economic flow.

This may tempt one to take the diametrically opposite point of view, that economics is really a completely artificial discipline and we should concentrate instead on the real value of things, as grounded in the bodily reality of human needs. But if we did that, we would also fail to understand the real causal power of events that take place within the circulation of abstract exchange value, as embodied in money. Crises are the most striking examples of the co-existence of different ontological levels. When an economy crashes, economic indicators may plummet within hours while the purely physical resources are not immediately affected. And when an animal dies, predictions based on the biological level of understanding are suddenly null and void, while facts on the chemical level remain the same.

On the other hand, if the physical substratum is destroyed, the higher levels have to go as well: no life without chemistry, and no economy without needs and resources. Generally speaking, the lesson is that we need to understand simultaneously the ways in which subsystems obey special laws of their own and the ways in which they depend on the larger systems of which they form parts.

## 2. The grounding of cognition: the outside and the inside story

### 2.1. An outline of the argument

When this general issue is seen in the context of cognitive linguistics, it raises an issue which I think cognitive linguists should address more explicitly than they have done up to now: the relation between cognitive facts on the one hand and functional and social facts on the other. The overall ontological position that is presupposed in the following is realism, which is sometimes called objectivism; but it should be added that there is an important difference between being an objectivist about the world and being an objectivist about meaning. An objectivist about the world (cf. also Searle 1995) believes that the world exists independently of his perception and understanding (although parts of it exist only because he exists, as part of the world). An objectivist about meaning believes that word meanings can be translated into mind-independent 'objective' categories—which is a different matter. I have no way of proving realism about the world, since I cannot escape from my own cognitive universe, but this does not prevent me from saying that this is what I believe, any more than lack of access to direct experience of other people's pain would prevent me from saying that I believe other people also feel pain.

Rather than actual disagreement with the realist position, what I am presupposing in the discussion is that it is not entirely clear to everyone in the cognitive linguistics community how the core domain of cognitive linguistics hangs together with the rest of the world. What I shall call 'cognitivism'[2] below is not so much a body of beliefs but a habitual perspective, in which cognitive models and processes are in focus and their links to facts outside an individual's cognitive system are somewhat hazy. To illustrate the problem, let me take up the classical notion of the semiotic triangle, dating back to the stoics and reinvented by Ogden and Richards, according to which *vox significat res mediantibus conceptibus*, i.e. words denote things by means of mental concepts.

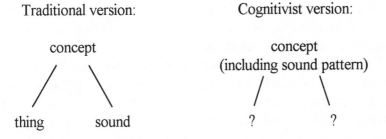

Traditional version:

concept

thing        sound

Cognitivist version:

concept
(including sound pattern)

?            ?

Saying that words denote things would be 'objectivism about meaning', so we have to put a question mark there. Further, as pointed out most explicitly by Langacker (1987: 78), the linguistically relevant aspect of speech sounds is not the physical sounds but rather the cognitive patterns of sound, so sounds really belong under the same heading as the concepts, as mental constructs. So we have to leave a question mark at that corner, too. The third corner, the mental one, is then the only one that remains. And it is by no means obvious how to get out of the circle of cognitive facts. After all, functions and social relations and descriptions of physical objects and experiential qualities can only be understood as products of the human cognitive system anyway, so a cognitive description can accommodate all these types of fact with equal ease.

The first prerequisite for making sense about the relation between cognition and context is to be clear about what constitutes cognition. Roughly speaking, the prototype of cognition that pervades the whole cognitive movement of which cognitive linguistics is a part, are higher-level processes, specifically those which involve symbolic-representational (i.e. intentional) content. As in other prototype concepts, there is much less agreement about the outer bounds of the concept than about the core, and many authors support a very wide definition of cognition—in part because rigid distinctions between 'higher' cognitive processes and the rest would go against the 'continuist' program within cognitive linguistics.

However, vague boundaries create problems when you go from discussing cognition to discussing its grounding: when the distinction becomes blurred between the outposts of cognition itself and those phenomena in which cognition is grounded, the grounding issue itself becomes blurred. When I speak about cognition below, I refer specifically to processes involving intentional content, i.e. the stuff of which conceptual models or representations are made.

In terms of this picture, cognition is causally grounded in the biology of the organism in which it belongs, and functionally grounded in the interaction between organism (including brain) and environment. Grounding, in other words, goes in two directions. Understanding cognitive facts requires an understanding of grounding relations both to the body that produces them and to the interactive context that constrains this process. (This context-oriented sense of grounding is related to the notion of 'grounding predications' as used by Langacker).

To show why the dual grounding is important, I am going to discuss the cognitive disturbances of schizophrenic patients (in section 2.4 below). This example is addressed at those people who may be inclined to think that the distinctions that I am arguing for are less important and compelling than I think, because the continuity is so smooth and continuous in 'normal' subjects that there is something forced about insisting on the discontinuities. But when things fall apart, as they do in schizophrenic breakdowns, it becomes literally a matter of life and death to be able both to identify the specific nature of the cognitive symptoms and to relate them to those biological and interactive factors in which they are grounded.

## 2.2. The dual relation between cognitive and non-cognitive facts

The first grounding relation has been the subject of focal interest in cognitive linguistics under the name of 'embodiment'. My point in this context is to emphasize the difference between 'ontological status' and 'grounding': you do not get at the full description of meaning by describing its locus in the body, specifically the brain. A description of the state of your brain may indicate that you are in a state of excitation—but it cannot tell us, however refined tools of neurological analysis may become, that you are worrying about the future of the Middle East. This is beyond the neurological vocabulary, so to speak, in involving reference to the embeddedness of mental processes in a wider context than the body itself.

This means that one cannot tell the full story of word meaning by exploring relations between words and neurological patterns. I emphasize again that this should not be taken as a criticism of attempts to find out what exactly the bodily grounding of word meaning is. The 'Neural Theory of Language' project at Berkeley (cf. Bailey, Feldman, Narayanan and Lakoff 1997) has made impressive progress in exploring how simulated cognitive systems can learn, organize and use concepts, cf. also Regier (1996). Among the recent achievements are Bailey's (1997) success in linking up features of verb meaning with the motor skills corresponding to those features, so that conceptual and motor organization go hand in hand in learning and use and Narayanan's (1997) success in showing how the same neurally implemented features can be used not only in perception and movement but also in inferences, including inferences based on metaphorical projections (as when whole economies rather than persons make 'giant strides').

The point in this context is that one can be excited about progress in this direction without having to assume that a neural theory of language can ever be a complete theory of language. Meaning stands on the shoulders of the whole motor, perceptual and conceptual powers of the individual and draws on all this to create something on a higher level of complexity that includes embeddedness in trans-individual processes. Of course everything about verb meaning must be represented in an individual's cognitive system, hence in his neural system, once the individual has learned the meaning of a verb. But that consideration applies to everything learnable, including, for instance, economics or geology—and from that it does not follow that everything we need to know about economics or geology can be learnt by exploring the bodily grounding of economic or geological concepts.

The essential aspect of what is missing, I have claimed, is the functional grounding of cognitive phenomena in human interaction. In order to explain what that means, I have to provide a definition of what function is. To begin with, functional relationships are different from cognitive relationships in that function is a type of effect: the function of an object is a privileged subclass of the effects caused by that object. Further, a functional role involves the relation between part and whole, such that the function of a part is that kind of effect that promotes the survival or persistence of the whole to which it belongs. This has both a Darwinistic application and a more everyday one. The function of wings is to enable the animal to fly—because that is the way wings help the animal to survive (and thereby also to keep the wings themselves around). The function of light bulbs is to shed light, because that is the way light bulbs contribute to the persistence of lamps—and ultimately also of the light bulbs themselves (cf. also Harder 1996: 88-93).

This functional relationship applies also to cognitive representations as a human accomplishment. Whether conceptual or purely perceptual, they have a functional relation to our practices in the external world: a mental image of a tree as caused by perception is useful because it helps us to avoid bumping into trees, thus serving its owner in ways analogous to biological organs like wings. Further, a functional relation is also what relates language to the world. The utterance *watch out for the tree!* may help us to avoid bumping into trees that our own perception was not alert enough to register. The difference between the functional and the objectivist link between language and the world is that in the functional approach the relationship with the world is not pre-established; it is continually created and maintained by the speakers because it serves a function.

From a hard-nosed scientific perspective the implication is that in addition to those forms of direct causal impact on mental representations that everybody assumes, such as photons impinging on the retina, we need to operate with the more complex type of causality that is involved in the functional feedback cycles. Their central feature is that cognitive and linguistic practices stay tuned because of them; if our categorization of what qualifies as food is faulty, we either improve our judgement or stay hungry, and if we use the wrong words in trying to explain what we mean, people will get us wrong until we get in line.

## 2.3. The nature of social facts

The most salient part of the functional context in which language and cognition belong is the domain of social interaction. To understand the functional grounding of cognition and linguistic meaning, it is necessary to understand what social facts are, and how they differ from individual mental facts. In wanting to stress the distinct role of collective as opposed to individual facts, I see myself as pursuing an aim that has also been emphasized by others working within cognitive linguistics, for example Sinha (e.g. 1988) and Geeraerts (e.g. 1992).

Returning to the distinction between brute and institutional facts that entered into the first discussion of speech acts (cf. Searle 1969), Searle (1995) develops a general theory of social facts. A crucial element is that physical items can acquire new properties merely by virtue of collective recognition that they have these properties. The status of president of the U.S. is assigned by virtue of the collective recognition of someone as having just that status, which again is bound up with certain recognized procedures for acquiring it. Searle discusses the whiff of magic or conjuring that is associated with the assignment of such status functions, but emphasizes that once they are there, social facts are just as real as the physical facts that underlie them. Clinton is president of the U.S. just as surely as he is a male human adult,[3] in spite of the fact that you cannot demonstrate that he has the property of being president by looking at his physical composition.

Social facts fit into the picture I have outlined by being partially autonomous of the physical substratum on which they are imposed. The autonomy is only partial, because you cannot impose the status of president upon a doughnut, on a baby, or a citizen of another country. They also fit in as examples of functional properties that can only be understood in terms of a top-down differentiation. We must have a collective body (in this case a nation) before we can have a president of that nation; and the role of the president in relation to the nation is analogous to the role of an organ in relation to an organism, cf. above.

This is crucial for understanding the place of individual cognitive systems in the ontology of social facts. To begin with, social facts are only possible by virtue of the existence of individual minds capable of representing such social facts to themselves. If no one could understand the concept of being president, there could be no socially recognized status of president. But although mental representations in individuals are necessary, they are not sufficient: an individual's representation of who is president is not an incontrovertible, autonomous fact for her, but depends for its status on what representations her fellow citizens have.

The main point of all this is that language itself, including its structural features, is a prime example of a social construct of this kind, one in which individual minds make possible the creation of properties whose ontological grounding transcends the individual mind. What is missing if you take language to belong inside an individual's cognitive system is the same thing that is missing if you place the office of president of the U.S. inside the cognitive system of an individual: the fact that both are dependent on the role of the individual as a member of collective body, in relation to which the elements of his own cognitive system must be understood.

This ties in with what was said about functional systems above: although an individual's language is totally included in his cognitive system, an essential property of it consists in the fact that it is adapted to the communicative environment of the individual. The most obvious illustration of the point of this description is the process of mother tongue acquisition: there is something going on which the child wants to become part of, and this ambition is realized by adapting its cognitive processes so as to become a member of the speech community. The individual's language is 'downloaded' from the interactive practices of the community, so to speak. That the downloading is made possible by the child's genetic predisposition (whatever its precise form may be) in no way invalidates the ontological dependence of 'my language' on 'our language'.

This picture would appear to be essentially compatible with the 'usage-based' view of language within cognitive linguistics; the functional feedback loops and the adaptive mechanisms that they stimulate would then provide the link between what at any given point would count as socially sanctioned *langue* and the usage on which it was based. In this constant process of distilling language out of usage there is room for variation between boundaries set by the criterion of mutual intelligibility and tolerance, as administered by the linguistic power structure (cf. Gärdenfors 1991). A key mechanism as pointed out by Henning Andersen (1973) is abduction: working backward from the usage to the principle behind it.

The picture outlined above contrasts on one point with that introduced by Croft (1995, 1996). Croft makes a distinction between 'grammar' as something that belongs inside the head of an individual, and 'language' which consists of the total population of utterances in a speech community. Croft's distinction serves to create a revealing parallel between the way change works in biology and linguistics, with 'grammars' being parallel to individuals and 'language' to populations: a change can gradually work its way through the population, in virtue of 'structural DNA-equivalents' being exchanged whenever speakers have communicative intercourse, changing the individual grammars one at a time.

However, one can retain the point made by Croft without having to accept that grammar as a property of language is a totally individual construct with no social status. A rigid separation does not capture the way in which the individual's grammar is synchronically embedded in social processes and norms (a more detailed discussion is given in Harder, in prep.). The individual's 'grammar', rather than being an analogy of a fixed individual DNA profile, reflects variability as a natural part of 'our language'. On some points, social norms and individual grammars are relatively firm, such as the meaning of *horse;* on others there can be variation, as with the meaning of *cool* (cf. Connor 1995). Similar patterns occur with other social facts: there is no variability about who the world champion of soccer football is, as opposed to the world champions of professional boxing. The discussion is important because it determines what the object of description of linguistics is. If grammars only exist inside the heads of individuals, we are left with idiolects whenever we do grammatical analysis, i.e. basically with Chomsky's object of description: the mental grammar of an individual speaker (apart from the fact that she does not have to reside in a homogeneous speech community).

In the picture that I defend, there is an affinity as well as a difference in relation to an important point made by Verhagen (1995). He pointed out the existence of types of meaning that could only be understood as means of coordinating cognition with other speakers (negation being one of the examples). Using Hutchins' (1995) account of navigation as an example of large-scale cognitive processes that must be distributed between different individuals, Verhagen demonstrates the crucial role of such coordination and by implication of the linguistic means of bringing it about. To this picture of linked cognitive processes I want to add the functional relationship between the cognitive processes of the collaborating individuals and the task they are working on. The whole coordinated operation is kept on the rails by functional 'feedback cycles' operating between each individual and feedback not only from other people involved, but also from the behavior of the ship that is being navigated (cf. also Clark 1996 on language use as a 'joint project').

## 2.4. Schizophrenia and the importance of social grounding[4]

The importance of keeping in mind and distinguishing between biology, conceptual representations and social interaction can be illustrated with the situation of schizophrenic patients. In the case of serious mental illness, the distinction between subjective conceptualization and reality out there raises itself in a way that makes any attempt at fence-sitting entirely frivolous. For such patients the question of using what Freud called the reality check as opposed to taking refuge in delusional fantasies is literally a matter of life and death; about ten percent of schizophrenic patients commit suicide.

The theory that I base this on (cf. Selzer, Carsky, Sullivan, and Terkelsen 1989) understands schizophrenia as having a biological basis. The onset of the disease is caused by something in the physiology of the brain; instead of producing the normal experiential sense of who you are and what it feels like, it produces two extremely unpleasant types of experiential qualities:

(a) part of yourself does not feel as if it belongs to you any more; thoughts feel and sound as if they come from the outside,
(b) the ordinary behavior of familiar people around you feels threatening and hostile.

This is of course extremely anxiety provoking and depressing, so as a secondary but closely connected reaction, schizophrenics develop anxiety and depression.

On the conceptual-representational level, based upon but partially autonomous of biological processes and pure experiential qualia, the patient will of course try desperately to make sense of the chaos that he finds himself in. So he tries to find a cognitive model that will allow him to make sense of this. One type of metaphor provides a match with the schizophrenic experience: external forces have invaded his brain and secretly taken possession. Since we know that the CIA perform covert infiltration processes, they may offer the best bid there is for an explanation: the CIA has subtle electronic equipment, access to military experiments with ESP, and so forth—so the patient in telling about his situation may tell the therapist that his mind has been invaded by CIA people who are trying to control him, and who are sending messages by means of inner voices, and everybody around him might very well be a CIA agent. As a purely conceptual model, it all fits very well; the only problem is that it is not true, and it will not help the patient to cope with ('function in') the real world of objects that he has to live in.

Being caused by biological processes in the brain, the primary symptoms can to a considerable extent be suppressed by medication: a physical agent for a physical malfunction. However, the patients are very often reluctant to take medication—because in terms of their mental model of the situation this does not address their problem. The therapist therefore finds himself with the task of getting the patient to comply. The most obvious solution is to address the cognitive level, that is, to try and change the patient's conceptual representation of the situation. But this is frequently a very difficult thing to do. In order to solve that problem the therapist needs to know what causes the persistent defense of the delusional conceptual model.

To account for this defense, we have to look outside the cognitive system and see how it functions in the patient's life. The central function, the one that causes the delusion to persist, is probably that it protects the patient's sense of integrity, his self-esteem. If your mind has been invaded by the CIA, there is nothing wrong with yourself; if that is not the explanation, however, then your self is not something to feel very good about. To make matters worse, pressure and anxiety appear to stimulate those biological processes that cause the primary symptoms (making it difficult to say what the 'ultimate' cause of the disease is). Thus a vicious circle may come into being, so that the more anxious and threatened the patient feels, the more desperately he clings to his delusions.

This means that there is a very important psychotherapeutic dimension in the treatment. First, it is essential to create a situation in which the patient can feel that his shaky self is treated in a friendly, supportive and non-threatening way, thus maximizing the chances that the patient is subjectively open to alternative conceptualizations of his situation. Secondly, once medication is doing its job, another task becomes paramount to the patient's chances: to achieve a role within a social group in which personal integrity and self-esteem can be reconstructed. The main instrument in this situation is the therapist, working through the interpersonal link between the patient and the therapist that is known as the "treatment alliance". The treatment alliance serves as a channel through which it becomes possible to support those aspects of the mental infrastructure which enable the patient to assume a role in normal social interaction: hooking on to real persons and real things out there, instead of withdrawing into an inner world of protective but ultimately destructive delusions.

In this context, the point of all this is that we have to understand conceptual structures not only as grounded in relation to bodily processes, but also in relation to the functional feedback cycles that they give rise to in relation to the environment. In the case of schizophrenics, failure to distinguish and interrelate these factors with sufficient care may be fatal.

## 3. Linguistic description

### 3.1. Meaning as interactive function

The argument above has concentrated on the level of principle, where a natural cognitive linguistic reaction would perhaps be: so what? We all know that language is used in social interaction, and that this in some general sense constrains the properties of language; and we already have a number of traditions that emphasize the social dimension of language, so what does such a 'me-too' ticket on this point do for cognitive linguistics?

I think it makes a difference on two points. The first involves the nature of and relationship between meanings. The functional-interactive dimension is not just a matter of external anchoring, but also of the way meaning is built up in complex utterances. This semantic dimension therefore needs to be recognized over and above the understanding of meaning in terms of conceptualization that is standard in cognitive linguistics. The second involves the status of syntax as that component which makes possible the automatic and efficient integration of fragments of meaning into whole utterance meanings.

The role of the functional-interactive dimension of meaning can be understood by reference to what in Langacker's terminology is called 'grounding', which as pointed out above is related to the second, external dimension of grounding that I argued for above. Langacker uses the term with respect to those elements that (instead of invoking the 'objective' viewing arrangement) link up with the subjective point of view of the deictic center, including the speaker. Part of the distinctive properties of 'grounding predications' have to do with conceptual subjectification, that is, the reorientation of the conceptual content towards the subjective point of view. However, part of the grounding process, I believe, is only understood if it is seen as invoking an actual interactive process, rather than a subjectified conceptual content. Definiteness thus requires the addressee to establish the actual situational referent, not only to adjust the conceptual content of the message itself.

Often it does not make much of a difference to see meanings as inter-active instructions, rather than as symbols of conceptual content. How-ever, the phenomenon of presupposition is one of the points where the difference shows. From a purely conceptual point of view it is difficult to see why some discordant combinations of elements should give rise to presupposition failure and others not. The fact that *the present King of France* gives rise to difficulties of a different kind from *colorless green ideas* is due to the difficulties in following up the instruction-to-identify that is coded by the definite article, and as a result of which the utterance is supposed to be grounded in the discourse context of the interlocutors. Cases where definiteness combines with conceptual content in a way that only makes sense in contexts that contain particular types of entities, are one kind of the situations where presupposition failure can arise. (I see the recent introduction of a temporal dimension in the conceptual repre-sentations in Cognitive Grammar as an important step in this direction, cf. Langacker 1998).

Just as definiteness as a grounding element takes scope over the whole noun phrase, in the organization of the clause (as also pointed out in Langacker 1991: 33-34), grounding predications come at the top of the clausal hierarchy. When this is viewed from a functional point of view (cf. the Functional Grammar of Simon Dik as elaborated by Kees Hengeveld, cf. e.g. 1989), it is understood as reflecting a logic in the clausal structure whereby a conceptual core is embedded in a functional-interactive periphery. The basic logic is the same as reflected in the speech act model F(p), where F stands for illocutionary force and p for propositional content (cf. Searle 1969); in the clausal context, 'declarative' or 'interrogative' may serve as examples of illocutionary nuclei.

This description reflects a sort of bipartition in clausal hierarchies between those elements that embed the clause in the functional context and the rest of the clause content. But bipartition as a model is a little simplistic, because the functional dimension operates not just at the top, linking 'normal' content to the context, but persists all the way down the hierarchy, embedding 'lower' elements in the functional context of the 'higher' elements. The relationship I am talking about can be understood as the reverse of that basic relationship which Langacker calls 'conceptual dependence'. Roughly speaking, when element A is conceptually dependent on B, B is 'functionally dependent' on A. To take an example:

(1)   *Did John beat Joe?*

Aspects of the syntactic hierarchy between meanings in the clause:

    interrogative (past (beat (John, Joe)))

If we work our way downwards in the hierarchy, the conceptual dependence of higher on lower elements can be paraphrased as follows: you cannot have an interrogative without a propositional content (or the question would be void of content); you cannot have a past tense without a state-of-affairs that the tense concerns (pastness only makes sense when it applies to something that is to be located in the past); and you cannot have a predicate such as *beat* without some arguments that it can be predicated of. The last stage corresponds to the billiard-ball model, cf. Langacker (1987): you cannot have interaction without billiard-balls, but conceptually speaking you can have the billiard-balls without doing anything with them—which is why Langacker rightly calls them (conceptually) autonomous.

But we may now reverse the argument in terms of the necessity of a functional embedding of lower elements in an interactive context specified by the higher elements. In terms of functional considerations, the argument terms are not fully autonomous. You cannot begin a conversation by saying, *John (...) Joe*; the two unrelated 'billiard-balls' without a predicate do not constitute a useful complex meaning, so the arguments alone are functionally incomplete. Moving upward in the hierarchy, you cannot (in English) have a pure state-of-affairs without tense in a main indicative clause, because a state-of-affairs must be paired off with an address in the discourse context, either in the past or in the present. One step further up, the propositional content (consisting of a state-of-affairs seen as applying to the present or past) can still not stand alone—in spite of the fact that from a purely conceptual point of view propositions are interesting enough, as documented by the attention they get in the philosophical literature. Propositions are defective considered as interactive messages, because there is little functional point in being provided with a bare propositional content, without knowing what job it is supposed to do: does the speaker want to tell me that the proposition is true, or does he want to raise the question of whether it is true? The moral of this is that function-assignment operates not only in relation to the discourse context, but also between linguistic elements collaborating in the clause.

## 3.2. The partial autonomy of syntax

However, the main service that the ontology presented above has to offer to the civil-war-ridden science of linguistics is perhaps to provide a way to capture the status of syntax as simultaneously grounded and having a life of its own. I believe that the 'continuism' of the cognitive position is responsible for some of the misunderstandings. I wholly agree with what I understand as the core of the cognitive linguistics position, namely that there is no purely formal syntactic level, aloof from the symbolic nature of language. The question, however, is what else there is to say about syntax; and that tends to be somewhat implicit in cognitive linguistics.

The notion of 'construction' is important in this context, both for what it says and what is does not say. It encompasses both lexical items, pure patterns of combination, and mixed forms consisting of idiomatic constructions with some remaining slots, and thus focuses (correctly, as far as it goes) on what all these elements share: an expression side, a content side and a distributional potential. What it does not make fully explicit, however, is the existence of a distinction of levels between 'item' properties and 'combinatorial' properties. Let me quote Steven Pinker on this point [the first extract comments on an experiment in which a group of children produced correct questions from a series of stimuli including *Ask Jabba if it is raining in the picture*]:

> The *it* of the sentence, of course, does not refer to anything; it is a dummy element that is only there to satisfy the rules of syntax, which demand a subject. But the English question rule treats it just like any other subject: *Is it raining?* Now, how do children cope with this meaningless placeholder? (1994: 42)

> A part of speech, then, is not a kind of meaning; it is a kind of token that obeys certain formal rules, like a chess piece or a poker chip. A noun, for instance, is simply a word that does nouny things; it is the kind of word that comes after an article, can have an 's stuck onto it, and so on. There is a connection between concepts and part-of-speech categories, but it is a subtle and abstract one...Nouns are often used for names of things, and verbs for something being done, but because the human mind can construe reality in a variety of ways, nouns and verbs are not limited to those uses. (1994: 106)

I believe that this is substantially correct, and that cognitive linguistics needs to make it clearer that it can handle that insight better than generative grammar does. The essential element is the role of a difference of levels within the context of a semantically grounded theory of language. As I understand the role of syntax within cognitive grammar (cf. also Langacker, this volume) the notion of partial autonomy is wholly compatible with it. By stressing the fact that autonomy is only partial, one avoids the basic generative fallacy that is part of Pinker's position, i.e. the postulation of a mental safe-deposit box for grammatical structure in which all contextual links are severed:

> Outside of a particular conversation or text, then, the words *a* and *the* are quite meaningless: they have no place in one's permanent mental database. Other conversation-specific words like *here, there, this, that, now, then, I, me, my, her*, we and *you* pose the same problems... (1994: 80).

In order to describe how I think the partial autonomy of syntax should be captured, I must describe what I see as the two central properties of syntax. The first is that it is the central task of syntax to permit speakers to create complex utterance meanings out of fragments. The unique distinction of human language (as far as we know) is that we are not limited to a fixed number of pre-fab utterance meanings: the existence of meanings of sub-utterance size means we can construct our own personal complex meanings.

The price tag, on the other hand, is that some assembly is required. And if addressees had the same processing load that some of us have when they buy things that they have to assemble on their own, that price would be too great. Therefore, as the second design feature of syntax, those combination patterns according to which we assemble meanings have to be extremely simple and general, compared with the semantic variety of the messages that we want to assemble by means of syntax. The automatic routines that permit us to assemble clause meanings without conscious effort must be vastly simpler than the diversity of different messages that we would like to operate with. If we look at the central area of syntax, we find an extremely limited inventory of 'chips' to play with; the number of phrase types can be counted on one hand, and so forth.

To understand the nature of syntax, therefore, it is not enough to view syntactic items simply as meaning-bearing elements. Rather, their role must be understood as bound up precisely with the task of assembling whole clause meanings. Syntax, in other words, operates on a different structural level than items, and in that sense syntax is partially autonomous of the items in themselves. In this, syntactic mechanisms are like monetary mechanisms—which need real goods to operate on, but whose operations cannot be understood in terms of the pre-economic properties of real goods.[5]

If we take the category of 'subject' in English, for example, there would be rough agreement among functional-cognitive linguists that it serves the function of indicating something like the primary clause-level 'topic' or 'figure'. But what do we do with Pinker's case *it is raining?* We can say, perfectly truthfully, that this is a specific construction, but that would not get at the way in which the subjecthood of *it* is motivated precisely at the higher, syntactic level, in terms of the harsh limitations that processability impose upon the number of syntactic patterns that we can operate with. In English, the role of the subject is so strongly entrenched in the combinatorial coding pattern that even types of state-of-affairs which have no candidate for clause-level topic/figure have to conform to that general coding strategy—which is motivated in terms of the system as a whole, but not for that particular clause type. The less pervasive the role of ('overt') subjects is in 'ordinary' clauses in a grammar, the fewer off-beat types of subjects you will get, compare the situation in, for instance, Spanish.

This type of higher-level regimentation is structurally analogous to the forms of apparent absurdities that you get in other systems with more than one level of organization. In an integrated transport system, for instance, you will sometimes find an empty bus going through its route, because the general running of the system is better served by having an occasional empty bus than by trying to devise a different timetable for every new situation that might arise. Some of us have experience with countries where the bus leaves whenever it is full, and where the driver goes home if no-one turns up—which is perfectly well motivated in the strictly local context, but bad for overall efficiency.

The special role of syntax can also be understood in terms of a cognitive skill that is needed over and above the ability to activate the conceptual content associated with lexical items. As pointed out by Gernsbacher and associates (cf. e.g. Gernsbacher and Faust 1994), the ability to suppress information as opposed to activating it (cf. 'spreading activation' as captured in connectionist networks), is an underrated but crucial aspect of mental competence. Avoiding the combinatorial explosion that would be the result of trying to combine concepts in all possible ways, automatic syntactic routines select the coded options, to the exclusion (= suppression) of other possibilities, with great efficiency.[6]

If syntactic ordering is to a large extent motivated by attunement to very general processing strategies, syntactic slots have a—usage-based, semantically motivated, and cognitively real, but partially autonomous—life of their own over and above the specific semantic content of the particular items that fill the slots. This is not denied in cognitive linguistics;

but neither is it pointed out with sufficient vigor to provide a clear picture of the distinct role of syntax in language.

## 4. Conclusions

I have argued that a more explicit orientation towards an ontology based on partial autonomy between different levels of organization, as a way to harness 'continuist' tendencies, would present some advantages for cognitive linguistics. I have further argued, as a case in point, that social facts as a specific ontological level should be included more explicitly in the worldview of cognitive linguistics.

I have tried to show that a more precise awareness of the specific nature of cognitive models as grounded on the one hand in neurobiology and on the other in interactive patterns is essential in order to understand cognitive disturbances such as those associated with schizophrenia—and hence, by implication, also the cognitive processes of normal subjects. An essential element in the picture was the complex form of causality that is the defining feature of functional roles, as maintained by feedback cycles that serve to stabilize the place of an element within a larger complex system.

Within the narrower bounds of linguistics, I argued first that functional-interactive grounding is not external to the understanding of syntax, but is one half of the basic mechanism of hierarchical combination in syntax—functional dependency being the inverse of Langacker's 'conceptual' dependence. Secondly, I argued that a notion of partial autonomy would provide the best way of capturing the integrated, semantically based picture of syntax that is favored in functional and cognitive linguistics, while explicitly leaving room for those less than direct correspondences between syntactic patterns and item meaning from which autonomists tend to draw the wrong conclusions.

## Notes

1. I am grateful to Jerome Feldman, Dirk Geeraerts, Theo Janssen, George Lakoff, and Gisela Redeker for their helpful comments on earlier versions of

this article. Needless to say, responsibility for imperfections in the present version is mine alone.

2. 'Cognitivism' is also used in other senses, notably one in which it is identified with the position of 'classical' artificial intelligence (cf. Searle 1992, Sinha 1996).

3. The ultimate foundation of status functions in Searle is in the individual mind, which entertains a belief of the form: WE take Bill Clinton to be president, where WE refers to the relevant collective body. While agreeing that this (rather than a series of assumptions of the form 'I believe that you believe...') is the proper format of the underlying assumption, I would emphasize the functional underpinning of this belief in the interactive practices of the community in which the president belongs—so that it is not a mental act alone that can assign status function.

4. I would like to thank Bent Rosenbaum, head of the psychotherapeutic ward in Risskov Psychiatric Hospital, Aarhus, for sharing his expertise on schizophrenia with me.

5. Dirk Geeraerts has pointed out that there is a difference between the two cases, in that syntax does not belong to a different ontological realm from the lexicon (unlike psychological as opposed to social facts). The similarity that makes me persist in using 'partial autonomy' in both cases is that syntactic properties can in some respects only be described with reference to other syntactic properties, rather than to item-level properties alone.

6. The emphasis on processability here is inspired by Hawkins (1994), in which a (universal) theory of word order is proposed based on a few simple strategies for recognizing the major syntactic constituents of the clause. Although the system is marred by its dependence on a notion of purely formal syntax, the pervasive isomorphism between content and expression in syntax means that the basic points survive quite well in a meaning-based grammar.

# References

Andersen, Henning
    1973    Abductive and deductive change. *Language* 49: 765–793.
Bailey, David
    1997    A computational model of embodiment in the acquisition of action verbs. Ph.D. dissertation, University of California, Berkeley.
Bailey, David, Jerome Feldman, Srini Narayanan and George Lakoff
    1997    Modeling embodied lexical development. *Proceedings of the 19th Annual Conference of the Cognitive Science Society, Stanford, August 9-11, 1997.* Mahwah, NJ: Erlbaum.

Clark, Herbert H.
    1996    *Using Language*. Cambridge/New York: Cambridge University Press.
Connor, Marlene Kim
    1995    *What Is Cool? Understanding Black Manhood in America*. New York:
            Crown Publishers Inc.
Croft, William A.
    1995    Autonomy and functionalist linguistics. *Language* 71: 490-532.
    1996    Linguistic selection: An utterance-based evolutionary theory of lan-
            guage change. *Nordic Journal of Linguistics* 19: 99-139.
Daly, Herman E.
    1996    *Beyond Growth. The Economics of Sustainable Development*. Boston:
            Beacon Press.
Dik, Simon C.
    1989    *The Theory of Functional Grammar*. Vol. 1. Dordrecht: Foris.
Fodor, Jerry A., and Zenon W. Pylyshyn
    1988    Connectionism and cognitive architecture: A critical analysis. *Cogni-
            tion* 28: 2–71.
Geeraerts, Dirk
    1992    The return of hermeneutics to lexical semantics. In: Martin Pütz (ed.),
            *Thirty Years of Linguistic Evolution*, 257–282. Amsterdam: John
            Benjamins.
Gernsbacher, Morton Ann, and Mark Faust
    1994    Skilled suppression. In: F.N. Dempster and C.N. Brainerd (eds.), *In-
            terference and Inhibition in Cognition*, 295-327. San Diego: Academic
            Press.
Harder, Peter
    1996    *Functional Semantics. A Theory of Meaning, Structure and Tense in
            English*. Berlin/New York: Mouton de Gruyter.
    1998    Syntax, semantics and processing. On the nature(s) of constituent or-
            der. *Acta Linguistica Hafniensia* 30, 167-187.
    in prep. A functionalist account of 'langue' and 'parole'. Manuscript.
Hawkins, John A.
    1994    *A Performance Theory of Order and Constituency*. Cambridge: Cam-
            bridge University Press.
Hengeveld, Kees
    1989    Layers and operators in functional grammar. *Journal of Linguistics* 25:
            127–157.
Hutchins, Edwin
    1995    *Cognition in the Wild*. Cambridge, MA: MIT Press.

Køppe, Simo
  1990    *Virkelighedens niveauer. De nye videnskaber og deres historie. [Lev-els of Reality. The New Sciences and their History.]* Copenhagen: Gyldendal.
Lakoff, George
  1996    *Moral Politics. What Conservatives Know that Liberals Don't.* Chicago: University of Chicago Press.
Langacker, Ronald W.
  1987    *Foundations of Cognitive Grammar, vol. 1: Theoretical Prerequisites.* Stanford: Stanford University Press.
  1991    *Foundations of Cognitive Grammar, vol. 2: Descriptive Applications.* Stanford: Stanford University Press.
  1998    Conceptualization, grounding and discourse. Lecture given at the summer school on embodiment, Odense University, June 1998.
Narayanan, Srini
  1997    Knowledge-based action representations for metaphor and aspect. Ph.D. dissertation, University of California, Berkeley.
Ogden, Charles K., and Ivor A. Richards
  1923    *The Meaning of Meaning.* London: Routledge & Kegan Paul.
Regier, Terry
  1996    *The Human Semantic Potential. Spatial Language and Constrained Connectionism.* Cambridge MA: MIT Press.
Searle, John R.
  1969    *Speech Acts.* Cambridge: Cambridge University Press.
  1980    Minds, brains and programs. *The Behavioral and Brain Sciences* 3: 417–57.
  1992    *The Rediscovery of the Mind.* Cambridge, MA.: MIT Press.
  1995    *The Construction of Social Reality.* Harmondsworth: Penguin.
Selzer, Michael A., Timothy B. Sullivan, Monica Carsky, and Kenneth G. Terkelsen
  1989    *Working with the Person with Schizophrenia. The Treatment Alliance.* New York/London: New York University Press.
Sinha, Chris
  1988    *Language and Representation.* London/New York: Harvester Wheatsheaf.
Stjernfelt, Frederik
  1995    We can't go on meeting like this. A cognitive theory of literature? The fall of the wall between linguistics and theory of literature. *Nordic Journal of Linguistics* 18(2): 121-136.
Talmy, Leonard
  1995    The cognitive culture system. *Monist* 78(1): 81-116.

Verhagen, Arie
  1995    Meaning and the coordination of cognition. Plenary lecture at the Fourth International Cognitive Linguistics Conference, Albuquerque, July 1995.

# Grounding, mapping, and acts of meaning

## Chris Sinha

### 1. Introduction: Two dogmas of reificatory semantics

What is meaning, what is it for a sign to be meaningful, how can meaning best be analyzed, and in what sense is linguistic meaning proper or unique to language? Cognitive linguistics offers answers to these questions that challenge two traditional dogmas of linguistic theory, philosophy of language, and cognitive science. However, although they have notionally abandoned both these dogmas, many cognitive linguists retain an ambiguous loyalty to some of their underlying presuppositions. I hope to convince them of the necessity to review their deep theoretical commitments, in order to rebut, once and for all, the charge that cognitive semantics entails a *Subjectivist* theory of meaning.[1]

The two dogmas are: (1) the Dogma of the *Autonomy* of linguistic meaning; and (2) the Dogma of the *Compositionality* of linguistic meaning. Both these dogmas are variants of a more general, fatal misconception of the nature of linguistic meaning, namely that "Meanings are Objects": a misconception of the nature of meaning that I shall call, following Zlatev (1997), Reificatory Semantics.

Obviously, no-one would seriously propose that meanings are the kind of *physical* objects that you can put in your handbag or hide under your bed—which is why the first dogma consists of variants on the theme that meanings are "mental" (or ideal) rather than "material" objects. Yet these supposedly ideal or mental objects retain, somehow, many properties of the impenetrable, massy objects of the thing-world—particularly their decomposability into smaller units or atoms, a notion consecrated by the second dogma. The Two Dogmas of Reificatory Semantics can be spelled out as follows:

*The Dogma of the Autonomy of Linguistic Meaning.* Meanings are immaterial Objects. The sphere of linguistic meaning is autonomous from the material world, existing in the realm of "mental objects" (mental representations), or in the realm of Durkheimian "social facts", or in the realm of ideal, Platonic and Fregean "senses".

*The Dogma of the Compositionality of Linguistic Meaning.* Meanings are decomposable into (immaterial) atomic Objects, actual legal combinations of which are the meanings of expression-items, which in turn can be combined with each other in certain ways to yield semantically valid (meaningful) expressions. The atoms themselves remain unchanged throughout their various combinations.

Both of these dogmas depend upon the acceptance of a certain view of, or metaphor about, linguistic communication, which is in essence Reddy's (1979) Conduit Metaphor for communication. The conduit metaphor sees language as a conduit or vehicle for the transportation of meanings from the inside of one person's head to the inside of another person's head; for this reason it has also been called the "telementation theory" of communication (Harris 1988). The version of the metaphor which I want to focus on as particularly relevant to the Two Dogmas of Reificatory Semantics can be called the "container-contents" metaphor of meaning and expression, where meanings are *contents* and expressions are *containers*. It can be pictured as if linguistic expressions are collections of pouches of marbles, the marbles being the atoms of meaning, and the pouches being the expression items containing the meaning-atoms. Semantics is then the theory of which marbles can legally be put into the same pouches, and which pouches can be gathered together; and syntax the theory of how the pouches are organized into ordered collections. (If you like, you can substitute handbags for pouches). It is rarely remarked, even by cognitive linguists who might be expected to notice it, that the container-contents metaphor of meaning and expression is almost built into the terminology of traditional linguistic theory, with its talk of semantic content, meaning-components, and selection restrictions.

## 2. "Ideas", other minds and the problem of representation

The provenance of the theory that meanings are mental objects or contents, and expressions are their containers, is of great antiquity—perhaps because the conduit-container metaphor of communication and language is so all-pervasive in ordinary discourse. The philosophical formulation of the theory is given by Aristotle: "Spoken words are the signs of affections of the soul, and written words are the signs of spoken words." Aristotle was a universalist who believed in what was later to be called the "psychic unity" of mankind. He was also a realist; he continued: "Just as all men have not the same writing, so all men have not the same speech sounds, but the affections of the soul which these signify are the same for all [universalism], as also are those things of which our experiences are images [realism]."[2]

Note then that for Aristotle, as Harris and Taylor (1989: 33) point out, "Words ... are signs or symbols of the 'affections of the soul' (i.e. what is stored in the mind); whereas the 'affections of the soul' are *not* signs or symbols of things in the real world, but *copies* of them (although *natural* copies and therefore identical for the whole human race)." Ferdinand de Saussure (1915, [1966]) conveyed exactly this idea with his celebrated drawing of a tree. There (in the world) is a tree, here (in my head) is an imagistic "idea" of a tree, I happen to label it *tree*, Saussure happens to label it *arbre, et voilà*, signs are arbitrary, but concepts are not.

The same theory of meaning is expressed in slightly different terms by John Locke: "That then which Words are the Marks of, are the *Ideas* of the Speaker: Nor can anyone apply them, as Marks, immediately to anything else, but the *Ideas*, that he himself hath."[3] Again, Saussure repeats, in almost as many words, Locke's formulation: "The linguistic sign unites, not a thing and a name, but a concept and a sound-image" (Saussure 1966: 66).

Note, now, that Locke's formulation immediately raises a problem, the problem sometimes referred to as Hume's problem, or the problem of Other Minds. If words stand for, or express, "ideas", how can I (as speaker) be, in fact, sure that you (as hearer), actually share the same "ideas" of things as I do? Aristotle's solution was "category realism": our ideas (categories of the mind) are reflections of objective reality. We all live in the same (objective) world, and have the same experiences of that world, and this means that our concepts (images) of the things that cause these experiences (affections of the soul) are also the same.

The problem with the Aristotelian story is that, as Saussure fully recognized and illustrated with a different example, Eng. *sheep* vs. Fr. *mouton*, not only do we not all have the same speech-sounds, but "equivalent" speech sounds sometimes map to different configurations of "affections of the soul". In this case, as is well known, the French (but not the English) term maps to the meat, as well as the animal from which the meat is butchered. Aristotle's elegant story is undermined, or at least problematized, by even the most seemingly banal linguistic relativity.

At this point there seem to be three theoretical options available. The first is to accept the relativity, and locate meaning not in image and concept, but in the semantic values constituted by the system of *langue*. This is, in essence, structuralism's solution. Since, however, structuralism never explicitly disavowed its other, ideationist, commitment, to meaning as mental object, its price is incoherence and contradiction.

Given the structuralist definition of language as consisting of *a system of relationships between meanings and sounds*, structuralism's problem was: what are meanings? Its answer was twofold: Meanings are, on the one hand, imagistic conceptual content mapped onto the oppositions constituting the system of expression (meanings are thus individual, mental and *prior to langue*); and meanings are, on the other hand, nothing more than a "potential" inherent in the systemic (paradigmatic and syntagmatic) oppositions which are defined in terms of expression itself (meanings are thus social and *defined by langue*). The first answer is the one Saussure gives in his illustration of the signifier-signified relation, in which the signifier (French *arbre*, English *tree*) is *arbitrarily* attached to the signified *concept*. The second answer is the one he gives in the passage where he discusses the non-identity of the semantic values of the English lexeme *sheep* and the French lexeme *mouton*.

The two structuralist answers to the question "What is meaning?" are two different variants of the Dogma of Autonomy. In the first variant, meanings are "mental objects" defined over individual psychology; in the second variant, meanings are "social objects" defined over "langue". Structuralism, as a general theoretical enterprise in the human sciences, not just a specific linguistic theory, was unable to produce a coherent account of the relationship between the individual psychological explanatory level, and the socio-cultural explanatory level, precisely because its original theory of meaning was contradictory, simultaneously embracing two different versions (one individual-mentalist, one social-collectivist) of the self-same Dogma of Autonomy. The contradiction was only ultimately resolved by excluding altogether reference both to conceptualization and to language-independent reality (this was the post-structuralist terminus of structuralism).

The second option is to develop, as does formal semantics, a rigorously formal view of the meanings of terms as determined by truth conditions on their application, excluding conceptualization from consideration. The apparent clarity this buys comes, however, at the price of divorcing meaning both from experiential and ecological reality, and from "messy" natural language; substituting for the former uninterpreted "states of affairs", and for the latter a fleshless skeleton of univocal terms and formal syntax. As Lakoff (1987) showed, most of natural language is inexplicable under this approach. As Putnam (1981) showed, it also brings with it its own irresolvable logical paradoxes.

The third option is what is plumped for by cognitive semantics: to elaborate and transform Aristotle's account of experientially-based meanings, and to supplement it with a further account of how metaphoric and metonymic mappings yield other kinds of meanings. Despite its disagreement with Aristotle's "classical" theory of categorization, cognitive semantics is more Aristotelian in spirit than are either (post-) structuralism or formal semantics. Its strengths (a recognition of the constitutive role of experientially based *human* cognition in meaning, and of the centrality of imagistic processes for such cognition) are similar to the strengths of Aristotle's theory. So, however, is its great weakness: an uncertainty and ambiguity about the status of images, concepts and meanings (are they the same? If not, how are they different? Are they independent of language, or constructed in language?), and a vulnerability to the Other Minds objection (how can we be sure that *your* meanings/concepts/schemata are the same as *mine*?).

Aristotle could avoid Subjectivism by appeal to category realism. Needless to say, cognitive semantics, having (for good reason) rejected classical category realism, cannot mount this defense. In short, the weakness of cognitive semantics, as long as it is implicitly based upon the Aristotelian theory that words stand for ideas, is its vulnerability to charges of Subjectivism. The challenge for cognitive semantics is to preserve its strengths while shedding its weakness.

Consider the basic problem raised by the Dogma of Autonomy. If you view meanings as objects inhabiting a different sphere (whether this be couched in terms of the Mind, or the Ideal, or the Culture), from the mundane world of things, your are immediately forced into the problem of how to get these immaterial objects somehow to reflect or represent the mundane, material world. This is the archetypal "Problem of Representation", the one that Wittgenstein (1921 [1961]) set out to solve in the *Tractatus Logico-Philosophicus*, and which he subsequently decided was both insoluble and the Wrong Question. How the Problem of Representation ties together the Two Dogmas of Reificatory Semantics into a philosophical Gordian knot I will examine later. For now, I shall simply mention the standard solution in philosophy of language, the "correspondence theory of truth". This states that a true proposition is one in which each expression item corresponds either to some real object(s) in the physical world, or to some real relation between two or more objects, such that the proposition truly "represents" a real state of affairs.

This is, of course, the standard Objectivist theory of meaning; we shall return to it below. For now, it is enough to say that the Problem of Representation (to which the correspondence theory of truth is supposed to be a solution) simply *does not arise* if we cease to view meanings as immaterial objects. Conversely, so long as we *do* continue to view meanings in that way, we shall be compelled to view Objectivism and Subjectivism as defining the basic parameters of the solution to this false problem. To Lakoff's and Putnam's arguments against Objectivism, I will add the following (expanding it below): the Problem of Representation *has no Objectivist solution,* since the putative Objectivist solution depends upon acceptance of the Dogma of Compositionality, which cognitive linguists have shown to be empirically false. Once again, this leaves us (as long as we remain entrapped in reificatory semantics), with Subjectivism.

Subjectivism apparently has some adherents in cognitive semantics, who believe not only that meanings are "in the head", but that the only real Reality is to be found in a mysterious entity called the Mind/Brain (as if the dualism underlying the traditional concept of "mental representation" can be spirited away by invoking a typological convention). There are many reasons for being unhappy about Subjectivism; not the least that it is widely considered to be incoherent. Fortunately, cognitive semantics does not have to embrace it, since it does not need *either* of the Two Dogmas of Reificatory Semantics, and hence need not pose the false Problem of Representation.

In claiming that the Problem of Representation is a false one, I do not mean to claim that there is no linguistic, philosophical, and psychological Problem of Grounding in a wider sense—that of how linguistic expressions get to mean something, and how acts of meaning both fit with the world and make a difference to the world. And by advocating a "non-reificatory" interpretation of cognitive semantics—that is, one in which meanings are no longer viewed as mental objects—I am not suggesting that cognition plays no role in acts of meaning. On the contrary, cognition plays a particular and specifiable role. This role is *mapping.* Mapping is a fundamental human cognitive capacity, one on which cognitive linguists have been shedding a great deal of light in their investigations of metaphor, mental spaces and conceptual blending (Fauconnier 1997). It is a fundamental hypothesis of cognitive linguistics that meaning involves *motivated mappings from conceptualization to expression.* This hypothesis underlies many investigations in metaphor theory, the role of iconicity in grammar, processes of grammaticalization and so forth; it is probably *the* fundamental theoretical postulate of cognitive linguistics.

Unfortunately, the cognitive linguistic thesis of meaning as mapping from conceptualization to expression sometimes gets confused with the quite different Reificatory Semantics doctrine of meaning-as-a-mental-object. This confusion, which is understandable, and perhaps endemic in any discussion of language as a "conceptualizing system", is illustrable by the following quotation: "Whereas objectivist theories of meaning hold that meaning exists 'in the world' and that language therefore derives meaning from reference to objects in this world, cognitive approaches offer an alternative: Meaning is hypothesized to exist only through reference to a *conceptualization* of the world" (Kreitzer 1997: 291).

If the point is to emphasize that expression is *motivated* by conceptualization, and not just *given* by reality, there can be little objection to the above formulation. As a more general statement about the theory of meaning in cognitive semantics, however, I think the formulation is ambiguous and problematic. Just what is problematic about it can be captured by asking the question: *If expression is motivated by conceptualization, what then is being conceptualized?*

There are, I submit, only two possible answers to this question:

- *either* (a) conceptualization is the linguistic organization of pre-existing individual mental content,
- *or* (b) conceptualization is the linguistic-conceptual organization of a referential situation in an intersubjectively shared universe of discourse.

I shall argue that (b) is the correct answer, thereby introducing reference (and *referential realism*) as a crucial dimension in cognitive linguistics, but also enabling us to develop a new, and different, understanding of *sense*. The reason for rejecting (a) as an answer is that it leads us straight back to the problems and paradoxes of Reificatory Semantics: If there is a mental content which precedes its linguistic organization in expression, what (if any) is the relationship between this content and the world outside language, towards which language points?

In cognitive semantics (to repeat), meanings are motivated mappings from *conceptualization* to *expression*. In standard Reificatory Semantics, meanings are mental *objects*, which are *defined* (in the standard, Objectivist account) in terms of their truth-valued mappings to an external world composed of discretely specifiable states of affairs.

Our discussion so far helps us to see why cognitive semantics is often either (mis)interpreted as, or accused of being, a Subjectivist theory of meaning. The Objectivist version of Reificatory Semantics shares with the "ideationist" variant of structuralism the view that meanings are mental objects. However, the Objectivist version of Reificatory Semantics introduces a third term into the theory: Meanings (expressed by linguistic utterances, canonically by simple active declarative sentences or propositions) are defined in terms of their (correspondence-mapping) relationship to non-linguistic reality. Objectivist semantics, as we know, therefore has problems with all non-canonical cases (such as performatives, or metaphors, or counterfactuals, or almost any kind of non-declarative and "irrealis" expressions; that is, perhaps most uses of language), which it tries to circumvent by treating these as derivative "special cases". At least, though, Objectivism can claim that it has a theory of how meanings relate to the world, while structuralism does not, since it can only talk (at best) about the concept-expression relationship.

The accusation which Objectivism makes against cognitive semantics is essentially the same as that which can be made against structuralism. The accusation is: Instead of fixing meanings to reality, cognitive linguists just identify them with schemata or conceptualizations, whose relation to reality is indeterminate. The implication is: Language is left just "hanging", as it were, to one end of the mapping of meaning to world, "ungrounded in" anything except, possibly, the human brain and nervous system. Unfortunately, some cognitive linguists concur with this argument, embracing a kind of neural solipsism (all that really exists is the Mind/Brain). If, however, we want to reject Subjectivism as decisively as we reject Objectivism, we need a general theory of meaning that departs from entirely different premises than the "meaning as mental object" assumption of Reificatory Semantics.

## 3. Intersubjectivity and referential realism

The alternative view of meaning which I shall advance is one in which meanings are not objects, but *acts* —in the general sense of Bruner (1994), as well as the specific sense of speech acts (Searle 1969, 1995). Acts of linguistic meaning, I shall argue, are *subjectively* constructed so as to make sense in an *intersubjectively shared* universe of discourse, which is continuous with (not separate from) the material world in which other (non-discursive) human activities are carried out. This is the shared world of *joint action, joint attention,* and *joint intention* (Shotter 1993). This means that, rather than seeing acts of meaning as being about transferring mental representations from one individual to another, I see them as being about foregrounding matters of mutual concern in a given communicative situation.

In contrast to the conduit metaphor, in which communication is about the "ergonic" (vehicular) exchange of "mental representations", the alternative "energeic" view sees communication as social and practical *action*; and where the former views Truth as the touchstone of meaning, the latter sees successfully achieved *joint reference* as the prototype of linguistic communication. The accounts that I shall offer of both cognition and semantics will therefore be more discursively situated, and context-dependent, than they are in either standard linguistic theory or many current versions of cognitive semantics. In brief, my argument is in part *against* one particular interpretation of cognitive semantics, in which meanings are held essentially to *be* concepts, or schemata, or any kind of mental representation; and in part *for* a different interpretation in which mental processes of conceptualization, schematization and perspectivization form the psychological *basis* for *discursive acts* of speaking and understanding.

Linguistic meaning is a social doing, an intersubjective accomplishing, not a thing. It would be impossible if human beings did not possess certain cognitive capacities, but to say that meaning is cognitively based is not the same as saying that it consists of mental objects "in the head". If we see cognitive semantics in the way I am arguing for, we may be able to gain new insights into that core problem of cognitive science, the *grounding* of meaning and of natural language. And the key to understanding grounding, I shall argue, is to understand *reference*.

John Stuart Mill may have been the first philosopher to give a hint that the "Other Minds" problem is a deceptive one, based upon the false premise that words stand for, or name, "ideas". He accepted that, in acts of meaning, we refer to the world by the mediation of our conceptualizations of it, but he rejected the further seductive conclusion that our communicative acts thereby *refer to our conceptualizations*. Discussing naming, Mill wrote:

> "If it be merely meant that the conception alone, and not the thing itself, is recalled by the name, or imparted to the hearer, this of course cannot be denied. Nevertheless, there seems good reason for adhering to common usage, and calling the word *sun* the name of the sun, and not the name of our idea of the sun. For names are not intended only to make the hearer conceive what we conceive, but also to inform him about what we believe. Now, when I use a name for the purpose of expressing a belief, it is a belief concerning the thing itself, not concerning my idea of it."[4]

Mill is making a crucial point here, one that was later to be taken up in speech act theory. His point is that communicating is not, at base, a matter of "representing reality", of passing "mental" surrogates for "real things" through a conduit of language from inside my head to inside your head. Of course, it would fly in the face of reason, as he says, to think that when we refer to something by its name, we thereby "conjure up" the thing itself. If we think in terms of the conduit metaphor, it is trivially true that ideas, not things, are the currency of communication. However, says Mill, communicating is not primarily about transferring representations. Rather, to communicate is to *act*, so as to make a difference to the universe of discourse which you and I share (our beliefs being one aspect of this). Linguistic reference works, to be sure, through the mediation of conceptualization. But that which we communicate *about*, says Mill, is not the concept, but the "thing itself".[5]

Mill, like Aristotle, is a realist; but (at least as I am interpreting this passage) his realism is based neither on the Aristotelian claim that our concepts reflect universal experiences of objectively real categories, nor upon the Objectivist claim that language itself can be made to "mirror" or transparently represent reality. Rather, for Mill, realism consists in the assumption that our linguistic expressions "point outwards" to the world about which we share and contest beliefs, desires and so on. Mill's realism is not, therefore, conceptual or categorical, but *referential*.

The primordial "pointing outwards" of reference implies a world whose *existence* is prior to any questions of the adequacy of our concepts. As Mill might put it, the existence of the "thing itself" is presupposed by whatever beliefs we might wish to communicate about it. However, and here is where I perhaps want to take the argument a step further than Mill, this "thing itself" only becomes a "thing signified" by virtue of *being referred to*. The act of referring is *intersubjective* in its fundamental structure: I refer to something *for you*, in such a way that *you can share* my reference. Now, what is referred to, on this view, is a world "outside the head": It is the world that I share with my communication partner. It is also, however, when reference is linguistic, the world which is *conceptualized in the language which I use to signify it*. In other words, we need to understand that linguistic conceptualization is an *active process* which is properly speaking *part of* linguistic reference. We conceptualize *in language, in order to refer to something, in a situation, for somebody*. Referential realism is based upon an understanding of meaning as *acting communicatively in an intersubjectively shared world or universe of discourse*.

Reference is irreducibly intentional, it involves the relationship of "aboutness" (Searle 1983) which I call *signifying*. Searle believes (if I can simplify his arguments considerably) that the signifying "aboutness" of a linguistic expression derives, essentially, from the same source as the "aboutness" of perceptions. So, claims Searle, my expression "the lamp is over the table" is *about* the lamp, the table and their relationship in space, in the same way that my perceiving a lamp is *about* the lamp which I perceive, and which is the "ground" of my perception. I think this is only half the story, at most, and that cognitive linguistics and its philosophy of language can gain a vital and important insight into why this is so from developmental psychology.

I will certainly grant that there needs to be a perceptible world (or surround) for reference to make any sense at all, and that our subjectivity is fundamentally *grounded* in this perceptible world—grounded in our direct perceptions and in our non-discursive organization of embodied experience. It is a basic tenet of cognitive linguistics that linguistic meaning is made possible by its *embodied grounding*. The principal, and best-known, part of the research program of cognitive semantics has been the investigation of the grounding of linguistic meaning in image schemas. More liberally, but perhaps even more in keeping with the "embodied cognition" thesis of cognitive semantics, we could speak of functional, action-based, force-dynamic image schematization; a formulation which emphasizes both the reliance of linguistic-communicative action upon the perceptuo-motor organization of physical action, and the active, online nature of the psycholinguistic processes permitting communication in speech and gesture (McNeill and Duncan, in press; Kita, in press). This formulation also emphasizes the developmental continuity between the organization of early object-directed action in infancy and language acquisition (Freeman, Lloyd and Sinha 1980; Sinha 1982), and the developmental continuity between prelinguistic, "proto-conceptual" categorizations of objects and spatial relations in terms which go *beyond* categorical perception, but which are prior to linguistic conceptualization proper (Mandler 1996).[6] It should be noted, too, that this formulation of "embodied grounding" is consistent with the general thrust of Piaget's epigenetic-naturalist account of the developmental roots of cognition in sensori-motor action, although it is specified differently and more fully than in Piaget's own account.

Embodied grounding, in both a psycholinguistic processing sense, and an ontogenetic sense, is one, but, I suggest, *only* one, fundamental prerequisite for linguistic conceptualization, or "thinking for speaking" (Slobin 1996). In order fully to understand grounding, we need to supplement an empirically rich analysis of the perceptuo-motor, actional basis of embodied grounding, with an empirically equally rich analysis of the developmental roots of linguistic reference in pre-linguistic communicative action. In doing so, we need to bear in mind that linguistic reference involves more than schematization-for-self. To *refer* implies the *picking out* or *figuration* of some aspect(s) of the schematized world, in such a way that the figured aspect is a *topic of joint and shared attention*.

Reference, it should be emphasized, is *not* intrinsically linguistic. While all linguistic conceptualization is referential, not all reference involves linguistic conceptualization. Linguistic reference has its roots in pre-linguistic episodes of joint attention, and pre-linguistic gestural reference. The ability to refer, while it may be assumed to be epigenetically based in innate initial states in the human perceptual and attentional system, is not present from birth, and its construction crucially implicates interactions between the infant and other human beings.

Although infants interact with adult caretakers almost from birth, and pay attention to objects and their dynamic relationships from 2-3 months, they do not initially coordinate interactions with persons with interactions with objects. It is as if, although infants understand that persons are special kinds of objects, they do not at first understand that persons have an attentional relationship to objects. From about 6 months, however, infants begin to follow the direction of gaze of an adult interactant (Butterworth and Jarrett 1991). From around nine or ten months of age infants "begin to engage with adults in relatively extended bouts of joint attention to objects ... In these triadic interactions infants actively coordinate their visual attention to person and object, for example by looking to an adult periodically as the two of them play together with a toy, or by following the adults gaze. Infants also become capable at this age of intentionally communicating to adults their desire to obtain an object or to share attention to an object, usually through non-linguistic gestures such as pointing or showing, often accompanied by gaze alternation between object and person" (Tomasello 1996: 310; see also Bruner 1975; Bates 1976; Lock 1978, 1980; Shotter and Newson 1982; Trevarthen and Hubley 1978).

The construction of joint reference in infancy is, I claim, a fundamental precondition for being able to signify semantic content in
language: Pre-linguistic signification in an intersubjective context of
shared goals, attention and communication, lays the foundation for
the discursive sharing of thought—the acquisition of linguistic meaning and the means for its expression.

The acquisition of language, in this view, is a process whereby human subjects come to appropriate the means afforded by the language
which they are learning, in order to linguistically conceptualize schematized content, and conventionally (but motivatedly) signify linguistically conceptualized content (for communicative partners) in expression. The learning of expression, and the appropriation of the discursive conceptualizations of language, are not two separate processes,
but a seamless whole process. This process is continuous with both
the development of pre-linguistic non-discursive schematization of
experience, and the development of pre-linguistic means for sharing
reference.

Linguistic meaning, then, is *continuous* with *both* the embodied
"having of a world", in schematized, subjective experience; *and* the
referential "sharing of a world", in intersubjective experience. Continuity (and motivation), however, does not mean the same as identity.
The speaking subject's significations "point outwards" to pick out
some aspect(s) of the shared universe of discourse for a hearer, but
they do so through the medium of expression, in such a way that this
expression organizes and signifies the conceptualization in language
of the picked-out aspects of the universe of discourse. Linguistic
conceptualization is rooted in non-linguistic and pre-linguistic schematization, but is not identical with it. Linguistic conceptualization
(and reference) is *conceptualization of the world signified, not of the*
*non-discursive schematizations which underpin linguistic conceptu-*
*alizations.*

Discursive or linguistic meanings are not "in the head"; they are
not identifiable with or reducible to non-discursive schematizations,
though non-discursive schematizations make them possible. Linguistic
meanings are *not objects*, either in the head or in objective reality.
They are *relationships,* but *not* between "mental objects" and "objects

in the world". The relationship which *is* linguistic meaning, is between linguistic conceptualization and the linguistic expression by which the conceptualization is signified and over which the conceptualization is distributed. *Meaning is a mapping relationship between a linguistically conceptualized referential situation, and a conceptually motivated expression, enabling the hearer to understand, in the context of the universe of discourse, the communicative act intended by the speaker.*

## 4. Meaning as mapping: sense and cognitive semantics

I have argued not only that reference is crucial to understanding meaning, but also that reference is an *act* accomplished by speakers in an intersubjective discourse situation. Reference, emphatically, is *not* a property of expressions in themselves. If we understand that it is *speakers* who refer, and that the reference of "words" to "things" is only secondary and derivative from the acts of speakers, we can also grasp the basic weakness of traditional reificatory theories of *sense*.

In Frege's philosophy of language (Frege 1892), and in the Objectivist tradition which he initiated, sense is defined as that which permits *true* reference, or correspondence, between expressions and extra-linguistic "states of affairs". The logical development of this approach, in some interpretations of formal semantics, leads to the counter-intuitive conclusion that the reference of a linguistic expression is not the state(s) of affairs to which it corresponds, but a *truth-value*. This peculiar and highly abstract conception of reference is part of the price paid by formal semantics for excluding human speakers and their psychological processes from its frame of reference. The other part of the price is its definition of senses as ideal objects whose relationship to human speakers and their psychological processes is left vague and mysterious.

Frege himself did not believe senses to be mental entities, and attributed to them an Ideal status in a Platonic realm outside both material and psychological reality. The motivation for his "anti-psychologism" was essentially the "Other Minds" problem. Individual speakers' "ideas of things", Frege considered, were too much influenced by opinion and by the vagaries of personal experience to function as a secure foundation for an Objectivist theory of meaning. Frege also suspected that natural languages were insufficiently compositional to fully exemplify his theory of meaning.

Frege's theory was not primarily intended, then, as a contribution to the empirical study either of natural language, or of the human mind. However, the logical irreducibility of Fregean sense to reference came inevitably to exercise a powerful grip on linguistic and psycholinguistic theories. At the same time, neither linguists nor psychologists could be content with the Platonic metaphysics of Fregean semantics, which seemed to preclude in principle the possibility of *sciences* of either language or the mind. If Fregean senses could, after all, and contrary to what Frege himself believed, be interpreted as "mental representations" (the building blocks of expressions in "mentalese"), then this would hold out the hope of a complete and formal account of human natural language competence. This reformulation of Reificatory and Objectivist semantics as a *psycholinguistic hypothesis* is fundamental to Classical, Symbolic cognitive science, and it is important to understand both what it entails, and why it is defeated by empirical evidence.

It is here that the Problem of Representation becomes central. Meanings, according to the Dogma of Autonomy, are mental objects (contents) which are exchanged between speakers as expression-tokens (containers). These mental objects represent the real world and its properties, and it is *because* the mental objects represent the real world and its properties, that linguistic expressions are able to refer to objects and relations in that world. Mental representation is a reflection or mirror of nature, and linguistic reference is derivative from the representational function of the mind.

Thus, in Classical, Symbolic cognitive science, a *double* mapping is postulated. The first mapping is between the "physical symbols" of "mentalese"—the Language of Thought (LoT) (Fodor 1976) inscribed in the "Mind/Brain", and "states of affairs" in the world; and the second is between expressions in LoT, and natural language expressions. The meanings (or senses) derived from the second mapping are held to be derivative from those defined by the first mapping. Both the structure of natural language, and the structure of LoT, are formally defined as an infinite set of symbol strings, generated by specified syntactic rules. "The world" is correspondingly defined as an infinite set of possible objects, in possible relationships (states of affairs).

As we know, the problem for an Objectivist theory of natural language semantics is to hook up the infinite set of legal natural language expressions with the infinite set of possible states of affairs in the world, a problem which is widely considered, on multifarious grounds, to be insoluble both in principle and in practice. The same objection, obviously, can be leveled against a hypothetical Objectivist semantics for LoT, but there is (it is claimed) a way round this. The (claimed) solution to this problem is to sideline it, or bracket it off, by postulating *a-priori* that LoT obeys the constraint that every semantically valid and syntactically legal string in LoT univocally represents a possible state of affairs in the world (even if this cannot formally be proved, and even if this is admitted not to be the case for natural languages). This "bracketing off" is what Fodor (1980) refers to as "methodological solipsism", and the postulate arrived at by the bracketing procedure can be referred to as the postulate of semantic coherence: Symbol strings in LoT are coherent with states of affairs in the world, even if a true correspondence mapping cannot be proved. The postulate of the semantic coherence of LoT is meant to save (Objectivist) realism for Classical cognitivism, in the absence of a demonstration of the possibility of a "directly" Objectivist semantics of natural language.[7]

Coherence is (presumably) epistemologically weaker than correspondence, but *ontologically* it entails the strong condition that LoT be implemented in "a *syntactically* driven machine whose state transitions satisfy *semantic* criteria of coherence .... the brain *is* such a machine" (Fodor and Pylyshyn 1988: 30; emphases in original). At this point, even if we grant the dubious a-priorism of the postulate of semantic coherence, the Classical cognitivist must next account for the second mapping: between the semantically coherent and univocal symbol strings of LoT, and lawful natural language expressions. To achieve this mapping, it is necessary that every semantically valid and syntactically legal expression in any natural language, including ambiguous expressions, should be translatable into at least one valid expression in LoT (in LoT, remember, it is a consequence of the postulate of semantic coherence that syntactic legality and semantic coherence coincide—there can be no ambiguous expressions in LoT).

Making classical cognitivism work as a psycholinguistic theory, then, entails the compositionality of the meanings of symbols, such that the representational format (or syntax) of expressions may be transformed, while preserving their semantic *content*, between a syntax coherent with semantic content, and a syntax which is incoherent with (or, in generativist terms, autonomous from) semantic content. It is this requirement which the rules of natural language syntax, and the information in the lexicon (supplemented perhaps by a nonsemantic pragmatics defined in terms of conversational implicature), are supposed to guarantee, by permitting an unambiguous interpretation of any given linguistic expression on the basis of *nothing but* linguistic rules and lexical semantic information.

Compositionality comes down, in the end, to the requirement that lexical meaning should be constant across combinatorial context, or at least that it should be so in as many cases as possible; and that where ambiguity arises (homonymy, polysemy) it should as far as possible be eliminable by reference only to that same combinatorial context (this is the function of so-called selection restrictions). Compositionality of meaning, even liberally interpreted, requires that appeal to referential, as opposed to linguistic, context should be held to a minimum in resolving ambiguity (or more generally, determining interpretation); that changes in combinatorial context should, if they do not yield constancy of meaning, *at most* yield *predictable* alternations between existing meanings, and *not* yield entirely new meanings; and, most obviously, that meanings should be "atomic", that is (in the general case) locally expressed by single morphemes, rather than distributed across different morphemes (except in special, rigid constructions like the French *ne ... pas* negative).

Cognitive linguistic research has conclusively demonstrated what Frege suspected: Natural languages are not compositional, if compositionality is defined truth-conditionally. The dependence of the interpretation of lexical items upon context goes far beyond a simple dichotomy between "indexicality" and "sentential context", to embrace both the conceptualized referential context and the discourse frame (Fillmore 1985, Lakoff 1987). Studies of conceptual blending and grammar (Fauconnier and Turner 1996) have shown that linguistic constructions frequently give rise to *emergent* meanings which (though cognitively motivated) are not predictable from the meanings of the individual constituents. Studies of the semantics of space have shown that conceptualization is regularly and emergently distributed across extended syntagmatic strings, rather than being localized at particular morphemes (Sinha and Kuteva 1995). If "compositionality" can be said to exist in natural languages at all, it has to be seen as one constraining principle among other competing ones such as blending, integration, conflation and distribution, rather than an all-embracing design-property (see also Fauconnier, this volume; Sweetser, this volume; Zlatev 1997).

If these results of cognitive linguistic research are well known, and the consequent empirical defeat of the Classical-Symbolic "Language of Thought" hypothesis is self-evident, why, you might ask, harp on about what many cognitive linguists must regard as old news? The reason is that an explication of the "LoT" argument, its intricate theoretical contortions and its ultimate empirical failure, helps to illustrate the general point which this chapter is intended to address: Objectivism and Subjectivism are natural (and equally erroneous) twins, conceived in the marriage between reificatory semantics and the traditional representational theory of mind. The "LoT" argument represents a retreat from a strictly Objectivist theory of natural language meaning, to an attenuated realism in which coherence replaces correspondence, and the Other Minds problem is addressed only as a methodological device for postulating a highly implausible theoretical constraint on cognitive neuroscience. The entire edifice of the "Language of Thought" theory collapses with the demonstration of the non-compositionality of natural language: If a Fodorean Language of Thought existed, it could not consistently be translated to or from natural languages.

The implications of this failure, I claim, are wider: A reificatory theory of meaning-as-mental-object *cannot* yield *any* kind of realist theory of meaning. If you start by treating meanings as mental objects "representing" real objects, you will never (however much you protest your "realist" credentials) emerge from the solipsist tunnel. Unfortunately, this is not unadulterated good news for many current approaches to cognitive semantics. The cautionary sting in the tail is that simply substituting "schema" for "symbol" does not change the import of the argument: *Any* theory which sees meanings as mental objects is condemned to a Subjectivist theory of meaning. If cognitive semantics wants a coherent realist (but non-Objectivist) theory of meaning, it will have to abandon the assumption that meanings are mental objects, and along with it the granting of primary psychological reality to reified entities such as "senses".

If my argument is correct, several issues which have seemed central in cognitive semantics are in fact superficial, or just symptomatic. For example, although it is crucial for generative linguistics to minimize the attribution of lexical polysemy (in order to maximize compositionality), it is *not* crucial for cognitive semantics to maximize or emphasize polysemy, and still less to assume that lexical polysemy reflects a deep, primary psychological reality. We would do better, I suggest, to view meaning *in principle* as involving many-to-many mappings between contextualized conceptualization and expression.[8] To the extent that such mapping relations become (in the histories of either languages or speakers) entrenched in usage, whether between conceptualization and lexeme or between conceptualization and construction, we can analyze these on divergent continua from one-to-one monosemy through polysemy to semantic vacuity; or from conflation to distribution; or from literalness to metaphoricity; or from novel blend to regular construction.

My point is not to argue for the abolition of the notion of "sense", but for its re-interpretation (see also Sinha and Thorseng 1995). Instead of seeing senses as mental objects, schemas, or nodes in semantic networks, we should view them as *relatively stable or entrenched patterns of mapping*, from contextualized conceptualization to expression, in the course of the dynamic construction of acts of meaning, in which the goal of the action is to successfully achieve (through linguistic means) joint reference in an intersubjectively shared universe of discourse.[9]

I have argued in this and the previous section that a turn away from a reificatory view of meaning-as-mental-object, and towards a practical-communicative view of meaning as communicative action, offers an escape from the sterile opposition between an unattainable Objectivist realism and an incoherent Subjectivist solipsism. I have also argued that the "foundational" realism which cognitive semantics should embrace is *referential realism*, understood not as an "objective" relationship between language and world, but as a *practical achievement* in an intersubjectively shared world *constituted* through its conceptualization and signification in language.

Referential realism may seem, especially to those familiar with Quinean "indeterminacy of ostension" arguments (Quine 1969), to be a weak basis for a theory of meaning. It is often held to involve nothing more than easily-defeasible "naïve realism". In the next and final section, I argue, on the contrary, not only that referential realism is psychologically and ecologically realistic, but also that it naturally (epigenetically-developmentally) merges into a *constructivist* approach to language and language acquisition. The starting point for this argument, which leads to a comprehensive, constructivist and realist theory of the grounding of linguistic meaning, is the "primordial discourse situation" of joint, intersubjectively shared attention.

## 5. Towards a constructivist cognitive linguistics

At a very minimum, for anything to be the focus of joint attention, it has to constitute a Figure against a shared and presupposed Ground. This *figuration* of attentional focus is the basis of all reference, and can be accomplished non-linguistically (by pointing, or showing, or looking); or through language, in more or less complex ways ("Train!" "Daddy, train!" "There's a train!" "A train is coming out of the tunnel"). Perhaps the most fundamental principle of *linguistic construction* is that referential situations are organized in terms of successive, nested and collocated, specifications and re-specifications of Figured aspects against Grounded aspects.[10]

The Figure is salient to the subject not only in virtue of some of its physical properties, but also in virtue of the subject's psychological mechanisms which are adapted to *perceiving as salient* those very physical properties. This is so even when the salience of the referent to the subject is involuntary (the child can't help but notice the brightly colored, fast-moving train). When *joint reference* (the inter-subjective *sharing* of Figure-Ground articulation) is accomplished, what has been achieved is the construction of a *primordial discourse situation*. The ability to intersubjectively co-construct such a situation, as we have seen, is mastered by human infants at around nine months of age. The acquisition and development of language consists in the elaboration of this ability, through the mastery of increasingly complex ways of constructing and construing reference in discourse situations that are increasingly constituted by language itself.

The voluntary, subjectively controllable specificity of the referential act increases enormously when it is accomplished through the mediation of complex constructions of linguistic expression. Natural languages, as we know from the work of Langacker (1987 1990) and many others, afford rich and varying possibilities for constructing and construing referential situations: Figure and Ground may be reversed, perspective may be shifted, and so forth. Fully developed linguistic conceptualization also permits reference to imaginary and non-physical entities and relations in "virtual" worlds, as well as the conceptualization of physical entities and relations in terms of "virtual" or "fictive" properties or relations (Talmy 1990). I shall concentrate, however, on the level of the "primordial discourse situation", in which physical referents are immediately perceptually available to the discourse participants. In the primordial discourse situation, the deployment of linguistic expression in constructing and construing the referential situation is supported and constrained by the following four factors:

- The physical properties and dispositions of the constituent aspects of the referential situation (in the real-world ecological surround).

- The perceptual and cognitive mechanisms of the communicator which are adapted to the "pick-up" and the schematic/figurative organization of relevant aspects or features of the world.
- The speaker's situatedness, and the speaker's awareness of the situatedness of the addressee, in the currently-obtaining Universe of Discourse.
- The constructional means afforded to the speaker by the language for construing and conceptualizing the situation.

The first two supports/constraints constitute the primary ecological life-world (*Umwelt*) of the human organism. Taken together, they form the basis of a psychology based upon *ecological realism*. Both the existence of a mind-independent reality, and the fact of its having real parts and real properties, are asserted. At the same time, there exist certain biologically based principles of perceptual, attentional and motor organization. These include, for developing human beings, prototype effects in categorical perception, caused by the computational properties of Natural Neural Networks; mechanisms for parsing motion, events and actions; and proto-conceptual categorizations based upon spatial relations and categorical roles in event structures. These organizing (schematic and figurative) principles are either innate, or epigenetically developed through organism-environment interaction (Elman *et al.* 1996; Plunkett and Sinha 1992).

Ecological realism (Fettes 1999) is in most respects equivalent to George Lakoff's (1987) experiential realism, with one difference: it pertains to the *pre-conceptual* and *proto-conceptual* level of cognitive organization, and not to conceptualization proper. Conceptualization, I am claiming, *depends* upon, and is schematically and figuratively *motivated* by, its embodied grounding in the ecological life-world, but it is neither *identical* with it, nor *reducible* to it (see Note 5).

If the first two supports/constraints together constitute one pillar, as it were, of grounding—*embodied grounding*—then the third constitutes a second pillar, one that I shall call *discursive grounding*. Its prototype, and the simplest structure realizing it, is unadorned *joint attention*: the intersubjective sharing of an indexically present, and mutually perceived, object or event. Its constructive elaboration involves the mastery of turn-taking, deixis of person and place, perspectivization, ellipsis, theme-rheme shifts, the incorporation of previous discourse segments, and devices for establishing coherence and cohesion. Such discourse construction principles, far from being secondary superstructures upon a mythic "pure propositional content", constitute the *basic functional motivation* of linguistic construction. They can be seen as providing a *communicative and cognitive bridge* between embodied grounding—the grounding of language in non-discursive schematizations—and linguistic conceptualization proper. My claim, then, is that the solution to the "Problem of Grounding" is twofold: there is a *dual grounding* of language and linguistic cognition, first Embodied Grounding, and second Discursive Grounding. And *both* of these "twin pillars" of human natural language flow, naturally and logically, from a commitment to, and an analysis of, linguistic meaning in terms of both ecological and referential realism.

We come now to the fourth support/constraint. This is inherent in language: in a quite fundamental sense it simply *is* language, viewed as a symbolic system. Since the first three supports which together make up the embodied and discursive grounding of meaning are also *constraints* upon what can be conceptualized and what can be expressed, natural languages are *motivated, non-arbitrary* symbolic systems. The fourth support-constraint is best conceived as the *specifically linguistic* mediational means, or semiotic vehicle, whereby the three other supports/constraints are integrated in the actual construction of acts of linguistic meaning. It is the system of mappings, from *articulated conceptualization*, to *articulated expression*, whose elucidation is the goal of cognitive linguistics. Linguistic conceptualizations (particular acts of linguistic meaning), and linguistic cognition (the cognitive capacity of subjects to produce and understand acts of linguistic meaning, or "think for speaking" in Slobin's felicitous expression), are, in this view, *language-dependent*: They depend upon the mastery of the symbolic means of linguistic expression.

This last proposal is by no means as self-evident and tautological as, at first sight, it seems. Many semantic theories hypothesize the existence of a universal, non-linguistic conceptual representational system, on the basis of which the specific semantic structures of any particular natural language are erected. Such theories are "ideationist" variants of the Reificatory Semantics that I have criticized throughout this chapter. Empirically, the hypothesis of a universal non-linguistic conceptual system is difficult to reconcile with evidence that (at least in the cognitive and linguistic domain of space) semantic development in children follows a *language specific* rather than universal course (Bowerman 1996). Not only does the adoption of the theoretical approach I am advocating render such a hypothesis unnecessary, but it in fact *precludes* it. There is, if this account is correct, *no possible developmental mechanism* which could secure (or ground) a conceptual-semantic system, in the absence of the acquisition of the means by which conceptualizations are expressed, and joint reference accomplished, in real discourse.

Language acquisition, in this view, consists essentially of two concurrent, parallel and mutually-dependent processes: the *semanticization* of the perceptuo-motor and proto-conceptual systems of schematic pre-linguistic cognition; and the *grammaticalization* of the signifying means for accomplishing joint reference. More simply, to use a modified Vygotskian formulation, language acquisition is the interactive, dual process of the semanticization of child thought and the grammaticalization of child speech.[11] In the course of acquiring language, and becoming a member of the surrounding speech community, the child develops the increasing ability to participate in acts of meaning grounded in a universe of discourse constituted by language itself. In this sense, it is not only the case that meaning grounds all of language; it is also the case that language, as a cognitively entrenched, normative means for accomplishing complex co-ordinations of reference in symbolically constituted intersubjective fields, grounds meaning.

## 6. Concluding note: the importance of development

The point of view that I have advanced and defended in this chapter is very similar (perhaps identical) to the one argued for by Peter Harder (this volume). Both Harder and I press a case for a "dual grounding" view of language and linguistic cognition, one which recognizes the centrality of *both* embodied grounding *and* functional or discursive grounding. As I see it, part of the underlying motivation for this view is a desire to escape from the restrictive scientific orthodoxy which says that you can have *either* an individual-cognitive, *or* a social-functional, view of language, but you can't combine the two (and we all know which one of them is supposed to be more "scientific"). Harder and I both argue, on the contrary, that you simply can't understand the one without the other (see also Itkonen 1997). Even more strongly, I would say (and I expect Harder would agree) that there simply would be no such a thing as human natural language, and linguistic cognition, were it not for its socio-cultural context. This proposition can be understood both in terms of the evolution of the human species, and in terms of the developmental processes underlying child language acquisition.

Cognitive linguistics is the first (at least the first successful) truly dynamic approach to human language and cognition. As a developmental psycholinguist, I would like to see this dynamic approach extended to a recognition of the centrality of the developmental perspective to our joint enterprise. The constructivist (or emergentist, MacWhinney 1999) perspective that I am advocating for cognitive linguistics sits naturally with a constructivist and emergentist approach to language development and cognitive development. Constructivism (emergentism) is the dynamic and materialist alternative to both eliminativist reductionism and Cartesian rationalism. It is scientific, but not scientistic; empirical but not empiricist; it recognizes the irreducibility of subjectivity without being subjectivist; it is realist but not objectivist.

We need, of course, more cognitive-linguistic inspired empirical studies of language acquisition. But we also need to incorporate the developmental perspective into the heart of our understanding of the human language faculty: not as one innate module (or subset of modules) amongst others, but as one aspect of an integrated yet complexly differentiated embodied neuro-cognitive system, functionally coupled and co-evolving with its socio-cultural surround.

# Notes

1. By "Subjectivist" I mean, in essence, the philosophical stance that our only access to the world is via our individual, private perceptions and ideas of it, and that only these private perceptions and ideas can therefore be said really to exist. "Subjective Idealism" was systematically expounded by Bishop Berkeley, after whom one of the campuses of the University of California is named. Immanuel Kant said that he had been awoken by Berkeley from his "dogmatic slumbers", and regarded it as his duty to combat what he regarded as the philosophical "scandal" which Berkeley propagated. Not all cognitive linguists regard Subjectivism as scandalous. A few embrace it and many more, I would say, teeter nervously on the brink of falling headlong into it. I agree with Kant, if not in his solution, at least in his diagnosis. See Section 2 on the "Other Minds" problem.
2. W.D. Ross (ed.) *The Works of Aristotle,* Vol. 1, transl. E.M. Edghill, Oxford, Clarendon Press, 1928, 16a.
3. *An Essay concerning Human Understanding* (1690), Book III, Ch. 2, section 2. Later (Book III, Ch. 11, section 5), Locke depicts language as "the great Conduit, whereby Men convey their Discoveries, Reasonings and Knowledge, from one to another." Cited in Harris and Taylor (1989: 109).
4. *Collected Works,* 1974, Vol. VII, pp. 24-25.
5. The theory of performatives is based upon the recognition that, in some (performative) cases, the meta-reference to the speech act does indeed, under appropriate conditions of authorization of speakers, bring into existence or "conjure up", the situation referred to in the speech act: for instance, "I pronounce you man and wife". There are many other secondary issues here, which I won't address yet; such as, how it is after all possible to have beliefs about one's ideas, such as to believe that one's understanding of the theory of relativity is incomplete; how imaginary entities figure in all this, and so on.
6. Jean Mandler, in the paper cited here, posits a pre-linguistic "conceptual level of representation" which is based upon "perceptually analyzed" image-schematic "meaning packages", which "language can put together in a variety of ways". I wish to resist this formulation, and signal this disagreement by using the term "proto-conceptual". I agree entirely, however, with Mandler and her colleagues that these "non-discursive schematizations", as I call them, go *beyond* perception (including beyond categorical perception). This is not simply a quibble: there is, I would argue, *continuity* between pre-linguistic cognition (functional-actional image schematic understanding), and linguistic conceptualization ("thinking for speaking"), but not *identity*. Identity would imply both that the acquisition of language leaves the proto-conceptual level untransformed, and that the semantic systems of all natural languages are re-

ducible to a universal non-linguistic conceptual system (whether modular or not). I explicitly reject such a hypothesis in the final section of this Chapter.

7. In effect, this amounts to "saving" Classical cognitivism from Searle's "Chinese Room" argument (Searle 1980) by accepting the argument but moving back one step and starting over again: a case of having your cake and eating it. It could be added, though, that Searle himself comes very near to exactly this kind of reasoning in proposing that the intentionality of linguistic reference derives from the intentionality of perception.

8. I am using this formulation as a shorthand for: the mapping relationship between a linguistically conceptualized referential situation, and a conceptually motivated expression, enabling the hearer to understand, in the context of the universe of discourse, the communicative act intended by the speaker. (See Section 3).

9. In (at least partial) support of this interpretation of "sense", I cite Karl Bühler (1933) [Innis 1982: 125]: "Plato called objects that manifest similarities [to linguistic meanings] *Ideas* ... That we have transformed the 'eternal and immutable' into 'intersubjective'...only needs to be said in order to exclude misunderstandings." A similar perspective is to be found in the writings of Vygotsky (1978, 1986).

10. Both developmentally and processually, Figure-Ground specification and re-specification is the basic psychological mechanism underlying the formal notions of predication and proposition. Although Figure-Ground and topic-comment (or theme-rheme) structuration are functionally differentiated during development, they initially coincide. The ontogenetically formative *communicative* context of "pre-predication" is that of joint action, but topic-comment separation and re-combination can also be observed in the solitary play of infants with objects before the end of the first year of life (Bruner 1975). Thanks to Jordan Zlatev for raising the important issue of predication in his comments on an earlier draft of this chapter.

11. "Speech" taken to be inclusive of visual-manual sign language signs. Slobin (1997 :313) points out that "some of the notions that are salient to small children are also salient in the process of grammaticization", but also emphasizes that language acquisition and diachronic grammaticalization processes should not be identified or assumed to be parallel: "Speech communities are at work (very slowly) in modifying grammars. Children are at work (quite quickly) in mastering *already existing* grammars." (p. 314).

# References

Bates, Elizabeth
  1976    *Language and Context: The Acquisition of Pragmatics*. New York: Academic Press.
Bowerman, Melissa
  1996    The origin of children's spatial semantic categories: cognitive versus linguistic determinants. In: John J. Gumperz and Stephen C. Levinson (eds.) *Rethinking Linguistic Relativity*, 145-176. Cambridge: Cambridge University Press.
Bruner, Jerome
  1975    From communication to language: a psychological perspective. *Cognition* 3: 225-287.
Bruner, Jerome
  1990    *Acts of Meaning*. Cambridge, MA: Harvard University Press.
Butterworth, George and Nick Jarrett
  1991    What minds have in common is space: spatial mechanisms serving joint visual attention in infancy. *British Journal of Developmental Psychology* 9: 55-72.
Elman, Jeff, Elizabeth Bates, Mark Johnson, Annette Karmiloff-Smith, Dominico Parisi and Kim Plunkett
  1996    *Rethinking Innateness: A Connectionist Perspective on Development*. Cambridge, MA: MIT Press/Bradford Books.
Fauconnier, Gilles
  1997    *Mappings in Thought and Language*. Cambridge: Cambridge University Press.
Fauconnier, Gilles and Mark Turner
  1996    Blending as a central process of grammar. In: Adele E. Goldberg (ed.) *Conceptual Structure, Discourse and Language*, 113-130. Stanford: Center for the Study of Language and Information.
Fettes, Mark
  1999    Critical realism and ecological psychology: foundations for a naturalist theory of language acquisition. Paper presented at the Ecology of Language Acquisition Workshop, Amsterdam, January.
Fillmore, Charles
  1985    Frame semantics. In: Linguistic Society of Korea (ed.) *Linguistics in the Morning Calm*, 111-138. Seoul: Hanshin.
Fodor, Jerry
  1976    *The Language of Thought*. Hassocks: Harvester.
Fodor, Jerry
  1980    Methodological solipsism considered as a research strategy in the cognitive sciences. *Behavioral and Brain Sciences* 3: 63-73.

Fodor, Jerry and Zenon Pylyshyn
  1988    Connectionism and cognitive architecture: A critical analysis. *Cognition* 28: 3-71.
Frege, Gottlob
  1892    Über Sinn und Bedeutung. *Zeitschrift für Philosophie und Philosophische Kritik* 100: 25-50.
Freeman, Norman, Sharon Lloyd, and Chris Sinha
  1980    Infant search tasks reveal early concepts of containment and canonical usage of objects. *Cognition* 8: 243-262.
Harris, Roy
  1988    *Language, Saussure and Wittgenstein*. London: Routledge.
Harris, Roy and Talbot J. Taylor
  1989    *Landmarks in Linguistic Thought*. London: Routledge.
Innis, Robert E.
  1982    *Karl Bühler: Semiotic Foundations of Language Theory*. New York: Plenum Press.
Itkonen, Esa
  1997    The social ontology of linguistic meaning. *SKY 1997 Yearbook of the Linguistic Association of Finland*: 49-80.
Kreitzer, Anatol
  1997    Multiple levels of schematization: A study in the conceptualization of space. *Cognitive Linguistics* 8: 291-325.
Kita, Sotaro
  in press How representational gestures help speaking. In: David McNeill (ed.) *Speech and Gesture: Window into Thought and Action*.
Lakoff, George
  1987    *Women, Fire and Dangerous Things: What Categories Tell us about the Mind*. Chicago: University of Chicago Press.
Langacker, Ronald W.
  1987    Foundations of Cognitive Grammar Vol. 1, Theoretical Prerequisites. Stanford: Stanford University Press.
  1990    *Concept, Image and Symbol: The Cognitive Basis of Grammar*. Berlin: Mouton de Gruyter.
Lock, Andrew (ed.)
  1978    *Action, Gesture and Symbol: The Emergence of Language*. London: Academic Press.
Lock, Andrew
  1980    *The Guided Reinvention of Language*. London: Academic Press.
MacWhinney, Brian (ed.)
  1999    *The Emergence of Language*. Mahwah, NJ: Lawrence Erlbaum.

Mandler, Jean
  1996    Preverbal representation and language. In: Bloom, Paul, Mary A. Pe-
          terson, Lyn Nadel and Merrill F. Garret (eds.), *Language and Space,*
          365-384. Cambridge, MA: MIT Press/Bradford Books.
McNeill, David, and Susan Duncan
  in press Growth points in thinking for speaking. In: David McNeill (ed.)
          *Speech and Gesture: Window into Thought and Action.*
Plunkett, Kim, and Chris Sinha
  1992    Connectionism and developmental theory. *British Journal of Devel-
          opmental Psychology* 10: 209-254.
Putnam, Hilary
  1981    A problem about reference & Appendix. In: *Reason, Truth and His-
          tory,* 22-28 & 217-218. Cambridge: Cambridge University Press.
Quine, Willard
  1969    *Ontological Relativity and Other Essays.* New York: Columbia Uni-
          versity Press.
Reddy, Michael
  1979    The conduit metaphor. In: Andrew Ortony (ed.), *Metaphor and
          Thought,* 284-324. Cambridge: Cambridge University Press.
Saussure, Ferdinand de
  1966    *Cours de Linguistique Générale.* New York: McGraw-Hill.
Searle, John R.
  1969    *Speech Acts: An Essay in the Philosophy of Language.* Cambridge:
          Cambridge University Press.
  1980    Minds, brains and programs. *Behavioral and Brain Sciences* 3: 417-
          424.
  1983    *Intentionality.* Cambridge: Cambridge University Press.
  1995    *The Construction of Social Reality.* London: Allen Lane The Penguin
          Press.
Shotter, John
  1993    *Conversational Realities.* London: Sage Publications.
Shotter, John, and John Newson
  1982    An ecological approach to cognitive development: implicate orders,
          joint action and intentionality. In: George Butterworth and Paul Light
          (eds.), *Social Cognition: Studies in the Development of Understand-
          ing,* 32-52. Brighton, Harvester Press.
Sinha, Chris
  1982    Representational development and the structure of action. In: George
          Butterworth and Paul Light (eds.), *Social Cognition: Studies in the
          Development of Understanding,* 137-162. Brighton, Harvester Press.

Sinha, Chris, and Tania Kuteva
    1995    Distributed spatial semantics. *Nordic Journal of Linguistics* 18: 167-199.

Sinha, Chris, and Lis A. Thorseng
    1995    A coding system for spatial relational reference. *Cognitive Linguistics* 6: 261-309.

Slobin, Dan I.
    1996    From 'thought and language' to 'thinking for speaking'. In: John J. Gumperz and Stephen C. Levinson (eds.) *Rethinking Linguistic Relativity*, 70-96. Cambridge: Cambridge University Press.

Talmy, Leonard
    1990    Fictive motion and change in language and cognition. Plenary lecture at the International Pragmatics Conference, Barcelona.

Tomasello, Michael
    1996    The child's contribution to culture: A commentary on Toomela. *Culture and Psychology* 2: 307-318.

Trevarthen, Colwyn, and Penelope Hubley
    1978    Secondary intersubjectivity: confidence, confiding and acts of meaning in the first year. In: A. Lock (ed.), *Action, Gesture and Symbol: The Emergence of Language*, 183-229. London: Academic Press.

Vygotsky, Lev
    1978    *Mind in Society: The Development of Higher Psychological Processes.* Edited by Michael Cole, Vera John-Steiner, Sylvia Scribner and Ellen Souberman. Cambridge: Harvard University Press.
    1986    *Thought and Language.* Edited by Alex Kozulin. Cambridge, MA: Harvard University Press.

Wittgenstein, Ludwig
    1961    *Tractatus Logico-Philosophicus.* London: Routledge and Kegan Paul.

Zlatev, Jordan
    1997    Situated embodiment: studies in spatial semantics. Ph.D. dissertation, University of Stockholm. Stockholm: Gotab.

# List of contributors

**William Croft**, Department of Linguistics, Manchester University, Manchester, UK. Email: w.croft@man.ac.uk

**Gilles Fauconnier**, Department of Cognitive Science, University of California, San Diego, USA. Email: faucon@cogsci.ucsd.edu

**Dirk Geeraerts**, Department of Linguistics, Katholieke Universiteit Leuven, Leuven, Belgium. Email: dirk.geeraerts@arts.kuleuven.ac.be

**Peter Harder**, English Department, University of Copenhagen, Copenhagen, Denmark. Email: harder@coco.ihi.ku.dk

**Theo Janssen**, Department of Linguistics, Vrije Universiteit Amsterdam, Amsterdam, The Netherlands. Email: janssen_thajm@let.vu.nl

**Ronald W. Langacker**, Department of Linguistics, University of California, San Diego, USA. Email: rlangacker@ucsd.edu

**Gisela Redeker**, Department of Language and Communication, University of Groningen, Groningen, The Netherlands. Email: g.redeker@let.rug.nl

**Chris Sinha**, Department of Psychology, University of Aarhus, Risskov, Denmark. Email: chris@psy.au.dk

**Eve Sweetser**, Department of Linguistics, University of California, Berkeley, USA. Email: sweetser@cogsci.berkeley.edu

# Index of names

# Subject index

# Cognitive Linguistics Research

Edited by René Dirven, Ronald W. Langacker and
John R. Taylor

Mouton de Gruyter · Berlin · New York

This series offers a forum for the presentation of research within the perspective of "cognitive linguistics". This rubric subsumes a variety of concerns and broadly compatible theoretical approaches that have a common basic outlook: that language is an integral facet of cognition which reflects the interaction of social, cultural, psychological, communicative and functional considerations, and which can only be understood in the context of a realistic view of acquisition, cognitive development and mental processing. Cognitive linguistics thus eschews the imposition of artificial boundaries, both internal and external. Internally, it seeks a unified account of language structure that avoids such problematic dichotomies as lexicon vs. grammar, morphology vs. syntax, semantics vs. pragmatics, and synchrony vs. diachrony. Externally, it seeks insofar as possible to explicate language structure in terms of the other facets of cognition on which it draws, as well as the communicative function it serves. Linguistic analysis can therefore profit from the insights of neighboring and overlapping disciplines such as sociology, cultural anthropology, neuroscience, philosophy, psychology, and cognitive science.

8 *The Construal of Space in Language and Thought.* Edited by Martin Pütz and René Dirven. 1996.

9 Ewa Dąbrowska, *Cognitive Semantics and the Polish Dative.* 1997.

10 *Speaking of Emotions: Conceptualisation and Expression.* Edited by Angeliki Athanasiadou and Elżbieta Tabakowska. 1998.

11 Michel Achard, *Representation of Cognitive Structures.* 1998.

12 *Issues in Cognitive Linguistics. 1993 Proceedings of the International Cognitive Linguistics Conference.* Edited by Leon de Stadler and Christoph Eyrich. 1999.

13 *Historical Semantics and Cognition.* Edited by Andreas Blank and Peter Koch. 1999.

14 Ronald W. Langacker, *Grammar and Conceptualization.* 1999.

15 *Cognitive Linguistics: Foundations, Scope, and Methodology.* Edited by Theo Janssen and Gisela Redeker. 1999.